BRINGING DOWN
THE KRAYS

15/5

BRINGING DOWN
THE KRAYS

Finally the truth about Ronnie and Reggie

by the man who took them down

BOBBY TEALE

with Alfie and David Teale

EBURY
PRESS

3 5 7 9 10 8 6 4 2

This edition published 2013
First published in 2012 by Ebury Press, an imprint of Ebury Publishing
A Random House Group company

Written with Clare Campbell

The Random House Group Limited Reg. No. 954009

Addresses for companies within the Random House Group can be found at
www.randomhouse.co.uk

A CIP catalogue record for this book is available from the British Library

The Random House Group Limited supports the Forest Stewardship
Council® (FSC®), the leading international forest-certification organisation.
Our books carrying the FSC label are printed on FSC®-certified paper. FSC is
the only forest-certification scheme supported by the leading environmental
organisations, including Greenpeace. Our paper procurement policy
can be found at www.randomhouse.co.uk/environment

Designed and set by seagulls.net

Printed and bound by CPI Group (UK) Ltd, Croydon, CR0 4YY

ISBN 9780091946630
To buy books by your favourite authors and register for offers visit
www.randomhouse.co.uk

*To our mother, Ellen Teale,
and to Christine Teale*

CONTENTS

Prologue: Facing Down the Past 1

Chapter 1: Lost and Found 5

Chapter 2: Part of the Family 19

Chapter 3: Down the 66 and Up the West End 31

Chapter 4: A Casual Violence 41

Chapter 5: Bungs and Bodies 55

Chapter 6: The Cedra Court Scene 65

Chapter 7: Puppies and Flowers 81

Chapter 8: The Party Comes to Me 89

Chapter 9: Dead Men Can't Speak 99

Chapter 10: The Turning Point 107

Chapter 11: Moresby Road – and a Trip to Dartmoor 117

Chapter 12: Beside the Seaside 131

Chapter 13: A Close Shave 145

Chapter 14: A Walk in the Woods 163

Chapter 15: The Set-Up 173

Chapter 16: David's Story 185

Chapter 17: Alfie's Story 201

Chapter 18: My Story 209

Chapter 19: Bringing Down the House of Cards 221

Chapter 20: Mum and Christine's Stories 233

Chapter 21: Secrets and Lies 245

Chapter 22: Into the Lions' Den 257

Chapter 23: The Deal 277

Chapter 24: Slipping Away 287

Epilogue: Forty Years On 293

Note 311

Acknowledgements 312

PROLOGUE
FACING DOWN THE PAST

I have spent a long time trying to forget who I really am. Look at me and you'd see an average guy as anonymous as the battered pick-up truck I drive and the plaid shirt I wear at weekends. I am a Canadian citizen with right of residence in the US, as good a neighbour and as law-abiding a citizen in our little slice of the state of Utah as anyone could wish for.

Most of my life I worked in the construction business. I still do. But once, a long time before, I had been someone very different.

The only bit of me which has stayed the same is my name, the one my parents gave me: Robert Frank Teale. Most people call me Bobby.

A few Christmases back, my daughter Paula bought me a large picture book as a present. It was called *Defining Moments in History*, and it included major world events such as Pearl Harbor and the assassination of JFK, plus quirky stuff like the invention of sliced bread. Sitting there in our home with all the kids opening their gifts around me, I skimmed through it until I came across a page that featured a photo of a horse-drawn hearse.

The name 'REG' was written on the side in big letters made out of flowers and the word 'RESPECT' was on the top, made out of more floral tributes. A huge crowd was following on foot and in an endless line of cars. The picture was taken in east London on 11 October 2000, so the caption said. I didn't recognise quite where it was, but I knew exactly who it was in the coffin on his way to the cemetery.

I felt a sudden torrent of emotion. Trying to hide it, I stood up and got the attention of the family, saying casually: 'See the man in this coffin? He was once my best friend.'

The kids were shocked. 'Who is it?' they asked.

'His name was Reggie Kray,' I said softly, 'and he was one of the most notorious criminals of his time – or any other time. He had a twin brother called Ronnie. They were cold-blooded murderers. They ruled London by fear. I helped to bring them down. In fact I very nearly stopped them altogether.'

'Dad, if you were his friend, does that mean you were a criminal too?' one of the kids asked.

I didn't know how to reply. There was a long silence. Eventually my daughter said softly, 'Dad, did you ever kill anyone?'

'The opposite,' I said. 'I tried to save people, and I suffered for it.'

I'd never told them a thing about who I used to be. This time, I don't know why, it was different. I wanted to tell them a little bit more.

'There was a cop who went after these people,' I explained. 'He was called Nipper Read. Do you know he told my mother, your grandmother, that without me it would have taken a hell of a lot longer to have nabbed the Krays and get them off the street and locked up?'

I did not tell them that, for a time, I'd been completely in their thrall. That I'd been overwhelmed at how glamorous and powerful they seemed. How I'd left my first wife and baby daughter to be with them, how I'd carried guns for them, carried a gun myself, witnessed beatings and shootings. Like I was a Cockney version of that guy in the movie *Goodfellas*, the one who says: 'As far back as I can remember, I always wanted to be a gangster.' Well, for a little while I had been a gangster. Or at least I thought I was.

I had been a part of 'the Firm'. Not the Kray firm, *the* Firm. There was only one that mattered.

Then something had happened which changed my life forever. I saw things that terrified and disgusted me, things that I would never want anyone to know about. I had to make a stand. I did something that put my own life in deadly danger and that of my beloved brothers: Alfie, a little older than me, and David who is a little younger. They did not know at the time just what I had done. I'd had to run away from my old life and let my family think I was dead. Could it really all have happened almost fifty years ago?

Anger and grief welled up in me. I slammed the book shut.

Over the years I'd mastered the art of cutting off emotionally from everyone. For months, I'd only managed to stay alive at all by acting. I thought I'd been so good at it. But maybe I wasn't any more.

Did I really want my children to know the true story of what happened? Did I want anyone in my new life to know? My children were now well out of school. They weren't stupid. I had long ago decided that I would have to tell them all of it when the time was right. When I had worked out what really happened and why. Well, now was the time.

After that first shocking reminder of my past, I began to research more about the London of my youth, tentatively drawing to the surface old memories I had suppressed for years. I trawled the internet. I was astonished at how much was out there on the Krays. What was it about them that exerted such a strong grip on the public imagination, even now, forty years after the height of their reign of terror? Late into the night, I'd stay up, discovering things I never knew about them at the time. But I also came to realise that there were a lot of things that my brothers and I had witnessed that nobody else knew about – and certainly had never written about. We were part of it. We'd been there.

This book could not have been written without the cooperation of my two brothers, Alfie and David. They were at the heart of everything and they were involved with the Krays well before I ever met them. Many of the stories contained in these pages were drawn from their detailed recollections, told to me either at the time or many years later when we were reunited. We have dug up some painful memories as we went over these events together during the course of writing this book. I have to thank them from the bottom of my heart for their support. Without them it would only be half the story.

There had been official cover-ups. There had been myth-making and distortion on an epic scale. There were so many lies. Now it was time for the truth.

CHAPTER 1
LOST AND FOUND

Where to start? Right at the beginning is as good a place as anywhere. This is a story about family – about loving, losing and being found again. One of the very earliest episodes in my life was being lost. I was just a baby. I was born in Islington in north London on 23 January 1942. The war was on. In fact it had been on for two and a half years when I had my first big adventure.

One evening during an air-raid alert the family had to go to the shelter with all the children, rushing to get in as the siren rang out. The smallest children, including me, were squeezed together into prams and pushed inside. When they did a head-count of the children inside, I was missing. My mother was frantic and screaming. A brave man went out and found me in the street and carried me to the shelter. That's how Mum told it to me, when I was old enough to understand. I loved hearing this story, particularly the part about how overjoyed she was to have me back.

A little later it was the time when the flying bombs were coming over London. It was just after D-Day. My first memories are of cowering inside the coal cellar on the occasions when we couldn't get to the air-raid shelter in time. The children were put inside a kind of upturned metal table with wire mesh round it, the idea being that if a bomb hit the house, the rescuers could dig down through the rubble and perhaps save any children protected by the metal basket. We were in there plenty of times but we never got blown up. My mother was shocked when I told her I remembered that in such detail. I must have been about eighteen months old.

Dad met Mum when she was young, about sixteen. Dad was twenty years older. He saw Mum the first time when she was riding on a London tram and hanging on to the handrail as it clattered along. She must have been very pretty. He was driving a flashy convertible, and followed the tram and waited for her to get off. That as far as I know was the first time they met. I always liked that story too.

Dad had always been a natural showman. Just before the war they'd lived in a big, mock-Tudor house in Chingford. He'd built a greyhound-racing track in Edmonton, promoted all-in wrestling. He'd made a fortune. Dad told me that for years he'd had a chauffeur to drive him round. But by the time I was born it was all gone.

Mum lost her first child, a girl, named little Nell. Eileen, Alfie, me and David came along soon afterwards. A few years later they also had George, Paul and Jane. So there were seven of us kids – although it was us three boys in the middle who made up the gang. We hung out together all the time.

Dad seemed to favour me a little more than the others; at least that's how it felt to me. I would sometimes get a beating from him with a cane. Even so I would think he still loved me. Dad would say, 'I've got to do this because my dad beat me in the same way.'

I wanted to show Dad I was brave; so one day when I was about eight years old I found a dead rat and I picked it up. I hid it behind my back and said, 'I'm brave, you know.' Dad looked at me curiously and said, 'I know you are, Bobby.' Then I showed him the dead rat I had in my hand. I was fully expecting to get praise for being so courageous. Instead I got a beating.

I was always trying to make my dad love me even more. I always thought I wasn't good enough to be worthy of his favour. I was going to spend a long while trying to make him proud of me. In the end it didn't matter too much. We had it tough but not as hard as some. The tougher things got, the more solidarity there was between me and my brothers. That was the comfort. That's what made the big separation, when it came later, so hard to bear.

The three of us – Alfie, David and I – were always very close. As children we would sleep in the same bed almost every night. Alfie would say, 'Witches' trick,' and we would all have to turn over simultaneously, our legs fitting together like a jigsaw because there was so little room in the bed. Before we went to sleep Alfie would remind us to say our prayers. This carried on right up to our early teens. When it was cold we would fill glass Tizer bottles with hot water to warm our beds.

By now we were living in the middle of London, in Lamb's Conduit Street, Holborn. The West End wasn't too far away. I was learning how to survive on the streets, how to earn money

– even if I got it wrong sometimes. One night I went to Russell Square tube station on Guy Fawkes Night to get a penny for the guy. It was very cold so Mum said I could put on her old fur coat. I wasn't getting much and I was just about to go home when this American soldier came along. He said he wouldn't give me anything for the guy but he would give me five shillings for the coat. It seemed like a good deal to me so I sold it, and ran home to give Mum the money. Well, she was not exactly pleased. She went out looking for the American but never did find him or the coat. It must have been worth a lot more than what I got for it. Mum never did tell Dad. I would have got a good beating if he had found out.

St Joseph's Roman Catholic was the first school I went to. It was on Macklin Street next to Covent Garden Market, and it was run by nuns. The nuns would give my brothers and me the cane when we were late, but I soon worked out a strategy to avoid this. I would pick up some flowers out of the market dustbins that still had some life in them and take them to the nuns to get their blessing. 'My child, how kind and thoughtful of you,' Sister Camilla or Sister Dominique would say to me, instead of punishing me for being late. But this kind of trick only got me so far. I never shone at school – I was always put at the back of the classroom so I was out of the way, especially when dignitaries came in to observe us. The clever girls were put up front. I hated the place. I didn't really learn to read, write, spell or even speak properly while I was there.

Then one day we discovered that Dad had another family living in Westcliff-on-Sea near Southend. He couldn't keep it hidden. We just heard Mum shouting: 'Go on then, you're always going off to see *her*.' It was the cause of a lot of argument between Mum and Dad. No surprise there. His other wife's name was Alice. He had other children although I still don't know how many. For some reason, I don't remember this bothering me too much. As long as he loved Mum and us best, and I believed he did, I didn't care.

Dad had lost everything after the war so he would duck and dive to get by. He was always into diamonds in a small way, but no one really knew what he was up to, not even us. Because Dad's attentions were divided and we always needed money, Mum would take in costume jewellery and we would glue cheap glass 'diamonds' on pieces to sell. We would all help out any way we could. In the summer we would go hop-picking in Kent. Six weeks working the hop fields and sleeping in wooden sheds.

As I grew up I continued to come up with new ways to help the family finances – as long as it didn't involve too much hard work. Alfie and David would do the same. There was a sense of 'all for one and one for all' in our little gang. We'd look out for each other whatever happened. I used to think I'd never keep a secret from my brothers. They'd know anyway, instinctively, I believed. Though of course one day that would all change.

But as kids, my brothers and I were all in it together. We would get rags, paper and cardboard and sell them to a man who would give us cash to help the family out. Sometimes we used the money to fund our escapades. More as an adventure than protest, we ran away from home when I was about twelve and got as far as Southend. We loved the Kursaal fairground, the sea and especially the big rock-candy sweets. Another time it was Epping Forest, always a big draw; climbing trees, getting lost… We would catch the Number 38 bus that took you right into the countryside and then all the way back to Holborn. That little jaunt got us a good beating off Dad.

By now I'd got a taste for wheeling and dealing and was getting much better at it. The street markets of the East End were the big draw. I would go down Petticoat Lane and Club Row with all the pets, pulling a pram-wheeled homemade cart loaded with junk – old clocks and gramophones and the like. I was about eleven years old at the time. The family tried to stop me because I would leave at five on a Sunday morning, rain or shine. The streets would be empty but I needed to get a good pitch and I knew that Mum needed the money.

Meanwhile I had started at Sir William Collins secondary modern school in Somers Town. I didn't last long. I couldn't stand it, and would just play truant. Alfie, David and I spent a lot of time playing in the bombed-out ruins when we should have been in class. The middle of London was still a big bomb-site. Everything was grey and brown and colourless and there was still rationing, although people were so poor it didn't make any difference. When I was eleven there was big street party for the coronation of Queen Elizabeth. Some people even watched it on the television, a novelty in those days.

You could tell better times were coming. But I could not wait that long. Street trading did not bring in enough for me, so eventually I started shoplifting and stealing bikes. I was a right villain, or thought I was. In fact there were lots of kids just like me.

Of course I got nicked. The case was heard at Chelsea Juvenile Court and I got sent to an approved school called Banstead Hall for nine months. It was horrible.

I went down with the mumps and Mum came to see me. She wore Yardley's pillar-box-red lipstick, a knitted jumper of the same colour and a flowery skirt. She was as immaculate as always, but I could see that the skirt had been mended several times over. She'd once worn furs and diamonds when Dad was rich but now she didn't have two pennies to rub together.

I was in bed in a hospital wing at the school. I had a fluorescent rosary in a little box on cotton wool and hidden underneath the cotton wool I had a half-crown coin. I gave it to her.

'I don't need it, Mum.' I told her. 'If I get found with it I'll be in trouble.'

Only then would she take it from me.

After six months I went on the run from Banstead Hall. After a few weeks of generally larking around, I needed money. This time I got a proper job – at Bentley's Oyster Bar on Swallow Street in Piccadilly. I was going to be a West End delivery boy. My bicycle had a big metal basket on the front.

One day a Rolls-Royce stopped in the middle of the road and the driver opened his door suddenly as I was coming up behind on my bike. Everything went flying, including me. The driver wanted to take me to the hospital. I was in terrible pain but I knew I couldn't go. After all, I was a fugitive from justice, a big-time criminal. The hospital casualty department would be full of policemen all waiting for me. In my head it was playing out like a gangster movie. Actually I was a petty bike-thief and a spectacularly unsuccessful oyster delivery boy.

In any case, my freedom turned out to be short-lived. I was staying at my aunt Mary's, my mother's younger sister. She lived opposite Great Ormond Street Hospital, round the corner from our old house. Not much of a hiding place. At the time Mum was living at Leigh-On–Sea, on the way to Southend. My aunt got news that she was ill, so off I went to see her. Good old Mum was in bed and not looking well. I stayed to help out as best I could. There was a lot of lace-curtain rustling in the houses nearby and I think some nosy neighbour must have noticed I was there. Two days later the police came knocking.

This time I was put into a real prison cell back in London – in Wormwood Scrubs – even though I was only fifteen years old and looked no more than twelve. It was terrifying. I couldn't stop crying. All the other cons would look through the peephole in the door of the cell to check out the crying kid.

Then I was taken to a detention centre, where I would await the juvenile court. The approved school had been so bad that I'd had to run away. This was much, much worse. I went through hell with regular beatings by a real sadist – the sort who got that kind of job just so he could take his sexual kinks out on young boys. I hated it, loathed it. I could understand that what I'd done was going to get me punished – but not like this.

My older brother Alfie came to see me. I told him what this man was doing to me and he was furious. I grabbed Alfie and said, 'Please don't do anything! When you leave he will beat the shit out of me.' Alfie understood and managed to hold his temper. I didn't get a kicking that time.

Eventually, two men arrived one morning to take me to court for the hearing. I was charged with stealing property worth forty quid. It seemed a long drive. I was handcuffed, sitting in the back of the car. One of them asked me: 'Why are you holding your stomach?'

'I'm in pain,' I replied.

'Did you see the doctor?' he asked. I shook my head.

He looked at me closely. 'How long have you had this pain?'

'A few days, after every beating.'

There was a folder on the front seat and the driver told the other man to take a look at it. He opened it immediately and read my notes. After a time the man reading the folder turned to me and said: 'They are going to stick you away in the worst place anyone could be put. I wish we could help. Sorry.' He was sympathetic but there was nothing he could do.

When I got to the court, in Dorking, Mum was there and when I saw her I just started to cry. I couldn't stop sobbing – so much that I had to be taken out. On the panel of the court there were two women and two men. I was sat outside the door while they were deliberating and I could hear the two women arguing with the men and saying they were not going to agree with their decision.

I know those two ladies saved my life. Instead of the 'worst place' possible I was sent to an approved school called Glamorgan Farm School, at Neath in Wales. It was the furthest I had ever been from home, but from that point on the beatings stopped – or at least they were not on as regular a basis as they had been at the detention centre.

Glamorgan Farm was on top of a hill. As soon as I got there one of the staff made it clear he fancied me and would follow me all over the place. If I were taking a shower and another guard was on the door, this man would come to the door and start talking to him, while openly staring at me. It was obvious what he was doing. I felt furious and desperately humiliated, but there was nothing I could do. He was a plump, short man called Mr Williams, and I hated him.

Boys at this school would sometimes get a chance to actually go off and live on a local farm and be paid for their labour. I volunteered and I must say I enjoyed it, especially the sense of freedom I experienced while driving a tractor up and down the Welsh hills. I was a hard worker and the farmer would let me and another boy have time out to go into the village to buy sweets and look in the shops. Then I was accused of stealing a watch – which I certainly had not. The watch later turned up. The farmer and his family said sorry and wanted me back – but on my side the trust had gone.

I was hurt and sad because I had hoped that this time I had found a job that I could be good at, but it was not meant to be. At this time of my young life, so much of it recently spent in various forms of detention, I desperately wanted control of my own destiny. I wanted to be free. But there was no more running away, even if I could. They'd caught me before and they would surely catch me again.

And so I finished my time in approved schools and was released. It was 1959. I was seventeen years old, with what might seem the experience of someone twice that age. I had been routinely beaten, abused and sexually preyed upon. Meanwhile I had learned how to stand up for myself. I thought I was tough. I thought I knew it all. In fact I was pathetically naïve. I still had so much to learn about the realities of the world.

I got work with a man who fitted out bars and pubs, but this didn't last long. Soon I gravitated to the West End of London and met an older lady by the name of Ruth, to whom I lost my virginity. I was seventeen and she was twenty-seven. She said she would show me all about sex, and she did.

About this time I also met a man known as 'Phil'. His full name, as I found out later, was Lieutenant-Commander Cecil Howard Filmer. He was quite a character, a Fleet Air Arm pilot war hero who'd been born in South Africa. He'd been an escapee from German prisoner-of-war camps. Phil had been at that camp in Poland, helping to dig the tunnel for the Great Escape, the story of which was later turned into a film. In the fifties he'd been a merchant ship skipper in the South Seas. Phil had a club called the Music Box which got raided one night for selling drinks to under-age kids, or something like that, and he lost his licence.

Now Phil was setting up a club called the Flamingo in a place called Sandown on the Isle of Wight. He asked if I would like to work as a waiter, along with a friend of mine by the name of John Quinn. We accepted and off we went south for the season. Phil was gay, but he never tried it on with me. He treated us as his sons and I am proud to have known him.

We all moved from Sandown to Shanklin and rented a flat on the esplanade. We started a beach summer rental business on two sites, hiring out motorboats, canoes and deckchairs. After the tourist season came to an end, that winter John Quinn and I joined the merchant navy. I became a steward on the *Queen Elizabeth*, the Cunard liner. It was all fine apart from a sexually predatory chief steward who used to chase the younger staff. I managed to 'escape' on to a freighter. I got my stuff together and went on board what looked to me like a rust-bucket ship that brought whisky from Scotland to New York.

I thought the ship would be heading straight back to London, but it had three more stops to make first: Philadelphia, Baltimore and Newport News in Virginia. At each stop we unloaded more whisky. On every trip from Scotland the ship had to carry one hundred extra cases of whisky to cover theft, breakages and bribes. I was told this was common practice. I soon learned I had come on board a ship with so many scams going on that I was not welcome, not at all.

I was asked many times by my other shipmates if I was going to sign up to stay on board. Like a fool, I said yes. About mid-Atlantic, coming back to London, I was asked again, did I intend to try to stay on board. Once more, I replied that I did. That night, when we were drinking whisky during a rough sea with the ship rolling all over the place, I started feeling very queasy even though I did not think I had drunk enough to feel that way.

As we were sitting there I made the mistake of saying I felt sick. Two men immediately got up and said they would take me up on deck. I was feeling so weak I went up the stairs with them but as soon as I got to the top of the deck I was overcome by a strong instinct that something was not right. I started to back off, saying, 'I'm OK, I feel OK,' even though I still felt terrible. But my instincts were right. At some unspoken signal they started to pull me and punch me with all their might, trying to drag me over the edge of the ship. Terrified, I seized hold of the steel handrail in a death grip, knowing if I let go I would be thrown overboard and that would be the end of me.

After a struggle that felt like it lasted for eternity but was probably only a couple of minutes, the two men eventually gave up. I watched out for them as I made my way unsteadily back to my bunk but they had probably gone back to drink some more. I did my utmost to avoid them for the rest of the voyage, keeping myself to myself. I found out later that one crewman goes missing and is never found again on almost all trips.

In spite of all that had happened, I had, I suppose, fallen in love with the sea. I loved being around small boats. I could never be far from open water. My dream was to live on an island. That part, at least, would come true.

But I got back to London with a sense of intense relief. I was about nineteen years old. I went home to Mum's house, in Holborn, desperate to see my family again. I knocked on the door but got no response. The lady next door looked out of her window and asked me who I was knocking for. I said I was looking for Mr and Mrs Teale. She told me they had moved, and slammed the window shut. I just stood there on the street, with my bags at my feet. I had never felt so alone.

I suppose I was used to this by now. Here I was, lost again. But I'd grown up a lot in the past two years. And so had the rest of London.

CHAPTER 2
PART OF THE FAMILY

I'd come back to London to find my family – and they were gone. It was devastating. I found another neighbour who said she thought they had moved to somewhere else in Holborn, but she was not sure where. Luckily I had a vague idea where my older sister Eileen lived, so I made my way there, eventually managing to track her down. It was such a relief to see a familiar face. She gave me a big hug and told me my family's new address.

There I found them: Mum, Dad, Alfie, David, George, Jane and Paul, my younger siblings. They were so pleased to see me that of course we had to have a party to celebrate. Alfie was still full of laughs but harder and more cynical somehow than when I'd seen him last. David had changed too. We weren't the mischievous kids running from the local coppers any more (and look how far that had got us).

After staying in London for a few days it was back off to Shanklin, to start fixing up the boats and deckchairs for the next season. I loved the winter and the deserted beaches and esplanade almost as much as the summer. There was one special boat that I spent a lot of time restoring. The old salt I bought it from told me it had been one of those that brought the British Army back from the beaches of Dunkirk in 1940. I renamed her *The African Queen*.

Did I want to watch the sunset, strolling on the beach through the surf? Or did I want bright lights, big city? I didn't know myself. But I did know that, even if the Isle of Wight was seemingly stuck forever in some pre-war time warp, London was changing fast. It was happening on the streets. Most of all, it was happening in clubs, the sort of places my brothers were going to.

Apart from nicking bicycles and going to reform school, I didn't know too much about big-time crime. But I was street-wise enough to have picked up the whispers. Our Dad used to tell stories about the old-time villains, the old West End firms run by men like Jack 'Spot' Comer, Billy Hill, Albert Dimes, the Sabini brothers. Their time was passing. In their place I heard there were a couple of new faces round Bethnal Green way, known as 'the twins'. They were supposed to be as hard as nails and had a reputation for extreme violence that had even managed to reach as far as the leafy squares of Holborn – even if it wasn't quite terrifying the Isle of Wight yet.

Mum and Dad came down to Shanklin for a day out now and then. I could see Mum could use a nice holiday so I told her that she, Dad, and the children should stay in a guest-house for two weeks and I would pay. Alfie and David came down too, full of stories about wild times in London and their smart and glamorous new friends. These included the infamous twins I was starting to hear so much about.

They were called the Krays. Reggie and Ronnie Kray. Because Ronnie commanded a little army of admirers, he was known as 'the Colonel'. Alfie was full of them.

'We've met some fellers from over in the East End,' he would boast. 'Big villains they are, the governors, you know what I'm saying? The real thing, they are, pretty much running all of London now. And we're their friends! We go round to their house, we know their mum and dad, the lot. Like family we are, already.'

I couldn't help but feel jealous. I tried to act uninterested but Alfie kept telling me more. 'Honest, Bobby,' he would say. 'If you go out with Ronnie and Reggie to a club or anything, everyone just gets out of the way and clears the best table for you. It's brilliant.'

The more I heard about it, the more I wanted to be part of it. I had so many questions. What are they like? How did you meet them? When am I going to?

I naturally looked up to Alfie. He'd been in trouble with the law like me; he'd grown up pretty fast and had been going down to clubs in Soho from his early teens. Mum worried, like she worried about all of us, but it was best she didn't know too much.

While I'd been putting out deckchairs, Alfie had already had the encounter that was going to change all our lives. It had happened in the summer of 1959. He had been having a drink in Soho, down in Jack Murray's bar, opposite the Freight Train in Berwick Street. It was about eight o'clock and absolutely dead when who should walk in but 'Mad' Teddy Smith.

Teddy was a face round the West End who Alfie knew only slightly. He had a reputation as a bit of a tearaway, especially when drunk, which was often. He was a sensitive soul the rest of the time and liked to think of himself as a writer. There were quite of few of those round Soho in those days.

Teddy suggested going to a club in the East End owned by some friends of his he thought Alfie would like. 'What's it called, this club?' Alfie had asked.

'It's the Double R, run by Ronnie and Reggie Kray,' replied Teddy.

Alfie had just about heard of the Krays. One day an old school-friend pulled up in a big car as Alfie was walking along the street and told him: 'You'd better be careful. You've got the Firm after you for giving Flash Harry a slap. He's one of theirs.'

The way Alfie remembered it, Flash Harry used to hang around the West End, a Mod before there were any. He wasn't a villain but he thought he was, and styled himself that way, bragging about who he was mates with.

'What's this Firm?' Alfie had asked.

'They're called the Kray twins and everyone is frightened of them,' the guy told Alfie. But back then Alfie couldn't give a monkey's.

There'd been stories about the Krays, of course – rumours, bits of gossip. They were older than us Teales, and had some sort of club in the Mile End Road. My brothers had no reason to give them a second thought. Anyway, did anybody go to east London for fun? Even East End taxi-drivers didn't go to the East End. At least it wasn't south of the river, where it really was the Stone Age.

But the way my brothers heard it, there was always action around the Krays, some kind of general hilarity, or punch-up or knife-fight – from which the twins would never once come out as the losers. So it was said. They'd been in and out of nick, apparently. And there was an older brother, too – Charlie Kray. He was married. The twins still lived with their old mum and dad in Bethnal Green.

Alfie was intrigued by the thought of going to the twins' club and having a chance to check it out for himself. So he and Teddy jumped in a black cab and went down the East End. They got to the Mile End Road and went into what looked to Alfie like an old tube station. When they got inside though, they could see it was absolutely beautiful, like the Astor Club in Berkeley Square, full of well-dressed men and women. It was so glitzy and glamorous – the decor, the velvet wallpaper, the chandeliers, the gay barmen with their smart bow ties… Everyone who was anyone in the East End was there. Wives sat there all done up to the nines, sipping cocktails with their families, everyone on best behaviour.

As Alfie stood there staring, drinking it all in, Teddy said to him: 'Come on, I'll introduce you to Ronnie.'

Alfie nodded. 'Yeah, I don't mind. Let's go over.' So they walked further into the club and there, at the centre of it all, sitting at the bar, was Ronnie Kray.

Ronnie was a little bit older than Alfie. He was heavily built with a fleshy, quite sensual face, and he was dressed in a navy mohair suit. He was sitting half turned so he could see the people coming in and survey the whole place as if from a throne. Reggie wasn't there. At the time he was away in prison, on a charge of demanding money with menaces from a north London shop-owner. Alfie later found out that in fact it was Reggie who had first opened the Double R Club when Ronnie himself had been away doing time for wounding with intent. The name of course was a tribute to his twin, to the two of them.

Ted said, 'Hello Ron! Here's a friend of mine, Alfie Teale.'

Alfie stepped forward and shook Ronnie's hand. 'Pleased to meet you, Ron,' he said. 'This is a lovely place you've got here.' Alfie felt pretty pleased with himself. He had no reason to feel in awe of Ronnie Kray.

'Thank you very much. Would you like a drink?' Ron said.

Alfie asked for a gin and tonic.

Ron asked Alfie where he lived. He replied that he came from Holborn.

'Oooh, Holborn. It's nice round there isn't it?' he said. The voice was high coming out of such a big body, but not overly effeminate. My brothers and I would be getting very used to the sound of that voice over the next few years. Alfie told him our mother had recently opened a club called the 66 in Upper Street and he said: 'Got a club, eh? I'd love to go there and meet her... Get him another drink. He's smart, very smart, you must come here again.'

Alfie was flattered. He *was* smart, despite having left school at fourteen and getting a job as a butcher's boy. Like me, he'd grown up fast and had found quicker ways to make money than cycling round Holborn delivering pork chops. By now he had a bit of experience as a petty thief, mainly in jewellery shops. He used to drive two Buicks at the time. He thought he was Elvis Presley. I used to catch him posing in the mirror, combing his hair and wiggling his hips whenever he came to stay with me.

As Alfie had revealed, Mum and Dad had indeed recently opened a nightclub. Their first one was called the Theberton Club near the Angel in Islington. I suppose it was a natural thing for Dad to do – he was always a showman, and Mum loved a bit of glamour. It was her stage and she was the star in the spotlight.

Everyone used to drink there. Small-time crooks, big-time crooks, market stallholders, coppers, the lot. It got very crowded so they soon moved round the corner to a bigger place called the 66 Club. It was above a clothes shop on Upper Street, a bit beyond Islington Green towards the Angel with the old Collins Music Hall just over the way. It was what you might describe as a little speakeasy. I was only there a couple of times but David and Alfie caught all the action.

Ronnie Kray obviously saw the possibilities in this new friendship with the son of these north London nightclub owners. By the end of that night in the Double R, Ronnie told Alfie directly how pleased he was that Teddy Smith had brought him there, what a shame it was that Reggie was away, and that it was good to see new people coming in. Alfie basked in the attention. He was twenty-one years old. Ron was five years older, a man of the world, a businessman, a face among faces.

Three days later Alfie got a phone call. It was Ronnie. Alfie had been expecting it. 'I thought I'd phone you up because I'd like you to come over to my house in Vallance Road and meet my mum and dad,' Ron said. 'You'll like my mum and dad.'

Alfie said: 'OK, Ron. What time?'

'Come over early,' Ron replied. 'I've got a bit of running about to do later.'

Alfie agreed to be there at nine o'clock. He was intrigued to know more about Ronnie Kray and his family. So the next morning he drove over to Vallance Road, parked his car round the corner, and knocked on the door. Ronnie's mum, Violet, answered the door and greeted Alfie warmly.

'Oh, you must be Alfie! Ron is over at the bath-house right now but he'll be back in ten minutes. Come in and wait in the kitchen and I'll make you a nice cup of tea.'

Alfie went into the kitchen and saw about ten or fifteen white shirts all immaculately ironed, hanging up on an old-fashioned indoor drying frame on a pulley. He sat amongst them awkwardly, drinking his tea, until eventually Ronnie came in.

'Hello, Mum,' he said, handing her the towels and soap he'd been using over at the bath-house. Then he turned to my brother. 'Hello Alfie! You met Mum then?'

Alfie said he had and what a lovely lady she was. Ron then turned to her and said: 'Make me a nice bit of breakfast, Mum. You'll have some, Alfie, won't you?'

Ron sat down with Alfie and started telling him about the caravans the family had got down at a place called Steeple Bay in Essex, where they often used to go at weekends. In the meantime Violet Kray rustled up two plates of smoked haddock and poached eggs with bread and butter. Alfie ate it up with relish, enjoying the company of his new friend. It already felt like he was part of the family.

Alfie started telling Ron more about our parents' new club, the 66. It was nothing like as luxurious as the Double R, of course, but it was a nice, clean family club. Alfie proudly told Ronnie how well it was doing.

'Oh, that's good,' said Ronnie. 'I must come up there and meet your mum and dad. Do you mind? We'll take a couple of friends up and have a nice drink with them. That will be nice, won't it?'

Alfie wasn't dumb. He knew what Ron had on his mind, and realised that he was thinking of the 66 for little private meets. But he couldn't see the harm in it. In fact, Ronnie quickly made the club his second home. My parents didn't mind either. Dad used to sit down with Ronnie and tell him stories about all the old gangsters he had known.

Ronnie was intrigued, saying: 'I knew a few of them.' And Ronnie did. When he was still a teenager he used to work for Jack Spot and Billy Hill. It was his apprenticeship. Jack Spot taught him the golden rule: 'Only nick from thieves; that way you'll never get nicked.'

So that's what the twins did – they moved in on anyone who was vulnerable. They called it a 'pension', a slice of every bit of dodgy business, every tickle, every bit of profit from a deal. Their main interest was clubs.

Clubs were everything in London at the time, the way the laws on prostitution and gambling had changed in the late fifties. Grafters [prostitutes] couldn't pull their punters on the streets any more without being arrested, they'd do it indoors, and at the same time you could now gamble in 'licensed premises'. You could make big money. To run one you just had to find some premises, get a drinks licence and square the local coppers. Then there was the little matter of 'protection' – keeping out troublemakers. But who was it making all the trouble?

If you had an interest in a club and had a criminal record you didn't want anyone knowing about, you were easy meat. Anyone who had their own reason not to involve the police could be got at. And that was a lot of people.

Putting out the deckchairs in the Shanklin sunshine, it all seemed a world away from my quiet life. But every time Alfie came out to visit me he would regale me with stories of going out with his new friend. Soon Ronnie was phoning him up all the time. He would tell him: 'Come on, we're going to the Pigalle, or Churchills, the Astor, the Celebrity, the Society, Danny La Rue's…' Alfie's favourite place, which he used to go to four or five times a week, was called Talk of the Town. It had a stage that came up out of the floor and swirled round. Alfie swore that the women in there were the most beautiful he'd ever seen.

Going out to a club with Ronnie was like being with royalty, Alfie said. If a place was full, an empty table, freshly laid, would magically appear. Service was instant. When that first happened to Alfie, he thought he was a big boy, one of the chaps, one of the villains. 'We'll pay for it later,' Ron would say at the end. But no money would ever change hands. And it went on from there. First it was protection, a club owner having to pay the

Firm to make sure there was no trouble. Then the Firm would become 'staff'. Then all of a sudden the place would be theirs.

Well, we, the Teale family, were in the club business, even if I didn't have much to do with it at the time. That's how Mum and Dad made their living. And now we were on the Krays' takeover list.

CHAPTER 3
DOWN THE 66 AND UP THE WEST END

So that's how my brother Alfie met the big bad Ronnie Kray. While I was scraping barnacles off the bottoms of pleasure boats, he was now one of 'the chaps', posing around the West End clubs with his new friends. Meanwhile, my younger brother, David, had also had his first big meet with Ronnie. It was at our mum's club, the 66, where he was looking after the door. It was David's job to let the right people in and keep the undesirables out.

One night there was some loud banging on the door at the bottom of the stairs. Our mum called out to David: 'We're closed.'

David opened the door to the street and said to the two men standing there, 'No, you can't come in,' and shut the door in their faces. But they banged and banged until eventually David was forced to open the door on its thick metal chain. Peering through the gap, one of them said to him: 'D'you know who I've got here with me? It's the Colonel.'

'I don't care who it is,' David replied. 'My mum said you can't come in so that's it. We're finished, we're closed.' And he shut the door again.

Just at that moment Alfie came downstairs to ask what was going on, and hearing the Colonel's name, he said very quietly to David, 'Oh God! You'd better open the door – it's Ronnie Kray.'

Poor David had to let them in and went and sat in the kitchen at the back, feeling very embarrassed. He didn't even know who Ronnie Kray was. Alfie quickly filled him in. The man who'd done the talking was Dickie Morgan, a friend of Ronnie's since his misdemeanour-filled National Service days. David had never heard of him either.

David was still the kid brother, really. Alfie was the grown-up. I had gone off to seek my fortune at sea and had now disappeared off to some island. David was barely seventeen years old and didn't know much. He knew so little he didn't know how much he didn't know.

Like me and Alfie, David had never really been to school. He went once or twice and hated it, mainly because he just couldn't understand what he was being taught. At the time he just assumed that he must be stupid. Certainly, that's what everyone told him.

Also like me, David had been sent to an approved school, after being caught selling stolen cigarettes. Joining the boxing club was his one release, but I know he had a hard time there, just like I did.

In the end he spent just over two years there. He got back to Liverpool Street station with his few possessions in a small bag, and made his way home to Theberton Street near the Angel, where our family then lived. No one made much fuss of him when he got back, apart from Alfie and Mum, who both looked up with a sort of 'Oh, it's you' expression when he walked in. David was fifteen when he came back, and had changed from being a child to a young man while he'd been away.

When he was about sixteen, David got a job as a waiter on a ship that took emigrants to Australia. When that ended, he came back to London and started working the door at our mum's club. And now he had just tried to turn away Ronnie Kray. Alfie did not hesitate to explain to our younger brother what a major mistake he had just made.

David got over his embarrassment and went back into the main room of the club, where he saw a man in a flash suit laughing and joking, sitting up at the bar.

'Come over here and sit with me,' he said. 'I do like it here. It's lovely and private.' Nervously, David perched on a bar stool next to Ron.

'Well done, son, you're a good boy,' Ronnie continued. 'You look after your mother, and if your mother says don't let anyone in, you don't. I need someone like you in our clubs.'

That was it. Ron stayed until about four in the morning, drinking brown ales one after another. After that he started coming up the 66 Club night after night, bringing people to meet my brothers. It was that way David and Alfie got to meet the rest of the Firm. It was that way they got to understand how he was the undisputed commander of this little army. They all called Ronnie 'the Colonel'. He loved it. Soon I'd be calling him that too.

He kept insisting that David come and see one of his clubs, but although David didn't know at first that Ronnie was gay, he was instinctively wary of his interest. His own sexual inclinations certainly didn't lie that way – in fact, he was already seeing a girl at the time. But Ronnie was like a stalker. He would lay siege to someone or something until he got it.

By now Ronnie was coming to our mum's club at least four times a week. At first it was all very friendly up the 66. Ronnie especially loved our old man and he was very fond of our mother too. He'd call her Nell. He thought our mum was like his and Reggie's mother, which she was. She was a very loving woman who adored her sons.

As much as Ronnie would come to the 66, so Alfie and David would regularly be summoned to wherever he was. If they didn't come immediately he'd send a car round for them. Sometimes it was to go to another club, sometimes to Vallance Road. Whatever it was the Colonel wanted, you couldn't refuse. It seemed Violet Kray liked the idea of my brothers being there because it made Ron happy. She would greet the two of them with: 'Oh, Ronnie will be pleased to see the pair of you. Come in the kitchen, and I'll make you a lovely cup of tea.' She would always steer them away from the room where the Firm would be meeting.

'Do you want a sandwich?' she would smile.

'Yes please, Mrs Kray. Thank you so much, Mrs Kray,' my brothers would dutifully reply.

About this time, Reggie was released from Wandsworth Prison on bail pending an appeal. So where do the Krays come to celebrate? To the 66 Club, of course. And that was where Alfie and David first met Reggie.

Reggie liked them both straight away. He was a lot like Ronnie, obviously. People thought he was the serious one, the not-quite-so-crazy twin who had ideas about running a legitimate club and entertainment business in a way that didn't always end with someone being hit over the head or smashed in the jaw. But it was Ronnie who had the power. It was Ronnie who was the real 'character'. He was the 'Colonel'.

Meanwhile I continued to stay happily down on the Isle of Wight working at the boat business. David and Alfie were now coming down to see me every couple of weeks, helping me with the work, and staying with me in the seafront flat that Johnny Quinn and I shared in Shanklin, above a place called the Radcliffe Restaurant.

They'd come over even more in the spring, as that was when I really needed help getting ready for the summer season. They got themselves officially registered as 'longshoremen', meaning that if ever a boat got into trouble, the coast guards could call on us for help.

While my brothers and I worked recovering deckchairs, or taking the launch out, we'd be chatting all the time about what was happening to them in London – about the latest doings of Reggie and Ronnie. I pretended not to be that interested, getting on with working on an engine or something without saying much. But in my mind I was becoming quite jealous. The way Alfie and David told it, there were lots of women, loads of booze and lots of partying. I compared it to my own existence. Trips round the bay.

It was around this time that the Krays made their big move Up West. London in the early sixties was all about gambling clubs. Changes in the law were supposed to clean up illegal gambling but the new laws made these clubs magnets for rake-offs and extortion rackets, as the twins had already found to their advantage. This time they were going to run their own place and no one would be stupid enough to try to stop them. It was called Esmeralda's Barn.

There was the East End, there was Islington, there was Holborn and there was Soho – in a straight line, east to west. That was our universe, the London we knew best. But there was a world beyond that, too: Mayfair, Knightsbridge, the West End. Alfie got an old-fashioned Armstrong Siddeley limousine and used to drive around west London feeling quite at home. But it wasn't all lords and ladies in that part of town.

Around Bayswater and Paddington, there were lots of villains and lots of grafters. The Vienna Rooms in the Edgware Road is where the old faces like Jack Spot and Billy Hill used to hang out – and where the Krays used to come and learn from the masters. And then there was Notting Hill, filled with streets and squares of crumbling tenanted houses. This was the territory of Peter Rachman, the infamous slum landlord.

To get in with the Krays – and you had to be in with the Krays – Peter Rachman had introduced them to a man called Stefan de Faye, who had a gambling club in Knightsbridge. The

Krays naturally enough just took it over. They had a new face around, a geezer called Leslie Payne who'd been a sergeant in the war. He was some sort of money-man adviser to the twins – what the Mafia in America called a 'consigliere'. He helped them to run their new acquisition, Esmeralda's.

The club was in Wilton Place and the twins just took over the management one day with its staff and membership none the wiser. David and Alfie used to go there a lot. The casino was on the top of three floors with a restaurant beneath and the Cellar Club beneath that. That was a disco for lesbians.

Reggie was away again (he was back in Wandsworth for six months, his appeal having been turned down) and Ronnie was not getting very far without him. He didn't have clue about gambling. The customers kept coming, however. I suppose they found it amusing to be in a place run by gangsters. The men were in evening dress, black tie, and the women were in pearls. But if Ronnie didn't like a punter, he'd be thrown down the stairs. It was all part of the entertainment.

As Alfie and David would tell me, what Ronnie really liked about Esmeralda's Barn was seeing what he'd call the 'flash cunts' losing money. Management was a joke, with all the decisions being based on Ron's whims. Punters would have no credit left but Ronnie would still let them gamble if he liked the look of them. The club attracted lots of well-dressed women with their boyfriends, most of them Guards officers because the Household Division cavalry barracks was just round the corner. Alfie and David would look at the women and wonder who they were with, and whether they could try it on with them.

They were pretty wild, the times at the Barn. There was one punter (whose face Ronnie later sliced open with a sword when he had failed to pay) who traded a gambling debt for a lease for Ronnie on a flat in Kensington. It was in Ashburn Gardens. It all seemed a long way from Bethnal Green. Ronnie set up there with his boyfriend, a face called Bobby Buckley.

But it wasn't long before Ronnie moved back to his mum's house. Then Reggie came out of prison once more and the twins started arguing again. Ronnie put a caravan at the back of Vallance Road on some old bomb-site. It was like a garden shed, somewhere to go and sulk when they'd had a row.

Meanwhile their business empire continued to grow. As well as running the gambling club, Leslie Payne's main job was to supervise the Krays' latest venture, an old fraud called 'a long firm'. Leslie was the brains behind it. One day Alfie was taken to the front room in Vallance Road to meet him.

Leslie looked the part, immaculately dressed and presented. He could have fronted anything. He was a smart, blond man of about thirty, with the good looks of an actor. He lived in south London, Tulse Hill, and had a family. He was going to teach Alfie everything he knew. And it turned out he was a master of his craft.

It was a simple scam, really. There was a front man who would set up a business. He'd find premises, a warehouse, and he would get stationery printed, set up lines of credit and a bank account and then begin to trade.

Alfie was one of the front men. He'd ring up a wholesaler and say: 'I'll have whatever it is in three colours, blue, green and white, and more in medium than large as that will sell more.' The man at the other end would rub his hands in anticipation of the big deal, not knowing he was never going to see a penny profit from any of it. Thirty days' credit was the usual.

At first the transactions would be for relatively small amounts, with the front man building up trust with the wholesaler. When the time was right the operation would place larger orders with the suppliers. The stuff would then be sold off in a matter of hours for cash at any price, because everything must go. A huge sum might be cleared in just one day. The warehouse would be abandoned and everyone would vanish.

At the end, when the whole lot went missing, Alfie would have to front it out and say he'd spent it all. He'd say he was a drunkard and a loser and he'd pay it back when he could. There was nothing the supplier could do.

There was another kind of scam, according to Alfie. Whenever the twins found themselves short of money, Ronnie would say: 'Let's get everyone over and declare a charity.'

Ronnie would then have a big party, getting all the rich people he knew to donate large amounts of money, which was supposedly for children or old people or some other worthy cause. But in reality it he'd siphon off a thousand or so of it straight into his pocket.

Big-hearted Ronnie liked to cultivate a reputation for sudden, spontaneous acts of charity – having first ensured the photographers would be there, of course. What my brothers were beginning to realise, if they hadn't done so already, was his equal capability for sudden acts of extreme violence. They were being drawn in. They weren't yet part of the Firm themselves, but were getting close to being so.

CHAPTER 4
A CASUAL VIOLENCE

Gradually, my brothers were being lured deeper and deeper into the Krays' twisted world. David told me stories about how Ronnie would arrive at the 66, walk through the door and hand him and Alfie a couple of guns – 'a Beretta or a Luger'. He'd have to look after them for him, hiding them in the oven, the fridge, or anywhere else he could think of.

It was a big thrill at first, according to Alfie. My brothers didn't know much about guns, although pretty soon they would learn. It was just a way of luring them in, into the Firm, although they never considered themselves a real part of it. It just seemed so cool to be strutting around with an automatic tucked into the waistband of a smart suit.

David admitted to me that he would often be tooled up if they went in a club, carrying guns for the Colonel in case he needed one. 'We just sit there having a drink, while the Colonel does the business,' he would tell me. 'It's only happened to me once when he actually asked me for it.' David told me Ron had got up from his table and as he passed him on the way to the gents, he had nodded to David to follow him. 'Giss that,' he had said, taking the gun from my brother – but he never used it. Not on that occasion, at least.

At the time I thought this kind of talk was fantastic. Any young man would, I suppose. I'd had been to sea and thought I was pretty tough, but this was like something out of the movies. I wanted to be part of it. David told me more: how Ronnie would tell them to go down to some club and cause havoc. 'Smash it up, start a fight, get drunk,' he'd order my brothers. Ronnie and Reggie would then come into the club they'd just trashed and say to the owners, 'We can deal with all that. You give us a little pension, we'll sort all that out. You won't have any more trouble…'

One day Ronnie told my brothers: 'Listen, you two! Go back down the West End and do anything you like. If you want to take clubs over, do it, if you want to take over all the porno stuff there, do it. If you want to take over all the after-hours drinking clubs, do that too. And if anyone tries to stop you, or threatens you, just come back to us in Vallance Road and it gives us an excuse to go and get them.'

It was exhilarating, exciting, head-turning stuff. My brothers relished telling me these stories and in turn I lapped it up. But some of their stories chilled me to the bone.

One night David was having a drink with Ron in a club when a rich fence they knew had a few too many and started laughing to himself about how he had kept a lock-up garage round the corner for years, which the police believed belonged to Ronnie.

Ronnie turned round to the man and, still smiling at him, said: 'Ten years you've had it? And the police thought it was mine? I reckon that's £10,000 you owe me.'

There was an uncomfortable silence while the man searched for the right response. Ronnie just stared at him, waiting, still smiling. Then right in front of David, Ronnie took out a gun and shot the man straight in the foot. As his victim started to scream in agony, Ronnie stood over him, laughing, as if it was nothing. David and the other men present backed away, shaken.

Minutes later the same man appeared, limping, beside David, who was now over at the bar trying to steady his nerves. 'Get us a drink?' he asked. Ronnie followed, calmly telling one of the Firm: 'Set him down on that chair over there. Give him a light ale and a whisky and then take him in the car and drop him outside the hospital to get fixed up.'

As the man left the club, Ronnie called after him, 'And don't forget my ten grand, will you?'

As well as taking over the 66 Club as a sort of neutral territory, Ronnie would frequently use David's car because he thought all the others he had access to were being watched. David became his driver a lot of the time, taking him anywhere he wanted to go. Ron loved having my good-looking younger brother driving him all over the place.

If Ronnie wanted something, he had to have it. David would get to know about that little aspect of Ronnie's personality, because unfortunately Ron wanted him. But it wasn't just people. It was anything. If there was a club he fancied it would just be: 'Oh look, this club would do us,' and that would be it.

He never mentioned money. One of the Krays' clubs, the Green Dragon in Stepney, had been taken over like that. Soon they were in there all the time.

David was in the 66 one night, when Big Pat Connolly – a member of the Firm who was effectively next in command after Ronnie and Reggie – came in and said he was wanted at the Green Dragon. So off David went to Brick Lane.

It was a private club, which meant you had to sign members in to keep your alcohol licence and stay legal. When David got there, Ronnie was sitting at a table, with his older brother, Charlie Kray, and some of the Firm. David didn't know it but Reggie was away again, in prison. They all sat down and had a drink. Ronnie asked David, 'What do you think, David? Lovely club, isn't it?'

'Yes Ronnie, it's lovely.'

With that, three drunks came stumbling in, signing their names at the door. Whatever they'd written, the girl at the desk wasn't having it. She came over to Ronnie and read him what they'd put in the visitor's book. The three of them had written 'Dickie Bird' as their names, and their addresses as 'Up a tree.'

Ron said, 'Oh, right.' He went up to them and had a word.

'You're not Dickie Birds, are you?'

'What do you mean, mate? Who are you?' one answered back.

'And you don't live up a tree, do you?' Ronnie continued, ignoring him. 'Sign your names in properly next time.' And with that – wallop! Ronnie took a swing, and like a cartoon, the three drunks fell over, one by one, into a heap on the floor.

Ronnie just sighed and, walking up to the bar while dusting his hands down, said 'Giss a drink, will you?' to the stunned barman.

That was David's first real introduction to the casual nature of Ronnie's violence. Nobody moved to stop him, nobody said it was wrong. He behaved like it was nothing to knock three men out stone cold. It was just another day at the office. David was beginning to get it. This was just how Ronnie was all of the time. Did it give life that extra edge? Or were he and Alfie going somewhere they really didn't want to go?

It carried on from there. That was the way Ronnie did things. If you were out of order in any way you knew what to expect. You had to be respectable, and respectful. There was only one rule, and that was that you did exactly as Ronnie said. And that was whatever happened to come into his head.

Another time, David told me, he was in Esmeralda's at closing time when Ronnie asked him to drop him and Mad Teddy Smith off at the Regency Club – a Kray favourite in Stoke Newington – which five years later would become infamous as the starting point of the Jack the Hat murder.

Smithy got in the back, Ron in the front. Coming along Shaftesbury Avenue, David noticed a police car was following them, and pointed it out to Ron.

Teddy said, 'I've got a tool on me, Ron.'

Ronnie answered, 'So have I.'

David couldn't believe what he was hearing. He gaped at his passengers.

'Just drive careful. Don't look round,' Ronnie said. His voice was calm.

David started to panic. 'Look, Ron, I can see them in the mirror, the Old Bill. They're going to pull us,' he said.

Ron said, 'If they stop us, I'm going to kill them.' He wasn't so calm now.

Terrified, David begged him, 'Please, please don't do that!' He was shouting.

Ron just kept repeating, 'No, I am… I really mean it.'

And he did. In that moment David saw himself being caught up in the middle of a police killing. They hanged you for that in those days. Drenched in sweat, his mind racing, David turned sharply off the main road to try to lose them. Eventually he managed to duck in and out of a few side-turnings and got rid of them.

Arriving at the Regency, to David's great relief, Ron told him: 'You know, I would have shot the fucking lot of them.'

David could only reply, 'Ron, you know you're not all the ticket! I'm off.'

As he left, Ron said, as if nothing had happened: 'Be round the house in the morning.'

And of course David was. That's how Ron worked. You had to do what you were told or else something very unpleasant would occur. Everyone knew it.

By now Ronnie was using the 66 Club like it was his front room. All the rules had changed to Ronnie's rules. There was a big cellar at the back, where David used to put all the beer. It was like a big strong-room, or a cell. Once you were in there you couldn't get out. All concrete, no windows. If anyone was out of order, Ronnie would put them in there and leave them there, often all night. Sometimes people ended up being kept down there for days. That was just a playful slap.

David would tell me about more extreme punishments too. There was a certain face who owed Ronnie some money. Ronnie had the hump with him. So he got some thugs to take this man on to the flat roof of the club and dangle him by the legs off the back of it. They held him off the side by his feet while Ronnie said: 'Now you know what's coming to you next time.' Then they put him down the cell.

But it could go either way in the twins' company. It could be terrifying one moment and hilarious the next. David once brought a very good-looking friend of his called Johnny into the 66 one evening. Ronnie noticed him immediately. 'Who's he?' he asked, the moment he walked in. Following a brief introduction David took Johnny up to the bar for a drink.

Suddenly Johnny started nudging David, and whispering in a panic-stricken voice: 'That man over there – he keeps looking at my arse. He's a back-passage merchant. I've got to get out of here.' By the time Ronnie started asking for him, Johnny was already in a taxi on his way home. He didn't know what a lucky escape he'd had.

This wasn't the only time David's friends had a close brush with Ronnie. One night the Krays were doing some business upstairs when three or four old school-friends of his turned up at the door of the 66. Knowing Ron wouldn't want them in that night, David tried to tell them to leave. As they were talking, Ron appeared at the top of the stairs to ask him what was going on. When David told them it was his friends and he was trying to get rid of them, Ron's mood suddenly went sour, and he snarled, 'Go on, open the door – I'm going to do them!'

Terrified that Ron would be as good as his word, David slammed the door shut in their faces. The following day David ran into his friends again near Cambridge Circus. They started to have a go at him, saying, 'That's a nice way to treat your old friends, to slam the door in our faces!' David told them the Krays had been there and asked them if they'd ever heard the name before. His friends said they hadn't. David told them that they were lucky to be alive. It was true.

Ronnie's capacity for violence, as the whole world would hear one day, was unusual to say the least. Years before, in prison on assault charges, he had been transferred from Winchester Jail to a mental hospital. Here the doctors decided he had suffered a schizophrenic breakdown, which powerful drugs might be able to treat.

The doctors missed the paranoid bit. Ronnie absconded with Reggie's help and managed to hide in a caravan on a farm in Suffolk owned by an insurance fraudster called Geoff Allen (whose house I would later visit). Mad Teddy Smith fetched and carried for him. It couldn't last long. After a few weeks he went back to prison and after a few months more, Ronnie was 'returned to society'. That was back in 1959. But his instability was always smouldering just beneath the surface.

In 1961 Reggie found himself arrested again, for housebreaking this time. But the woman who had filed the charges failed to identify him in court and the case was dismissed. They had a big party. There was always a party. Then a few weeks later they were charged with 'loitering with intent to steal' – by trying the doors of cars somewhere in Hackney. As if they'd do that. Again they got off, claiming police harassment. There was another big party that night, 8 May 1961, at Esmeralda's Barn.

Ronnie proposed a toast to 'British Justice' and all the journalists and photographers were given champagne. The Krays for the first time were national news. The papers the next day carried a big article about 'the celebrated boxing twins', which was what they were famous for at first – they had once had some success as boxers before their criminal record and dishonourable discharge from the army brought an end to their careers. The papers proudly proclaimed their declaration to 'go straight'.

And this time it seemed Reggie really seemed to want to go straight. He spent much of the summer at a place called Steeple Bay, on the Thames estuary in Essex, where the family had a caravan. I'd get to know about it one day. There was girl called Frances Shea from Hackney who came down for weekends. Alfie knew her brother, Frankie Shea. She was sixteen and Reggie was twenty-seven. She seemed to offer Reggie the opportunity to make a different life.

But it was clear to Alfie that Ronnie, who disliked all women except his mother, saw Frances as a threat. She would tell his brother what time to come home in the evening – just like Charlie's wife, Dolly, did – much to Ronnie's disgust. The way he saw it, that's what all women did.

The next summer, 1962, the twins opened their latest club. It was called the Kentucky, and it was located in Stepney, just across from the ABC Empire cinema at 106a Bow Road. It was supposed to be a posher version of the Double R, which had shut down when its drinks licence renewal was refused. The East End was suddenly getting a bit trendy. But to prove it you had to get faces in – proper faces, not just some old boxers like the Krays were always being photographed with. They wanted pop singers, film stars, people their old mum had seen off the telly.

They employed their old army chum, Dickie Morgan, to cruise the West End to persuade celebrity customers to head east. From what Alfie told me, Dickie was dreadful at it. My brothers were meant to do the same, to get faces in. David managed to get Colin Hicks (Tommy Steele's brother) and two tap dancers from America called the Clark Brothers. They used to sing as well, but Ronnie never gave them any money. Once they complained about the lack of pay and Ronnie said: 'Here, give them a fiver for their cab fare home.'

But the club did come good one time. The premiere of the film *Sparrers Can't Sing* was held at the Empire in Bow Road, on 27 February 1963. The whole Firm was told to attend, including their wives. Alfie and David were there too, of course. Princess Margaret was meant to be present, but Lord Snowdon turned up without her. People were told she had flu. Maybe her bodyguards wouldn't let her go down the East End.

There were jellied eels and mash at Queen Mary College over the road, then it was all back to the Kentucky Club so everyone could have their photos taken with the twins. Not Lord Snowdon, sadly. Perhaps he'd been warned off. All the women, including the film's star, Barbara Windsor, were done up in furs and diamonds. She wasn't that famous then but soon would be. My brothers told me she was laughing that dirty laugh of hers and trying hard not to swear too much.

Frances Shea was there with Reggie along with James Booth and George Sewell, the male stars of the film. Alfie had persuaded Victor Spinetti, the actor, to come. The singer Lenny Peters out of Peters and Lee was there, but there weren't the really big stars that Ronnie wanted. I don't know who he was expecting. Did he really think Elizabeth Taylor was on her way to join him and Reggie for a brown ale?

Ronnie went mad. It was his big night. It just wasn't big enough. They went back to Esmeralda's Barn in Knightsbridge for even more drinking.

In any case, the Kentucky did not last long after its turn in the spotlight. Just like the Double R, the police objected to the renewal of the club's licence. The Kentucky closed. But pretty soon Ron took the 66 Club off our mother. He promised to buy it: 'I'll sort the money out later,' he said. But of course he never did.

Dad was too old to make much of a fight of it. Mum was heartbroken. She loved the business and she wasn't yet forty. It was the family's living and there were still loads of young ones to support. It would have been a nice little earner, just at the time the London club scene was booming. But now it was lost to us. And because my brothers and I were off doing our own stuff, making our own way in the world, we couldn't badmouth the Krays too much, despite our private reservations about what had happened.

By this time the Double R, the club in the Mile End Road, was long over (the licence was not renewed by the local authorities), but Ronnie still had the Green Dragon in Stepney and Esmeralda's Barn in Knightsbridge. And now he had the 66. He felt safe round our mother's and he was on the plot, in the area that he wanted, on the way towards the West End.

Alfie told me what Ronnie used to say about Mum's club. 'This is perfect for us,' he would smile. 'A nice straight, clean little club, the ideal place to make a meet.' His enemies didn't know about it – it was a place no one would dream of looking for him.

Meanwhile Alfie had got into the club scene himself as a partner in a place called the Two Decks in Rupert Court, on the south side of Shaftesbury Avenue in Soho. I never saw it, but I know he'd fitted out the place like a ship, with portholes, brass lamps, that sort of thing. And I was the one who liked boats. He got some big names in there, he told me: Danny La Rue, Frankie Howerd, Victor Spinetti, Shirley Bassey, Brian Epstein. He did well with it.

Alfie confessed to me how much of the time he'd spend drinking away the profits in company with some serious Soho drinkers – like the painter Francis Bacon, the actor John Hurt and the composer Lionel Bart. He told me he'd never let Ronnie near the Two Decks. If he had found out about it, he would have moved in, just as he and Reggie always did. To make the point, Alfie told me the story about what happened with his tailor friend, Paul of Berwick Street.

Ronnie was always admiring my brothers' suits. So one day he told Alfie he wanted some suits made and asked him to arrange for Paul to come round to his flat and to bring some samples of material. David was there too, followed by Ronnie, Charlie and a few other members of the Firm. At that time Reggie was away.

Sitting down in Alfie's front room, Ronnie ordered about twenty-five suits, telling Charlie to pick out two or three for himself as well some for the rest of the Firm. Paul was very pleased, thanking Ronnie and arranging fittings for the following week.

So the next week everyone was back at Alfie's flat again. Alfie watched Paul getting the suits out of the boot of his car. He then laid them out one by one over the back of Alfie's sofa, with the labels marking out who each one belonged to: 'Ronnie', 'Charlie', 'Teddy' or whoever. Paul then fitted the suits on each member of the Firm, tearing the arms out of the jackets the way tailors do and hanging each one up carefully on the dado rail afterwards. Two weeks later another fitting was arranged, at which point Paul politely asked Ronnie if he could have some money as a deposit in order to finish off the work.

Ronnie's expression turned murderous and, picking Paul up by the throat, he snarled, 'Don't you ever ask me for money again. If I feel like it, I'll send Alfie round with something for you. Now just get the suits finished!'

Ronnie and Charlie got their suits. But Ronnie never gave Alfie any money for Paul – and my brothers lost the best tailor they ever had.

CHAPTER 5
BUNGS AND BODIES

By 1963 Ronnie had got tired of Vallance Road and the caravan round the back, and had moved into an apartment in a block of flats called Cedra Court in Upper Clapton. Our mum and dad were already living there – they had got a flat through the Freemasons. My parents found Ronnie a gaff there, number 8 on the first floor. Reggie got a flat on the ground floor. A face called Leslie Holt lived upstairs. That nice, respectable block of flats was going to see some very strange goings-on.

Ronnie was fantasising about being a legitimate business-man. Reggie was actually doing something about it, making plans to go into betting shops and restaurants – even a 'security' firm. The money-man Leslie Payne had really got them at it. But the first thing they needed to do was button up the police even tighter. Even if they had vague intentions of going legit, the Old Bill were all as crooked as the criminals they were ostensibly trying to catch. In those days you couldn't run a club unless you gave a bung to the local police or they'd close you down. That's what our dad did when he was still running the 66, all the time, just in order to stay open.

So the Krays needed my brothers all the more. They had David and Alfie running all sorts of errands. Moving people, moving guns, moving money. After we'd lost the 66, Alfie had to set Mum up in a new business, a pie and mash shop in Stoke Newington. Perhaps it was just as well, because under the new management the 66 was now the Krays' back office, ideal for discreet meets with the Old Bill.

But these were not just the local coppers from the Upper Street nick. This was West End Central and the Yard. My brother David saw it all for himself. He was in the 66 early one afternoon when two men rang the doorbell. David let them in. He'd already been told they were coming by Ron. 'I've got someone coming in tomorrow, I've got a meet here,' he'd told David. So when the men asked him, 'Anyone in?' he knew who they were talking about. He also understood full well that they were plain-clothes coppers.

David gave them each a drink. He told them there was no one here yet, but they should wait and the Colonel would be along soon. David knew that Ron was in fact waiting in the pub over the road on Islington Green, downing drinks, watching the door to the club to see if anyone was being dropped off or if anyone else was with them, hanging about outside.

When Ron was sure it was just the two of them, he came in. David heard him asking them outright: 'Got any tapes on you?' – meaning were they wired up.

After that David stayed out of it. Of course he did. Whether they were paying for information or grassing up someone they wanted put away, he knew it would be more than his life was worth to get involved. While the three of them talked, he busied himself behind the bar, getting ready to open the club a few hours later. They'd do all their business before then, before anyone came into the club, and the Old Bill would creep out before anyone saw them.

That's how it was generally. My brothers never really knew what the twins were doing at the beginning and didn't want to know. But then of course they did know, by which time they were too excited by it, or too frightened, or both, not to do what Ronnie wanted.

Ronnie was in the club at lunchtime another day with another couple of cops, and David saw him giving them a packet, a white envelope. They went on talking for a while and then Ron got up, went over to the bar, put his hand in his pocket and got out a wad of notes. He pulled a few out, walked back over and put it down on the table in front of them, saying: 'There you are, you'd better cop that as well.'

David explained to me how it went. The police needed bodies as well as bungs. Money was lovely but the coppers had to get their books right. It was no use the Krays giving them loads of money and no one getting nicked. They'd pass envelopes of cash – but they'd also inform on anyone they wanted to see out of the way. If the Krays did a job with someone who then didn't give them the lion's share of the readies, a couple of weeks afterwards the former partner would find himself arrested.

Some of the coppers out of West End Central were especially corrupt. Their line was: 'I will help you, and I will leave you alone. If you're going to be raided I will let you know in advance. But

I need a pension for that – and to satisfy my governors, I need a body once a month.' So that's how it worked for the twins.

The Krays would get whatever information they wanted from the police – who was doing well, who might be in need of a little visit, who was going to get nicked and who might be talking to the coppers about the twins' business. It was a way of spreading fear: 'You talk to the police about us and we'll be hearing about it pretty quick.' So much of their operation depended on information – and informers – which is why they were so paranoid about anyone informing on them. Having coppers on the payroll was the best insurance policy. Sometimes David would go on special meets way outside London to make the pay-offs. One day he would find himself heading for the airport with a suitcase of cash.

David told me in detail afterwards what had happened. It was spring 1963. David was asleep at about eight or nine o'clock with a girl called Lucy on the couch at the 66 Club when there was a bang on the door. Big Pat Connolly and Charlie Kray walked in and told David he had to take some money to Ronnie in Jersey. He thought they were joking but he soon realised they were deadly serious.

They told him to go to Vallance Road. He went there and waited for about five hours before Charlie eventually came in and said: 'I've got a packet here with some money in it. And an air ticket. Keep this on you, whatever you do. Get a case and put some clean shirts in it for Ronnie' – Ronnie liked shirts – 'and get a cab to Heathrow. When you get to Jersey, someone will be there.'

David couldn't help feeling quite excited. He didn't know exactly how much money there was in the packet but he knew it must be a lot to warrant a personal courier to take it to Ron. He caught the plane to Jersey and waited for an hour but no one turned up to meet him. He knew Ronnie wouldn't want to be kept waiting so he started to panic. The last thing he wanted was for him to think he had absconded with the money.

Luckily he remembered Charlie saying to someone at Vallance Road that the hotel was near a castle. David jumped in a cab, keeping close hold of the packet, and asked if there was a hotel nearby that was also near a castle.

The cab driver said there was and took him there. Running up the steps into the reception David asked, 'Have you got a Mr Kray staying here?' The girl said, 'Try the bar.'

David walked in and saw Ronnie and Dickie Morgan sitting on a sofa with another man and a girl. He didn't recognise either of them. Ronnie glanced over at David and said in an offhand way to the others: 'Get David a drink, will you?' David felt pretty furious – he'd come all this way and Ronnie was treating him as if he'd just come from down the road. But of course he didn't say anything.

Ronnie then asked David, 'Have you got that packet for me?' My brother handed it over mutely. Ron left the bar for a moment and the girl turned to David and breathed a sigh of relief, saying 'Thank God for you, Dave!' She gave the impression it had been an anxious wait for the money. Ronnie returned, took out a wad of notes and gave them each some cash. Afterwards when they all started drinking and talking, the man said – cool as you like – that he worked at Scotland Yard. This was some sort of high-class pay-off and David had been the courier for the money.

So then David, Ronnie, Dickie Morgan, the policeman and the girl – a grafter who'd clearly been brought over to entertain the policeman – all proceeded to have a lot to drink in the bar, then they moved back to Ron's room and carried on drinking there. By the end of the night, the police officer was very drunk, the girl was happy and Ronnie seemed to be OK. The girl kept saying, 'Good for you, Dave,' to my brother, because he had brought the money.

Dickie and David, however, were just tired. Returning along the corridor from the bar with more drinks, Dickie, who'd had enough of the evening, slipped away to his room. David asked Ron where he was supposed to sleep. Ron kept saying: 'We'll sort it out later.' David didn't feel particularly comfortable with the situation but what could he do?

So they all kept talking and drinking in Ron's room for a while longer. Suddenly the copper passed out on the chair, fast asleep. Ronnie gave the copper a nudge with his foot so he slipped to the floor and Ronnie could take his seat. David again asked Ronnie where he should stay the night and this time he pointed to the girl who was lying on the bed and said: 'Just get in there and give her one.' David didn't know what to do. The girl was willing and he wanted to, but he naturally didn't like the idea of Ron being in the room while they did it.

But the girl kept asking him, so eventually David got into bed and had sex with her. It was only when it was all over and he looked round that he saw that Ronnie had been watching the whole thing from the chair, masturbating. David felt quite sick with disgust at what he'd got involved in.

At that stage it seemed Ronnie was bisexual, or perhaps he didn't even know what he was. Later on he had affairs with all sorts. But at this stage it wasn't widely known that he was gay. Certainly David didn't know at first. To him the image of a gangster and a 'pouf' just didn't go together, so it just hadn't really occurred to him. Later, Ronnie was to take David into his confidence and tell him a bit more about his sexuality. He said he had liked women when he was younger, but that one particular experience had put him off for life. He said he'd taken a young woman back to Vallance Road with him one night. After having sex he'd fallen asleep, only to wake the next morning to find himself, the woman and the bed all covered in her menstrual blood.

Jumping up in horror, he ran out of the room like a madman, going over to the bath-house six times that day to wash himself. He said he could not forget the disgust of that moment and how dirty it made him feel. He claimed this completely changed him, and that after that day he absolutely hated women. He said he could not even speak to his own mother for days.

When this incident occurred Reggie was having one of his spells in prison. Ronnie told David that while Reggie was away, he had been mucking around with Teddy Smith one day. Teddy climbed on top of him and Ronnie said something changed in him and he felt different. From that point he knew he was gay. That was what he told David, anyway.

Reggie was also difficult to read sexually. There was one night when David pulled a bird (a grafter again) and suggested the three of them went back to Vallance Road. The girl was up for having both of them and David thought Reggie wanted it too. So the girl and my brother went into Reggie's bedroom at the back of the house and got into bed. But after David had had sex with the girl, Reggie said he'd changed his mind, and let it go. Neither of my brothers ever saw Reggie sexually with a girl, ever, before he met Frances Shea – the teenager from Hackney he went on to marry.

Anyway, after the first night in Jersey the little group stayed at the hotel drinking for three days – though my brother insisted on getting his own hotel room on the second night. On the plane coming back there was another man and a woman, a supposed honeymoon couple, but they were clearly police. Everywhere Ronnie went, they were there watching. Ronnie insisted they all sit separately on the plane.

Three months later, David was sent out to Jersey again but this time there were two male officers from the Yard there. The Krays wouldn't trust anyone. Once Ronnie met someone in a rowing boat in Victoria Park in Hackney to make sure he wasn't wired up. All that paranoia about informers was because they depended on spies and informers themselves in other firms and in the police.

By now there were other things going on in my brother's life than doing errands for the Krays. That summer, 1963, David had come to see me again on the Isle of Wight to help out with the boat business – and to tell me more about the endless Kray parties in London. Along the way he fell in love. He saw a young girl walking along the boardwalk in Shanklin and that was it. She was called Christine. Meanwhile Alfie had also met his future wife, Wendy. Our mother predicted it wouldn't last for either of them, so David said to Alfie: 'We'll prove them all wrong and have a double wedding,' and they did. They both married on 26 September 1963, in Russell Square Registry Office. One after the other: David to Christine and Alfie to Wendy.

After the ceremony my brothers put their new wives in a taxi to go shopping in Oxford Street and they went round the pub. That night we all went to Talk of the Town in Leicester Square for a big party. And for once it was without Ron and Reg who were now ever-present in my brothers' lives.

CHAPTER 6
THE CEDRA COURT SCENE

The Krays' crazy world was the only one that mattered. I desperately wanted to be in on it myself but I was not there yet. It was like nothing could go wrong for the Krays at this time. The Barn in Knightsbridge shut down when too many cheques bounced but the twins had the other spielers and the long firms bringing in the cash. Their ambitions were bigger than ever. Ronnie was out of his own mum's way now, living in the same block as flats as our mum and dad, Cedra Court in Upper Clapton. It could get pretty wild there at times. The parties would attract all sorts, celebrities and villains, with people coming and going into the small hours.

Ronnie loved blue films. David told me about a party one night at Ron's flat. Everyone was watching them and getting very drunk. The film kept breaking and everyone started booing. It was funny really.

There were a lot of girls around too. Reggie used to say to Alfie: 'Go and get some women.' Alfie was a real ladies' man; he was the one bringing the birds back. But Ronnie would be saying: 'No, go and get some boys.' So half the time poor Alfie didn't know where he was.

One of the girls was very pretty, but looked very much like a boy, slim-hipped and short-haired. Ronnie took to her immediately, whispering in her ear, and leading her to the bedroom. Suddenly Alfie and David heard the girl crying out, not in ecstasy, but in distress. David walked over to the door and called out to her, asking her if everything was all right. Ron was furious, telling him to 'Fuck off out of it.' But David guessed what was happening – that he was forcing her to have anal sex.

Ten minutes later the girl came out of the room, screaming that she wanted to go home, that Ronnie was 'mental' and she didn't want anything to do with him ever again.

Ronnie did what he liked. There were so many incidents that should have alerted my brothers. Not only was he going more and more insane, but he was also getting increasingly sexually voracious, if that were possible. They were always being sent out to find him boys.

Ron was after David too, right from the beginning. He was always touching him but David wasn't frightened of him then and would just tell him to leave him alone. He kept him at bay by getting him rent boys instead.

It all nearly came out in public. The Cedra Court scene with all those celebrities and politicians trooping through Ronnie's flat was far too wild to keep hidden. On 12 July 1964 the famous newspaper headline appeared in the *Sunday Mirror*: 'Peer and a Gangster: Yard Inquiry'. The story went that a senior Scotland Yard detective was investigating connections between an 'underworld thug and a well-known member of the House of Lords'. A week later there was another front-page headline when the *Mirror* ran a story entitled 'The Picture We Dare Not Print'. It was a stunt really – a story about a photograph of the peer and the gangster sitting on a bed with a 'beatnik youth'. Well, it's true, they dared not print it.

The photo was of Ronnie and Lord Boothby. Lord Boothby was the Conservative peer who appeared frequently on the telly and in the newspapers. That's what the foreign magazines said at the time, even though you couldn't say that here in Britain. The boy on the bed was Leslie Holt from Cedra Court, rent-boy and cat-burglar. But it didn't come out until years later that the Prime Minster and Home Secretary had been involved in the cover-up, and that the Commissioner of the Metropolitan Police had terminated the investigation. The government were really frightened, worried that Ronnie was trying to get his picture taken with Sir Winston Churchill. So Boothby got a heavy solicitor and the *Mirror* ended up paying him £40,000, an enormous sum of money in those days. It didn't even go to court. But it was all true, what the paper had said. Boothby told people that he'd used the libel money to buy a house in France. In fact he gave much of it to Ronnie.

There was also a Labour MP on the scene at the time, named Tom Driberg. He was another homosexual. He loved the set-up at Ronnie's and was always round Cedra Court. It was Mad Teddy who introduced the Krays to Driberg because Teddy was sleeping with him. Teddy was like a scout for the Krays, searching for people who might be useful. The Krays then met Boothby through Driberg.

The two of them were very different personalities. As Alfie described them, Boothby was big and blustering, whereas Driberg was small and sickly-looking, like you wouldn't want to get too close to him. Both got a real kick out of being friends with the Colonel. And of course having these powerful connections on both sides of the political spectrum was tremendously advantageous for the Krays. They were controlling the police and now they could control the Establishment too.

David told me about one night when he and Alfie went to a party down in Brighton. It was a big house, full of MPs, including Boothby and Driberg, as well as Ronnie and Reggie. Everyone was terribly drunk. Mad Teddy Smith was there too, with Driberg, who had a gold cigarette holder and was walking around like the Queen with his drink balanced in one hand.

My brothers discovered that Driberg used to tell Mad Teddy about the houses of rich friends he could burgle. He and Boothby would send Teddy or Leslie Holt out on housebreaking missions to turn over anyone who had crossed them.

It was around this time that the Krays got involved in a mad scheme to fund the building of a new town in Enugu, Nigeria. Ronnie had been introduced to the project through his new political connections and Leslie Payne encouraged him to take it on. David was driving Ronnie round for meets and he heard about it all first-hand. Payne had set up an investment vehicle for this building development in the newly independent African nation. Ronnie got flown out to Nigeria, where he was treated like royalty and given VIP treatment. He thought the deal would be his ticket to greatness. It all went wrong. The project collapsed, Payne was arrested in Nigeria and had to be sprung out of prison with a big pay-off. Boothby would later claim he'd only got involved with Ronnie because he'd been approached to be an investor in the Nigerian project. It was lies, rubbish. He got involved because they were sharing boyfriends.

Alfie knew the truth of it. He was taking round money from Boothby so Ronnie would keep quiet. Lots of money. Alfie saw it all.

On two separate occasions he was asked by Ronnie to go and get £5,000 from Lord Boothby for him. That was his share of the *Mirror* money. The way he had to do it was very complicated, but Ron insisted. He had to walk from Vallance Road to Aldgate East, get a taxi down to Victoria Station, jump out of the taxi and walk round to Eaton Place, a little way from Victoria.

He then had to go to No 1, press the bell and go in and get the money – an envelope stuffed full of cash. The first time he went, Boothby asked Alfie if he'd like a drink, but he told him: 'No, thanks, Ronnie is expecting me back straight away.'

On the way back he had to go through exactly the same routine, all the while making sure he wasn't being followed – getting a taxi at Victoria to Aldgate, and then walking down to Vallance Road. Ronnie got no money from the newspaper libel case, officially anyway, but this was his share.

After that Ronnie's appetites just got wilder. And so did the parties. It was like he was untouchable. When Alfie was driving him round, Ronnie used to tell him to stop the car in Piccadilly and go up to some boy and get him in the back of the car. Then Ronnie would take him back and sleep on the floor with him in the kitchen of Alfie's house in Millman Street, Holborn. Wendy and Alfie would sleep in a big double bed in one room with their two sons beside them, while Ronnie would order Wendy to make up a bed in the kitchen for him and the boy. Wendy hated it but they were too scared to refuse.

This wasn't the first time my brothers' wives got dragged into Ronnie's dark world. Just before it was shut down, Ronnie was in Esmeralda's one night when he called David over and said he wanted to go to his place – 'to get away from everyone'. You couldn't say 'no' to Ronnie so David jumped in a cab with him and they drove over to his flat in Bloomsbury. David was living there with his wife, Christine, and by now they also had two young children.

When they got there, Ronnie told him he wanted to spend the next three days, as he put it, 'getting off booze and drugs', seeing how he'd cope without his Stemetil. This was the powerful drug he had been prescribed after he had been diagnosed with schizophrenia, used in the treatment of psychotic illness. He said that it was something he had to do, but insisted he had to do it with David. Never mind the fact that Christine and the kids would be there too. He told David, 'I have to get away from the Firm.'

Knowing Ronnie's moods, David was terrified. But there was nothing he could do but let him stay. Christine wasn't happy about it, of course, and neither was David. But what could he do? Was this guy his friend? Was he his boss?

The flat was just one room. Ronnie slept on the end of the bed with David's two children in cots either side of the bed. For the first day he was perfectly well-behaved, calm and reasonable. By the second he was starting to get twitchy, becoming very easily irritated. It was clear he was struggling without his medication and by the third day he'd had enough. Looking pale and sweating heavily he told David: 'Take me back to Vallance Road.'

David later told me Ron seemed edgy, neurotic and constantly thirsty. He knew then his nerves had gone. Ronnie was very dependent on his pills. He had about six private doctors, all of them crooked, who he paid to give him whatever he felt he needed at the time. Paradoxically, these were the only people Ronnie ever actually paid. Everyone else, including his barrister, was always told: 'I'll sort it out later.'

Dropping Ronnie off outside, David went to park the car. By the time he got back to the house, Ronnie was having to restrain Reggie from going for him. 'I'm going to kill him,' was all he kept saying. Ronnie had effectively disappeared for three days – and Reggie blamed David for it.

Luckily Reggie calmed down and David got back into his good books, continuing to run errands and drive cars for both twins. Reggie was still after Frances Shea at the time. She was the sister of a good friend of Alfie's named Frank Shea. Frankie ran a used-car business on Pentonville Road where Reggie used to take his cars. Frances was a beautiful girl – stunning, according to Alfie. She looked like the young Brigitte Bardot. But once she was with Reggie, she seemed petrified all the time.

While Reggie was after Frances, David used to drive round and collect her for him, so he got to know her quite well. David thought she seemed quiet and bookish. She very rarely smiled, always had a long face and it was as if she was weighing you up when she looked at you. She was probably frightened to speak for fear of saying something she shouldn't.

Her father and mother couldn't stand the twins. When David dropped Reggie round to see her, Reg had to wait outside for her because her father hated him so much. He wouldn't let him into the house even after the wedding.

Reggie used to tell David to put her in the back of the car when he was picking her up, but sometimes she'd try and sit in the front with my brother. If she did, David would get it from Reggie afterwards: 'I'm going to fucking kill you!' He may not have been quite as volatile as his twin but Reggie's moods could still turn on a sixpence.

Relations were also strained between Frances and Ronnie. Whenever they got to Cedra Court she would ask David: 'Is that pig there?' She meant Ronnie.

In spite of Frances's view of Ronnie, the twins weren't about to say goodbye to one another. They were on a roll after the Boothby business. The police – the straight ones, that is – seemed to just give up. It seemed like nothing could touch them – not the law, the politicians, the media, anything.

After the 66 Club got too small, the Krays found a new home for the Firm. They set up at a place called the Glenrae Hotel, a Victorian mansion in Finsbury Park. It was at 380 Seven Sisters Road, not far from Cedra Court, and had a drinking club in the basement. They'd sent in the Firm as 'staff'. Billy Exley, an old boxer, became the Glenrae's barman. The real owners didn't have a chance. All the regulars cleared off. The twins were back in the club business.

Most of all, though, they wanted to be back up the West End. There was a face called Hew McCowan who had a big flat at Marble Arch full of fruit machines. That was his business. There were non-stop parties, all-nighters, to which David and Alfie were always invited. He was already in the Krays' sights because David had introduced him to Charlie the year before, and as a result he had been tapped by Leslie Payne for that Nigerian scheme. McCowan had a club called the Bon Soir in Gerrard Street, which he was doing up and was planning to reopen at Christmas. He was going to rename it the Hideaway.

The Krays decided they would like twenty per cent of the profits. They summoned McCowan to the Grave Maurice pub in the Whitechapel Road to do a deal. McCowan refused. That was unwise. Now they demanded fifty per cent. The twins booked a table for ten people on the opening night of the Hideaway and of course their party failed to appear. But Mad Teddy Smith did show, two nights later, and smashed up some lamps, saying: 'You know who my friends are.' Well, everybody knew who his friends were. That was meant to assure cooperation.

But instead, as David heard it, McCowan had gone round to West End Central Police Station and accused the twins of demanding money with menaces. Next thing we knew, Charlie Kray was telling David the twins had been nicked and he had to go and visit Ronnie in Brixton Prison. David didn't want to go or to get involved at all. But he had no chance of staying out of it. He'd have been done himself if he had said no.

It turned out that a new copper was on their case. Ronnie, Reggie and Teddy Smith had all been nicked at the Glenrae Hotel by a detective superintendent from the Yard called Leonard 'Nipper' Read. We'd never heard of him. They didn't get bail and they were all on remand.

So David, on Charlie's instructions, went to see Ronnie in Brixton. The Colonel said to him: 'Listen boy, I want you to do me a favour. Go round and see that cunt McCowan and tell him if he don't drop the charges, him and his whole family will be done.'

David was shocked. It was one thing running little errands for the Krays but to actually threaten someone himself? He said, 'Ron, I can't. Please don't make me do this.' But Ron just answered: 'Go round and tell him!'

So that night David went to McCowan's. He told him the twins had given him a message for him to drop the charges or he'd be in a lot of trouble. McCowan said: 'I've got the police on to it now.' He didn't seem to get it. Anyway he was brave – but very foolish. There was no way the police were going to win this one. No one dared back up McCowan's accusations.

Nipper Read went round all the other Soho club owners but they all said the same thing. There was never any trouble from the Krays. There had never been any threats – McCowan was drunk, jealous, making it all up. The twins used the Boothby money to pay fancy lawyers and employ a private investigator to dig dirt on McCowan – of which there was plenty.

The jury was got at, too – not once but three times. All the witnesses who had initially been brave enough to speak up quickly changed their minds. Charlie was going round to Boothby's gaff all the time to keep him onside. Boothby even asked a question in the House of Lords on the Krays' behalf. On 6 April 1965, the jury gave their verdict, after ten minutes' deliberation. Not guilty.

That afternoon they all came back from the Old Bailey in triumph to Vallance Road to celebrate. There were photographers, reporters, loads of people – it was like a big street party. Everyone was congratulating them.

Like always, the twins got what they wanted, and soon they had a tight hold of the Hideaway. They renamed it 'El Morocco'. David thinks that was Ronnie's idea. He'd become a big fan of Tangiers and his flat at Cedra Court was done up like some Middle Eastern oasis. Charlie Kray took the club over through a holding company. There was yet another big party. For Ron it was simply a way of saying: 'Up yours' to the Establishment. Alfie and David got into trouble that night; in fact they got barred for chatting up the cigarette girls. But it wasn't for long.

The good times continued, with the Krays at the heart of the sixties nightclub scene. David told me how they were in El Morocco one night when Ronnie pointed out the actor Edmund Purdom (who was very famous at the time) to him. 'See him? I want you to meet him here tomorrow at ten and bring him over to Vallance Road,' he said, like it was the most normal thing in the world to pick up a film star and take him to a little terraced house in the East End. So the next day he met

Edmund Purdom as arranged and took him over to the Krays' house. Ronnie called out, 'Mum, make us a cup of tea?'

When Violet came in with the tray she couldn't believe her eyes.

'Is that really him? In our house?' Ronnie introduced her to him. When Violet had gone out, Ronnie handed the actor two hundred pounds, saying, 'Give it back to me when you can.'

But it wasn't just film stars that David got to drive around. He was in El Morocco one night when Ronnie gave him orders to pick up someone the next day – someone who was to become far more famous than any sixties matinee idol … but only after he was dead.

Ronnie told him: 'Right, Dave, go out tomorrow morning and pick Jack the Hat up at Aldgate at 10 a.m.' David said 'All right,' without the faintest idea as to why. The next morning he found Jack standing on the corner waiting for him. He told him to drive down Commercial Road, do a left and pull up. Jack then said: 'Don't move from here. I won't be a minute.'

Jack McVitie was an armed robber, getting a bit pissed a bit too often, taking too many of the drugs he was peddling, but otherwise inoffensive enough. He wore that trilby hat to hide a bald patch. He was very sensitive about it.

David waited patiently in the car, glancing up in the mirror a few minutes later to see Jack running towards him with a bag in his hand. He'd just robbed a bank. David couldn't believe it. Jumping into the car, Jack shouted: 'Get off the manor, I've just done a bank!'

David had just acted as an accessory to a bank robbery without even knowing about it. He never got a penny for it. Later he said to me, 'I was just used, stupid gofer that I was. I didn't dare complain or Ronnie would just tell me to shut up or he'd give me a slap.'

David told me about another crazy night when he and Alfie were summoned to go round to see the Colonel at Vallance Road about seven in the evening.

Alfie got out of the car and David went to park round the back. Ronnie came out, all suited and booted and said: 'Where's your car? I want you to drop me somewhere.' So they went back to the car, and Ronnie jumped in the front, Alfie got in the back, and David took his place behind the steering wheel.

Ronnie was wearing a camelhair coat. He told David he needed to go to a meet in a pub in Stoke Newington. When they arrived, Ronnie said something to the geezer behind the bar and went upstairs while Alfie and David waited downstairs. They stood there for about an hour until Ronnie came back down and told them, 'Take me back to Vallance Road. The three of them duly climbed in the car and David drove them back.

When they got there, Alfie and Ronnie went in ahead of David. Ronnie took off his overcoat and David heard him say to Alfie: 'Put that in the yard. Watch how you go with it … very gently.' Only then did my brothers both realise the coat was full of explosives.

Ronnie just grinned when David asked him about it. He said: 'If any of them had gone for me, the whole pub would have gone up.'

Turns out Ronnie knew someone who'd been in the army and was an explosives expert. Presumably it was him who had made up the coat for him. If my brothers didn't know by now, it was as clear as day how crazy Ron was going.

If Ronnie was getting more unpredictable by the day, Reggie seemed to know exactly what he was doing. On 19 April 1965, he married Frances Shea. It was a huge deal, the East End wedding of the year. The fashion photographer David Bailey took the wedding snaps. They went to live Up West to start with. That lasted a couple of weeks before Reg moved them to the flat in Cedra Court directly below Ronnie's, which he had specially done up with smart modern furniture.

But Reggie wasn't happy. And nor was Frances. As my brothers witnessed it, Reggie would take Frances out at night to some club where the Firm were – and all the talk was of villainy. She'd just stare into space. David said he thought she was just permanently terrified. Reggie would come back to Cedra Court and just leave her on her own, while he went upstairs to where Ronnie was partying.

She cried her eyes out night after night. Mad Teddy could make her laugh, and Alfie and David could cheer her up. But she hated the Firm and hated Ronnie. The Shea family knew and they loathed Reggie for it. In the end she left Reggie after eight weeks.

David caught some of the storms. One night Reggie came round to his flat with Dickie Morgan for a drink. They came knocking on the door about two o'clock in the morning. David was asleep, but he got up and found them a bottle of gin and sat down to talk. Dickie went home after a while but Reggie and David sat up together after he'd gone. Suddenly Reggie started to cry, saying, 'You know what, we're going to get a lot of bird when they get us.'

David told him, 'Look Reg, why don't you get out of it? You're well-known, you've got a few quid, why don't you and Frances get away by yourselves?'

Reggie looked back at David, and said, 'I can't do it, Dave. I can't. I'm a part of Ronnie, and he's part of me. I know it, I can see it. If he goes down, so do I. We're going to do lots and lots of bird. I know Ronnie's losing it but I can't do anything.'

He stayed that night and David took him back to Vallance Road in the morning. Reggie asked him not to say anything about what had passed between them to anyone: 'Keep this just between us,' he told David. But Reggie's marriage was over before it had even started. Ronnie had made sure of that.

Meanwhile, I had met a girl of my own. Her name was Pat Reader. She came from a wealthy, influential family on the island. We decided to marry quickly. But there would be trouble ahead.

CHAPTER 7
PUPPIES AND FLOWERS

So who were the Krays? Were they the loveable charity promoters the press depicted them as? Were they part of the new working-class aristocracy of pop stars and photographers? Certainly they were getting their photos taken with all the right people. The twins had always courted celebrities because they thought being in their company brought respect. Ronnie's madness was deepening but his craving for fame was growing too.

One night Ronnie told David: 'Come over this evening, you're going to meet Sonny Liston.' He was the heavyweight champion of the world, here in London on a European tour. So David went over to Vallance Road to pick him up. There were crowds of people in the street and loads of photographers. The twins wanted to be respected, not just feared. That's what all that charity and celebrity stuff was about, all those photographs of them with boxers, singers and film stars – all that trouble to make sure the press were tipped off when there was some gift to a kiddies' hospital. David and Ronnie went with Liston to the Grave Maurice in Whitechapel Road. God knows what he made of that.

The US big-fight game was crooked. So Ronnie asked him whether he would take a dive. Liston said: 'I'm one of eleven kids. The gangsters put me on a pedestal. Who am I going to look after? Them? Or the mug punters?'

Then David drove Liston to the Cambridge Rooms, a pub on the Kingston Bypass that the twins had set up as a sort of smart supper club. It was a big, big party that night but the club itself didn't turn out to be a big success. It was just another place they'd moved in on. They wanted the suburban set to come but in the end it was just the Firm. The place folded. People talk about the Kray club 'empire' but in fact it was more like squatting. They would just move in on someone's business and say it was theirs, just like they did to our mum's club. Then they would move on to the next place when they'd messed it up.

Another night in January 1964, the year before Reg married, David went to the Palladium with the Krays to meet Frank Sinatra's son, who was over here on a British tour. The word was that Sinatra wanted him to be seen with the Krays so that people would know not to mess with him. Nineteen-year-old Frank Sinatra Junior had been kidnapped on 8 December 1963 for two days at Lake Tahoe in Nevada. His father had paid a ransom of $240,000 to secure his release. Clearly, having a perceived connection with the Krays would be an insurance against something like that happening again.

The twins never got to see the show though. Ronnie just shook hands with him, said: 'How nice to meet you,' and that was it. They went off to the pub. But the brothers were really working hard at the connections. Reggie wanted to manage pop groups. Charlie Kray even took over the Sammy Lederman show-business agency, which brought American acts to London. Charlie didn't really have a clue, though, and eventually Sammy just became another hanger-on for the twins. Some of the Kentucky Club crowd stayed loyal – the actor Ronald Fraser, Barbara Windsor, a few others.

The twins ached for the big time – and they never quite got what they wanted. But there really were some big stars in their orbit.

One night David met Judy Garland, who was living in London in 1964. There were only about ten people there that night in Madge's (the Lion in Tapp Street, Bethnal Green, also known as the Widow's). Judy was tiny, no bigger than about five foot two according to David. He thinks she was half-pissed at the time, but she came over and perched on his lap and started to sing along with one of the records on the jukebox. I've no idea why she picked my little brother but it's a night he'll always remember.

The way he told it, at some point in the evening Ronnie said: 'All right, put it on,' and lined them all up to do the dance from *Zorba the Greek*. He was obsessed with it. As I was about to find out myself, the Zorba routine got a bit irritating after the twentieth time.

Then there was Ronnie's sentimental side. That was just as hard for my brothers to take. Neither Ronnie nor Reggie could read or write properly. They used to get Teddy Smith to do all their Christmas cards for them – about five hundred a year. A lot were to other gangsters, say in Scotland, or in prison. But

Ronnie also used to send cards to the families of those he'd just got rid of, or cut up. 'Send her a card' was a code Alfie and David learned to recognise instantly. Sometimes it was a bunch of flowers, or a bowl of fruit to someone's sister or mother. They'd put the stamps on the cards and post them.

David gave me an example of this when he told me about the time when Ginger Marks got done. Ginger was a car dealer supposedly shot dead by an unknown killer in Cheshire Street, Bethnal Green, late on the evening of 2 January 1965. His body was never found. Soon after he disappeared, his wife came round to see Ronnie in Vallance Road. She said that she was really worried about her husband's disappearance and that the children were pining for their father. She asked Ronnie if he knew what had happened to him, and he said: 'Oh, I think he's just gone away on business somewhere, I'm not sure.'

After telling Big Pat to 'give her a few quid', he looked thoughtful for a moment and then walked out into the passage. Calling Big Pat Connolly, Ron told him: 'Walk down the Lane [Petticoat Lane was just across the road from where they lived] and buy a puppy, will you?' When Pat got back with the puppy, Ron took it round to Ginger's children, saying: 'Here, this will take your mind off your dad.' It's as if he really believed that a puppy would make it up to them.

Ronnie could be like a kid sometimes but his mood could turn to one of extreme violence in an instant. And he could be very cunning, taking great care to hide his tracks. Alfie told me the story of one memorable occasion when he saw this first-hand.

Ronnie had ordered a chap down the East End to be cut to pieces. He needed an alibi while this was happening – so he told his inner circle, including Alfie, that they were all going to go horse-riding in Wiltshire for a couple of days. Alfie had no idea why they were going until later. It turned out that the police had got Vallance Road under surveillance, and he wanted to put them off the scent while his dirty work was being carried out. Ronnie had apparently treated the surveillance like it was all a bit of a joke. He had taken a tray of tea and biscuits out to the police, saying, 'You must be freezing out here. Don't worry, take your time. I'll send someone out for the tray after.'

So Ronnie had said to Alfie: 'We all need some fresh air, so we're going to go to the country for a day or two.' Alfie was told to watch they were not being followed. They were not. It was a beautiful sunny day and Ronnie was leaning his arm on the open car window as they headed towards Salisbury, when all of a sudden, a wasp flew up his shirt-sleeve and stung him on the arm.

'Pull the car up, pull the car up,' he screamed.

Jumping out of the car, Ronnie tore his jacket off and undid his cufflinks, effing and blinding at the wasp as it flew out and straight back into the car. Rushing into the woods, Ron grabbed a great big lump of wood, almost a tree trunk. Climbing back into the car, he started smashing the interior to pieces in his attempts to get revenge on the wasp. Eventually, much to Ron's fury, the 'fucking thing' flew away, unharmed.

By this time Alfie was helpless with laughter, annoying Ron even more. 'It hurts, you know, Alfie,' he whinged. Determined to wind him up even further, Alfie waited a few minutes in silence before asking him: 'Did you read that piece in the paper about a woman being stung by a bee?'

'What happened?' asked Ronnie grumpily.

'She died, Ron, she died.'

'Get me to a hospital, Ted!'

Alfie had only been joking but it was now too late. The car had to be turned round and an emergency trip made to the nearest casualty department. By the time they got there, Ron was complaining, 'My arm is killing me – I can hardly hold it up!'

One injection later they were back in the car.

Ronnie could be so childlike. This was why he loved Alfie and David, and he really did for a while. Because they used to lark about and weren't as scared of him as the rest.

Ron definitely had a unique sense of humour. They'd be driving along and Ronnie would suddenly shout out: 'Oi, bollock-chops, what's the time?' Or 'Soppy-bollocks, come here!' 'Bonzo' was another, and 'Basil'. One of his favourite catchphrases was, 'Smashing, innit?' It was all very funny – when he wasn't actually smashing somebody in the face.

Anyway, there was Alfie on his way to Wiltshire, with Ron and several other members of the Firm. By the time they got to the hotel, the Ship Inn at Wilton, Ronnie was getting very agitated. He wouldn't sit down, or go to the bar where they were all having a drink. He was immediately off at the phone box in the lobby.

Several phone calls later he came back, visibly relaxed. He started smiling away and telling them: 'It's all done.'

'What is, Ronnie?'

'Don't you worry. Just a bit of business with Charlie.'

Then he got up as if he had just thought of something and went back and phoned someone, presumably Charlie.

'Send some flowers from Ron and Reggie,' Alfie heard him say.

Alfie understood then for the first time why they were there. They were to give him an alibi – for a stabbing, some piece of horrible violence, revenge for something, money, a debt or even just a show of strength to someone they wanted to intimidate.

'Lovely! Back tomorrow, ta ta,' said Ronnie. Then, turning back to Teddy and Alfie, he said, 'Come on, let's go and have a drink.'

Standing at the bar they heard an upper-class voice ask: 'Come down from London?'

Ronnie answered: 'Horse-riding, yeah, we're going horse-riding tomorrow.'

The man at the bar was a well-dressed, grey-haired geezer – a bit of a colonel type (but not the Colonel).

'Funnily enough, that's what I'm doing too. Are you going on the same ride?' he asked.

'Yeah, I think so,' said Ronnie, starting to get interested. 'You live down here?'

'Yes,' answered the man. 'I'm the local magistrate.'

'I bet that's an interesting job, isn't it?' asked Ron.

'What line of business are you in yourself?' asked the magistrate.

'We're in clubs... we own clubs,' said Ronnie.

'That's very nice. Well, look forward to seeing you in the morning then.'

As Ronnie walked back over to the table, he was gleeful. 'Cor, that's fantastic... I hope we all get nicked when we get back to London so we can sue the police... We've got the best alibi ever!'

An hour later, after a few more drinks, Ronnie suddenly turned round to Alfie and said: 'What I want you to do tomorrow is smash his horse with a big stick when he gets on it so it will gallop and he'll fall off and break his neck.'

Alfie was bewildered. 'What are you talking about? I'm not smashing a man's horse!'

Ron looked at Alfie with disappointment.

'You won't do nothing, will you?'

Two minutes earlier the magistrate had been Ron's lucky ticket. Now suddenly he was to be 'smashed' as if he were of no more significance than a fly. It was at times like this my brothers realised what a complete psychopath Ronnie was becoming – if he wasn't crazy all along.

Dad always had some kind of business on the go. This is his betting shop.

This is him with his beloved motor car outside Edmonton dog track.

Dad (left) and the many trophies they had down at the dog track.

The family. (L-R: Me and friend, David, Alfie, Dad, Wendy, Mum, Christine and friend)

Me, having fun in the sun on the Isle of Wight.

The boat we took Ronnie out on and used to dump his holdalls.

Alfie, working hard!

While I was messing about with boats, David and Alfie were playing it cool in London.

Alfie and friend Jack looking the part.

Alfie (back left) and David (back right) celebrating their wedding day with their lovely wives and the family.

Ronnie and Reggie with brother Charlie (second from right) at The Kentucky Club. (Keystone/Getty Images)

The Krays with Judy Garland and her husband Mark Herron. (Keystone/Getty Images)

L-R: Actor George Sewell, Reggie, Barbara Windsor and Ronnie at the El Morocco nightclub. (Larry Ellis/Express/Getty Images)

CHAPTER 8
THE PARTY COMES TO ME

Summers at Shanklin came and went. I was happy enough, busy with the boat business. I liked the winters too, with the empty beaches and only the seabirds for company. But Alfie and David would keep turning up, full of their stories from London. I got the impression sometimes that they liked the peacefulness of the Isle of Wight as much as I was pining for the action in the big city. But now I'd got Pat. And she was pregnant.

Pat wouldn't get rid of her baby, whatever the pressure from her parents. I was proud of her for that. We would have to get married. I think that horrified her mum and dad even more.

The big wedding had to take place as soon as possible, for obvious reasons. Alfie was my best man. We married in August 1964. It was in the local newspaper. It was a fabulous wedding, no expense spared. The two bridesmaids had their dresses flown over from France. The wedding reception was held in one of the biggest and grandest hotels in Cowes. We were driven around in a huge Humber Super Snipe like the one Winston Churchill used to have.

Pat's parents were very grand. They had made a fortune out of lampshades, of all things, and didn't think I was nearly good enough for their daughter. That was made clear. Who was I and who were my brothers? Some sort of market traders from London.

They were extremely condescending towards us until they met our old man – who, like Pat's father, was a Freemason and could be very grand himself when he wanted to be. They couldn't get one over on him however hard they tried.

I was very much in love with Pat. We bought a house in East Cowes and I thought we would live happily ever after. I was proud of her for standing up for our unborn child and not having an abortion. Our daughter, Traci, was born in March 1965.

But things would soon go bad in our marriage. I suppose I have my brothers to blame for that. This is how it began. One day, soon after Traci was born, David rang up and said he had some friends in London who wanted to come and meet me. They've got some business on the island, he told me. That's right, it was the Kray twins. 'It'll be a pleasure to meet them,' I said.

Soon afterwards, Alfie and David came down as usual to give me a hand working on the boat-hire business. They told me there was some hold-up with the twins, but don't worry, they'd be down. So one sunny day we were all working on the beach, when a car pulled up in front of our site in Shanklin. A man got out from the front passenger seat, looking like a smart businessman, not a day-tripper. He had a driver but otherwise he was on his own.

Alfie walked up the stairs from the beach and on to the esplanade to greet him. I saw this from the water's edge as I was pulling in one of our small motorboats and getting the tourists out of it and on to the shore. Alfie starts calling out to me: 'Come up and meet Ronnie.'

All that time, I'd been hearing about the wild times in London, the big Kray party that never ended. The party I never thought I'd get to see. Now I'd got what I wanted. The party had come to me.

Alfie's still shouting: 'C'mon, Bobby. Hurry up. Ronnie Kray wants to meet you!'

I ambled up the wooden steps, looking like a bit of a beach bum really in shorts and sunglasses. I was in no hurry – or at least I didn't want anyone to think I was. Alfie and David had gone ahead of me. There's this guy in a dark suit standing there, grinning his head off. No Reggie, just Ronnie. Reggie sends his apologies. There was backslapping, playful sparring. My brothers were his best mates. Then he turned to me.

'You're Bobby, are you? I've heard such a lot about you, all good things. This is a nice little business you've got here for yourself, haven't you? We must come over here again soon.'

Now I'm going through the 'great to see you, Ronnie' routine and all the rest of the horseplay with my brothers. My first impression was of someone confident and commanding – but definitely on the make. He was looking around him, taking in everything – me, the boat business, my brothers – as if he were working out what he could get out of what we had. The way he strutted around it was as if it all already belonged to him. I had heard he had a very violent streak, that his mood could change in a second and that he was feared by everyone, but I had not at that time heard he was gay.

At first I didn't look at him as some kind of crime king, although I'd heard enough stories about him from my brothers. I thought he was just another villain out to make a pound note. I can't say I was overly impressed. I learned quickly how to get a read on Ronnie, a skill that later helped to me to stay alive.

As soon as Ronnie saw the speedboat, he wanted to go out in it. It was a jet turbine we'd bought brand-new from the Earl's Court Boat Show. It was the fastest speedboat on the island at that time. Ronnie loved it.

When he came back from the speedboat trip he stepped out – and immediately sunk down in the mud till it covered his shoes. He looked confused and unsure of himself while trying to keep his balance as he made his way back to shore. It was hard not to let him see us all laughing. As Ronnie always needed a drink we went to a pub called the Folly Inn. But it was fifteen minutes to opening time. Ronnie started banging on the door. We could see the staff inside the pub so Ronnie walked off, marching several feet away and swearing for two or three minutes. Then, unable to control himself, he stomped back to the pub and started banging on the door again.

The staff inside looked furious and shouted back, 'Not till 5.30!' Five minutes to opening time they gave in and Ronnie rushed inside and ordered a gin and tonic and instantly downed it before ordering another. This was before any of us had managed to get a drink for ourselves.

I remember thinking what an oddball he was. I had no idea then of how Ronnie was to take over my life, the same way he had with my brothers. Years on we would all wonder to ourselves how we ever let him do this to us. But that's how it happened with Ronnie; it's what he did to everyone.

A couple of weeks later I came up to London to stay with Mum for a few days. There was a summons to go to Madge's, the Lion in Tapp Street. The place was packed. I managed to push my way to the bar and got a gin and tonic and then Ronnie, who was standing at the end of the bar with a young boy, spotted me and waved me over. There were some other faces with him who I did not know. I shook hands with Ronnie and he introduced me to his boy and to Scotch Jack Dickson, a huge man.

Then Ronnie waved to someone in the crowd and that's when I thought I was seeing double. Next thing I knew I was shaking hands with a slimmer version of Ronnie.

'This is my brother, Reggie,' Ronnie said. 'This is Alfie's brother, Bobby. One of Nelly and Alfie Teale's kids, who have the 66 Club on Upper Street.'

'Oh yes, I see,' said Reggie. 'Let me get you a drink… What are you having?'

'Gin and tonic,' I said. And that's how it all started. Reggie wanted to ask me about the Isle of Wight so we chatted for a bit, mostly small talk. I remember him asking me, 'Can you drive, Bobby? Perhaps you could drive me around sometime?'

'I've got to go, I have a meet to go on,' I said. In fact the truth was I was too skint to pay for another drink.

'OK,' Reggie said. 'I hope to see you later.' It was hardly big-shot gangster talk. But then it never was.

A few weeks later, Reggie came down to see me on the island. He got especially excited when I told him that me and

Johnny Quinn were in the habit of taking a team of footballers into Parkhurst Prison to play the inmates' team.

From then on Reggie would find any excuse to come to the island. For example, not long after Pat and I got married, they were visiting Colin 'Dukey' Osbourne, who was doing time in Parkhurst for firearms offensives. I took them up to the prison and waited outside the gates for a couple of hours. I'd invited Ronnie and Reggie to come to our home for dinner afterwards. And they'd accepted. I couldn't believe it. It was so flattering.

It was a Sunday. Our house was a three-bedroom, two-storey semi on Oaktree Drive in East Cowes that Pat and I had bought new for two thousand quid when we got married. Ronnie sat in the living room with one of the Firm, and Reggie and another one of the Firm sat at the dining-room table. I don't remember their names. The conversation wasn't exactly sparkling. All through that dinner I was on edge because I thought Pat would speak her mind about this lot turning up and behaving – well, as I was finding, they usually did behave quite well in company. The talk, such as it was, was of villains and general villainy. The twins were polite enough with no swearing.

The Krays were always polite in front of women, so Alfie had told me. It was the way their mum had brought them up. The Firm mostly grunted: 'Yes Ron, right Ron.' It was hard to keep the conversation flowing.

In fact Pat said very little. Ronnie was just looking around and taking in things. We got through it somehow and it seemed to be a success, and I felt I was getting to know them better. It all looked good as far as I was concerned. Everything my brothers had been telling me for so long seemed true – the Krays were big-time villains. They had it all: glamour, clothes, money...

Pat was not that impressed. But I was overwhelmed. What had I been doing on the dozy old Isle of Wight all these years? OK, so David and Alfie were a bit too ready to jump when told to but so was everyone else, I could see that. I wasn't frightened of the twins, though, not me. I was going to go for it big, make up for lost time.

My brothers knew the score; they'd been at this game for five years already. They'd become wary. Me, I was starstruck.

Out of the two of them, Reggie especially seemed to need a friend – someone to draw him out of always being in Ronnie's shadow. Being with me helped him to do that. Ronnie could see Reggie and I were hitting it off, and he'd get pretty angry about it. But I understood it, sensing instinctively that Reggie admired me, not in a sexual way, but as one young man some-times looks up to another. In another life a part of him would have liked to be me, I think – to have a wife and child and a nice little boat business on the Isle of Wight.

But Ronnie had other plans for him, and for me too. I soon learned the kind of thing they had in mind for me. Reggie asked me how far out I could go out with my boats, as they might need me to help them get someone out of Parkhurst Prison and off the island. It all seemed like a movie, a big adventure. I was loving every minute of it.

Not too long after this, Ronnie sent two men over to the island with a couple of large, heavy black holdalls. They told me: 'Ronnie told us to come over with these. He wants to get rid of all this rubbish – just papers and documents and so on. He wants you to sling it in the sea. It's all weighted down ready for you.' So I took the bags out to the deepest point of the Solent, where the current is at its most dangerous, and I threw the holdalls into the water. The men left without a word of explanation. Was it a body? I wasn't going to ask.

And by now I would do anything for them, the more villainous-seeming the better. This was better than putting out deckchairs. More and more frequently I was coming to London to run little errands for the twins – Reggie especially. Then came a really big moment. Reggie asked me to carry a gun for him. I was to have it on me, concealed, while he went into some club or other, 'in case I need it'.

A gun! I was made. This was proper villainy. It was a six-shot revolver, I don't remember which make. I held it for ages, felt its weight, pushed in the shells, flicked the safety catch. I was on the Firm.

I had to tell Alfie about it. 'I carried a gun for Reggie today, y'know,' I said casually. I was trying to be so cool but I had to show my elder brother that I was as much, if not more, a member of the Firm than he was.

He was not that impressed. 'Be careful,' he said, 'that's what they do, the twins. They get you at it then you can't get out.' He told me the police had already marked him and David as associates of the Krays, and that as a result their usefulness to the twins – in, say, doing the driving or carrying a gun to a meet – was not quite what it used to be. I didn't believe any of that. Reggie had asked me because he liked me and trusted me.

But my marriage wasn't going to stand it. Pat had Reggie competing for my attention. She hated it, getting more and more jealous as time went on. To be honest, we had been arguing for a while. Reggie's arrival in my life only worsened what was already a relationship heading for the rocks.

The few days that I went home to East Cowes, the rows got really poisonous. Traci was just a baby. How could I do this? What the hell was I playing at hanging round with these creeps?

It was Pat and her family who started the divorce. Her family couldn't wait to see the back of me. Reggie put up the money for my solicitor's bill – two thousand pounds. 'Leave her behind,' he'd tell me. 'Women, what do they know?' Reggie was only too pleased to stump up the money to buy me out of a marriage that was no longer working. His own marriage had failed, so why not mine?

That part of my life was over: a wife, children, a home of our own. I was back running with a pack. I was on the prowl again. I came back to wicked old London, to be part of the big Kray party.

Alfie had already warned me about getting in too deep. But the one thing you couldn't do was say 'no' to the twins. If they asked you to do something, you did it. Alfie said it was starting to get dangerous. I thought it was overwhelmingly exciting. And so in that early spring of 1966 I became the coolest gangster in London. Or so I thought.

I had to learn the proper talk, learn to get a read on Ronnie's moods – when to flatter, when to duck out of view. Reggie was emerging as my friend but it was Ronnie giving the orders. I was sent down to the West End at one time with Ronnie Hart (the twins' cousin) to 'kill' someone. We were both tooled up. But I can't even remember who we were meant to murder. Ronnie Hart had no more intention of killing this person than flying to the moon, and neither did I.

I'd never killed anyone and never would. But you had to go along with it, pretend you were going to. When we came back that time we just said we couldn't find him and Ronnie had already forgotten about it. If you'd asked him the next day why he wanted us to kill whoever it was, he wouldn't even remember.

I bounced around, staying with Alfie in Holborn or with David and Christine in their ground-floor flat in Upper Clapton near Stoke Newington, not too far from Mum and Dad. It was at number 51 Moresby Road, an anonymous suburban street of Edwardian terraced houses. I felt safe there. Nothing bad could happen at David's place. Not with his kids there. That's what I believed, anyway.

CHAPTER 9
DEAD MEN CAN'T SPEAK

It was a normal spring evening the night it happened. I was round at David's gaff. His wife Christine was preparing supper in the little kitchen and Alfie was with us in the front room watching TV. I think it was that US show *The Fugitive*, about an innocent man who escapes from prison. It was a big deal at the time.

Early in the evening the phone rang in the hall. David went out to answer it.

'Who is it, Dave?'

I already knew the answer. We all did. Almost every night Reggie or Ron would phone up to ask us to come out drinking. If we said no, they'd just send someone round to get us anyway. It was 9 March 1966, a Wednesday, the day after David's birthday, so we all still had a bit of a hangover and didn't want to go out. We just wanted to watch telly. Have a few drinks.

'So, is it the usual?' I asked him. 'Of course it is,' David said. It had been Reggie on the phone saying that we should come over for a drink at the Widow's. No special reason. Just get over.

We all looked at each other. Better do as he says. David's car was outside the flat – a grey, two-door Ford Popular. Not flash.

The three of us got in and headed for Bethnal Green. David did the driving, with Alfie and me in the back.

We got to the Widow's. Reggie was outside in the street with the rest of the Firm, all of them milling around under the railway bridge beneath the street lamps. There was something funny going on, we could sense it. We all got out. There's Reggie walking towards us, saying to David quite matter-of-factly: 'Where's your motor?'

David nodded towards it.

Then Nobby Clark – an old safe-cracker and founder member of the Firm – said to Reg: 'What motor are you going in?'

Reggie replied, 'I'll go with these.' He indicated us.

We got back in the car. Reggie jumped in the front. He said to David, 'Come on, kid, we've got to get off the manor.' Reggie was excited, but spoke as if he was just arranging any other piece of business. David stepped on the accelerator hard and we screeched away.

At first no one spoke, but eventually Alfie asked Reg, 'So, what's the matter?'

Reggie said, calm as anything: 'Ronnie has just shot Cornell.'

'Who the fuck's Cornell?' It was David who asked. He didn't know and I certainly didn't.

Alfie had a bit more of a clue. George Cornell was some face who'd done rough stuff for the Richardsons, the scrap-dealing brothers who ran crime in south-east London with a sadistic ruthlessness that outdid even the Krays. His real name was George Myers. The word was he'd once beaten the shit out of Ronnie in a fist fight, the only one who ever had. The

Christmas before there'd nearly been a shoot-out at the Astor Club when Cornell was supposed to have referred to Ronnie as a 'fat pouf'. For him to come drinking in Whitechapel had been taking the piss.

Reggie was sitting in the front passenger seat complaining about why Ronnie had to do Cornell. Reggie was always moaning about what Ronnie had or hadn't done. The way he went on, it was like it was some domestic tiff.

So where are we all supposed to go? I was thinking. Nobody's saying.

David's driving very carefully, looking out for the Old Bill. Reggie says, 'Where are we going to go to now?' We all remain silent. Then Reggie tells David, 'Go up Lea Bridge Road way.'

The Krays had no hide-outs, whatever anyone might have suggested later. It was all far less planned than that. We were heading out of the East End, up Cambridge Heath Road, back past Cedra Court and David's flat in Moresby Road, past the dark Hackney Marshes and on into the suburbs. Nothing much else was moving; the streets were as quiet as a graveyard.

David thought he knew where we were going. He'd driven the twins this way before. It was a place called the Chequers in Walthamstow High Street, a favourite of the twins, run by an ex-policeman called Charlie Hobbs. There was a poker club called the Stow, round the back.

Reggie was still mumbling away, complaining that Ronnie 'should have organised this better'. The twins never organised anything. Everything happened because there was no fear of the consequences. Both of them acted on their impulses.

We got to Walthamstow and went into the pub. The governor glanced up at us and quickly opened a flap in the bar counter, and we all marched into another bar room that wasn't normally used. Ronnie was already there too and he came towards us when he saw us enter. It was very chaotic in there. The calmest one was Ronnie. At least it seemed to be.

He asked us as we came in: 'Do you want a drink?' I suppose at that moment, we could have used one.

While we had driven Reggie, Ronnie had been driven to the Chequers by Scotch Jack Dickson, so I found out a little later. We all gathered in the back room. You could feel the tension and excitement fizzing in the air. Everyone was talking at once and no one was making much sense. The radio was kept on in the background so we could listen to the news bulletins.

Ronnie went into a lavatory and changed his clothes and started to wash his hands in a sink. When I first saw him that evening he had been wearing a dark suit, shirt and tie. Now he looked more like a clown with a pullover too small for him and trousers too short. He had put on some of Alfie's clothes and looked absurd. If Ronnie had been a woman, he'd have been a size sixteen, while Alfie would have been a ten. So now he looked like Max Wall in his trousers.

We all gathered in an upstairs room when we heard on the radio there were road-blocks all over the East End and that someone was being rushed to hospital after a shooting in the Blind Beggar Pub on Whitechapel Road, just down the street from where we'd picked them up at the Widow's. There was laughing and whooping when they all heard that. The Firm were revelling in it, with Ronnie as the ringmaster.

Ronnie said: 'I hope the bastard's dead.'

At midnight the radio news came on again, telling us again that a man had been shot. This time it said he had died in the ambulance. Everyone started talking excitedly and I heard Ronnie say: 'Always shoot to kill. Dead men can't speak.'

So what the fuck had actually happened? Eventually it came out in a lot of fractured conversations around me. I could put together most of it – and the details were going to be common knowledge soon enough.

The events started when Ronnie gets a message that George Cornell was in the Beggar. He thinks that's a bit of a liberty. He gets Scotch Jack (John) Dickson to drive him there in his Cortina from the Widow's, along with Scotch Ian Barrie.

Ronnie enters the bar of the Beggar brandishing a 9mm automatic pistol. Cornell is sitting on a bar stool sipping a light ale. Scotch Ian fires two shots into the air and everyone dives for cover. And Ronnie calmly puts a single bullet into George Cornell's forehead. He didn't die straight away.

The talk in the Walthamstow pub turned to where we were going to go now. People started moving to a flat up the road above a parade of shops owned by a regular at the Chequers, a brewery driver called Roland Tarlton, who had set up an improvised bar in his front room with space for thirty or more revellers to carry on drinking. However, soon after a group of us arrived, his wife came in from her night shift and started screaming for us all to get out. You couldn't argue with her and there was a baby in the next room.

So then Reggie turned to David and said, 'Right, Dave, we're going to stay round your house tonight. We can't go near the East End. You're a straight boy. The Old Bill don't know your place.'

Alarmed, David said quickly, 'You can't. We've only got two rooms. My kids are there. And Christine has got another baby on the way.'

But David couldn't stop them. The Krays insisted on bringing everyone back to his family flat in Moresby Road. We didn't know it then but we'd all be trapped there for weeks.

I got there with Alfie, David and Reggie at about one in the morning. All of a sudden there's a knock at the window. I look up and there's Ronnie. I didn't know what David had told Christine about what was happening. But I knew she would not be pleased. He must have given her some old chat. Then Ronnie demanded: 'Can't she get up and make us some food? I'm starving!' So David had to ask Christine to make some cheese sandwiches.

Alfie was sent out to get more booze even though by now it was the middle of the night. He'd done that a lot over the last few years, coming back from Madge's way after hours with crates of the stuff – gin, whisky, beers, tonic, cigarettes. Madge had told him one time: 'Where's the money? What does Ronnie think I am, a fucking charity?'

Christine started trying to get some sheets and blankets together, but it was ridiculous. There were so many of us there was no room to move. There were about ten, twelve people sleeping on the floor.

That first night Ronnie and Reggie started arguing so badly that Alfie and David had to dive in between them. Eventually

Reggie said, 'Fuck you, I'm going,' and went out with Nobby Clark. It wasn't very long before he came back.

Meanwhile Ronnie announced: 'I want to have a bath.' David told him Christine was in bed and he'd have to walk through the bedroom to get to the bathroom. It was not what you might call ideal. David also explained to Ron that they had an old-fashioned heater that would take a while to warm up. Ronnie put half a crown in the slot and waited. To us it was all completely mad, but I realised then that for Ronnie this was just an ordinary night.

People were coming and going after that. Ronnie came back in after his bath and after Reggie had returned with Nobby he and Ron started arguing again. It was like we were dreaming.

The next morning David was woken by Ronnie putting his head round the door and asking, 'Can Christine make me some tea?' It was about 8 a.m. but he'd been up with the sparrows. He then informed David: 'We're going to have to stay here for a bit.'

David looked scared and told him, 'The Old Bill will come round. They're bound to. I've got my wife and children here. I don't want it, Ron, I don't want it.'

Ronnie said, 'Listen, Dave. Dead men can't speak, can they?' We all heard that.

So we all got up and had some tea. We needed more supplies – cups, plates, food, everything. Christine and David were allowed out to the shops in Upper Clapton Road but not without one of the children staying behind as a hostage. 'They won't come in while the kids are here,' Ronnie said. He meant the police. He said that twenty times at least.

He was clever like that. Christine was terrified. Then our eleven-year-old younger brother Paul came round the next morning from our mum's house nearby to see Christine and the kids without knowing what he was walking into. He wasn't going to be allowed to leave.

Ronnie had taken a pencil and piece of paper from one of David's kids' little notebooks. He'd made some sort of list and was constantly scribbling on it. I managed to see it and realised it was full of the names of people he wanted to get shot of.

There was a rival firm in Clerkenwell. Someone from that was going to go. Leslie Payne, the money-man, was also on the list. They had fallen out big-time by now. There were people from south London. Ronnie would leave the list around for a day, then the next morning he would tear it up and start again. He couldn't put any of our names on it as we were all in the house with him.

Ronnie seemed quite relaxed on the surface. He seemed to trust us all. But if one of us wasn't around for a day or two, he would want to know the reason why. We all knew exactly where we stood.

Insane as he was, Ronnie was completely in charge.

CHAPTER 10
THE TURNING POINT

The days passed. I was now very aware of Ronnie's 'dreaded list'. I realised that the list contained the names of people that he wanted to kill; that he was going to kill. As soon as I saw it, I knew something had to be done. The Krays were out of control. They had the East End buttoned up too tight and someone had to undo it. And, slowly, I realised that someone had to be me... It took just one moment for the scales to fall from my eyes. All the Colonel's 'glamour', if he ever had any, was as nothing now. I had spent the last six months fawning on them both, being so flattered that the twins seemed to think well of me. Now I'd heard Ronnie boasting about how good it felt to kill. And now he and Reggie were hiding behind children. I felt physically sick.

But what could I do right there and then? We were all effectively hostages, with David's wife Christine and their two young kids. Also there was our eleven-year-old brother Paul. Now all of us were in the power of this paranoid schizo and an armed mob who would do whatever they were told to do.

Ronnie knew it. We were all like his human shields. He knew the police were never going to come in shooting because of all the kids being in the place.

But there was something else that happened in that flat, too – something that would make me act in a way that would change my life for ever.

It was the third or maybe the fourth day. Ronnie announced that he wanted Paul to sit on his lap. I told Christine under my breath that if Ronnie made a move to the bedroom for what he'd call a 'lie-down' with Paul I would shoot him dead there and then. I could only imagine what he had in mind for my little brother. The room was dark so I went to the kitchen and got my own gun, a 9mm, from where I'd left it on the top of the fridge. Christine saw me and, hearing the click of a bullet going into the chamber, she grabbed my arm and started pleading, 'No, no, Bobby! Please not here, not in front of the kids!'

But I'd made up my mind. I loaded a full clip. If Ronnie made a move on Paul, that would be his last. I was intending to unload the gun on him. Christine grabbed my arm, still begging me, 'Please, please don't do it!'

I said something like, 'OK, Chris, it's OK.' But it wasn't OK, not in the slightest. I hid my gun under my coat and, taking a deep breath, I pushed by her and stood in the doorway of the living room. Ronnie started to walk towards me until we were face to face with each other. He had his arm on Paul's shoulder. He told me he was just going to lie down for a few minutes. I didn't move out of the way. He could see I was not going to put up with it so he said: 'Bobby, you silly boy, I just need to lie down.'

But he did not push by me, as I thought he would. He just stood there and talked on, with his eyes half-closed. And then, after what seemed to be the longest time, he turned and went back to the couch and sat down, putting Paul on his lap again. He closed his eyes, and seemingly went to sleep. I went and sat next to him and now I had my gun out under my coat, pointed at his heart, with one bullet in the chamber and the safety off and my finger firmly on the trigger.

I intended to empty the six bullets into him if I had to. I also knew that if I did let Ronnie have what was coming, I would not get out alive. The Firm all had guns on them. Scotch Ian Barrie, Albert Donoghue, Ronnie Hart, Scotch Jack Dickson, loads more of them – they were all in the place. They'd shoot me down before I could make it to the door. Not to mention how I would get Paul out alive. Well, I waited, but Ronnie didn't move. Thank God. He must have sensed something.

Then suddenly Paul got up and went into the kitchen. Ronnie turned away and appeared to forget all about him – and me. He waved at Paul and said something like 'Nice boy'. Remember, Ronnie was always doing this – acting on some mad impulse then going off in another direction. It was like the time he'd told me and Ronnie Hart to go and kill someone and then forgot all about it.

But this wasn't like that. He had made a move on Paul and he would surely do so again. Maybe he wouldn't back off next time. Now I really did know I had to do something.

I made some kind of excuse that I had to go outside for a while. I think I said my mother needed help in clearing up the flat. Ronnie would appreciate me going out to help our mum. My stomach was churning but I had made up my mind what I was about to do, even though I could hardly believe it myself.

I phoned Scotland Yard from a phone box near my mum's flat at Cedra Court. You had to put pennies in when you got an answer. Inside it smelt of piss, stale sweat and fag-ash. I'd get to know that smell pretty well. Mixed with the smell of my own fear.

It was an old-fashioned dialler. The number was famous – it was in all the TV police shows and on the radio. Whitehall 1212.

The switchboard answered. In went my coins. One, two, three, four. Big old pennies. My hands were trembling.

I asked to speak to Mr Butler. I didn't know his full name, but I knew he was an old enemy of the Krays. He had first got on the twins' case in 1960 as a Flying Squad detective investigating clubland rackets and the Double R in particular. I knew he was someone important at the Yard.

The woman at the other end of the line said: 'We have two Mr Butlers. Which one do you want?'

I was so nervous I couldn't speak. For a second, I was sure I'd been followed. I hung up in a panic and – not knowing what else to do – went home to see my mum, who welcomed me with tea and affection as ever. She never knew exactly what was going on and we would never worry her with the uncomfortable truth, although she must have known some of it.

I sat in the kitchen and had a cup of tea and we talked, mostly about Dad and how she was going to leave him. God bless dear old Mum. We had heard her talk this way so many times before. I would always say something like: 'You should,

Mum. You've put up with him for far too long.' But I knew she would never leave him.

Eventually I drained my cup of tea and said, 'Right. I've got to go and do some stuff.'

I gave Mum a kiss and out the door I went, back to the phone box where I had funked phoning the police a little while before. I was going to have another try.

This time I would do it. It had started raining, just a light drizzle. I got the Yard on the phone and asked again for Mr Butler, saying this time that it was 'regarding the Krays'. It sounded so heavy, so official, as if someone else was saying that, not me.

'Oh, you must mean Superintendent Tommy Butler,' said the female operator.

'Yes, him,' I said.

After a short time a gruff male voice came on the phone and said, 'What can I do for you?'

Taking a deep breath, I said the seven words that would change the course of the rest of my life. 'I have some information about the Krays.'

He said, 'I'll set up a meeting, just wait a minute.'

I suppose he was recording the call. About a minute or two later he came back on the line and said, 'Can you get to Bouverie Street just off Fleet Street by two this afternoon?'

'Yes,' I answered.

He told me to walk down the right side of the street from Fleet Street and asked what I would be wearing. I said a blue rain-coat, and he said, 'We will see you at two this afternoon then.'

'OK,' I replied, and hung up.

It was about one in the afternoon and I had just about enough time to get from where I was to Fleet Street. All the time I was thinking: 'What if I'm being followed?' So much was going on in my head. I could not stop seeing images in my mind of all the people in David's flat. I thought that perhaps I should just turn around and forget the whole thing. But I knew that if our family was to make it through all this, this was the only way it might work. As soon as I felt I was not being tailed, I finally walked down Bouverie Street with all its newspaper offices.

I turned my raincoat collar up, not because it was drizzling, but because I wanted to hide my face. I think it just made me look more conspicuous. That's how it felt. I felt like everything about me was screaming *this man is going to grass up the most violent criminals in London*. Look at him, what a mug. He's signed his own death warrant.

There was one man I could see on my side of the street, but he was some way away. As I looked over to the other side, I could see three men walking parallel to me and looking over at me. Then one of the men crossed the road and started heading towards me at the same time the man on my side of the street neared. Soon the two men were on either side of me. This was it. My heart was pounding.

One said to me: 'Did you phone?'

'Yes,' I said.

They asked me to open my coat. The two men started to help me off with it in the middle of the street with the other men over the road, just watching. I still couldn't quite believe what was happening. By now, it was raining hard, and drops of water were running down the back of my collar, icy little rivulets, like sweat creeping down my spine. I'd get to know that sensation very well.

The two men searched me from top to bottom and walked me to a car a little way away on the other side of the street. One opened the back door and told me to get in.

It was a mid-size black car. A Rover 3-litre I think. There were two men sitting in the front seats. As I got in the back, one of the men from the street came and sat next to me and closed the door. I was wet and holding my raincoat and in a bit of a shock at the turn of events. The man in the front passenger seat turned to me and held out his hand, saying 'I'm Tommy Butler.' I shook his hand. He said, 'And you are…?'

I said, 'I'm Robert Teale. Bobby.' Then he asked me what I wanted to tell them about the Krays.

I said, 'I know a lot, I have a lot to tell.'

Tommy Butler stared at me, appraising me. 'Do you know anything about the Cornell killing?'

'Yes,' I said.

'Who killed Cornell?' he asked directly.

'Ronnie Kray.'

'Do you know that for a fact?'

'Yes,' I said.

'Where are the Krays now?' he asked.

'In my brother David's flat.'

'What's the address?'

I told him – 51 Moresby Road, Stoke Newington – and who else was in the flat with them, namely most of the Firm members, my brothers Alfie and David, my younger brother, Paul, only eleven years old, David's wife who was pregnant and David's two very young daughters.

'A lot of people are coming and going, and they are armed to the teeth,' I told him. There were at least two shotguns that I had seen, one of which was a pump-action repeater. The Firm were certainly tooled up with handguns. And, although I certainly wasn't going to tell the police this, I too had a gun.

'Our family are all very afraid,' I said. 'Ronnie has got a list of people he intends to kill.'

Butler asked, 'Are any of my men on the list?' After a moment I said, 'No.'

I told him that Ronnie wouldn't let the young children leave because he'd said that the Old Bill wouldn't come in with guns blazing with women and children in the flat. I also explained that David had told Ronnie that he did not want any of them to stay at his place, but Ronnie had said, 'We are staying anyway and that's that,' or words to that effect. Then I said to Tommy Butler: 'Just be careful when you raid the place because of Christine and the kids. Please.'

Butler sat there for a while, mulling over my information. Then he said, as if he hadn't heard a word of what I had just told him: 'We had no idea how powerful they are becoming. They are hard to keep track of when they move all the time. Everyone is so terrified of them that we can't get anyone close to them to work with us.'

I wasn't sure what he was getting at so I said: 'I'll be leaving now,' and went to get out of the car. I felt like I'd said everything I needed to say.

'No, not yet,' Tommy Butler said, restraining me. 'We need you to let us know what's going on.'

I didn't like the way this conversation was going. 'Aren't you going to arrest them?' I asked.

'No,' he said. 'It's not as easy as that. We need more information.' Then he asked me, 'Will you go back in and get us what we need?'

What had I done? Maybe I was stupid to think one call, one meet would be enough. I don't know what I really thought when I first went out to make that call to Scotland Yard. But by the time I'd made it, I really believed that they would raid the flat in Stoke Newington, arrest the Krays and the rest of the Firm and that my family would be safe.

I thought for a minute and said, 'I will as long as all my family are kept safe and left out of it.'

Butler said nothing for a minute and then he answered, 'OK, I promise we will do everything we can. So don't you worry. But just remember you are doing a very dangerous job for us. Be very careful or you will be dead.'

As if I needed telling.

Then Butler continued, pointing to the man sitting next to me, 'This is your contact. His name is Joe Pogue. Memorise his name by thinking of the word "rogue". Now you need a code name that you will remember.'

I decided on the name 'Phillips'. I chose it as a tribute to the man who had been so kind to me when I was starting out: Commander Cecil Filmer, who I used to call 'Phil'.

Now it truly was time for me to leave. I looked at the faces in the car and wondered again: 'What the fuck have I got myself into?'

Joe Pogue gave me a number to memorise so that I could call at anytime. 'Stay in touch,' he said. I left the car and walked back to Fleet Street with a few men standing on both sides of the street just looking at me.

I kept my head down and moved as fast as I could without running. I felt the men on the street were trying to see my face. I knew, or thought I did, that the Krays had paid informers within the police – but had no idea how high they went. I couldn't run, I couldn't hide. I'd crossed the line. And now I must go back into the jaws of it and most probably get myself killed. I was in a daze.

I got a bus going towards Islington but needed more time, so I got off and started walking. Then I got a cab to Stoke Newington, got out in the High Road and walked the rest of the way to Moresby Road. I thought I was being watched all the way.

I finally got to the door of my brother's flat. I couldn't see a soul around. I tapped on the window and a face peeked out so fast I didn't see who it was. The door was opened by Christine, who didn't say a word but gave me a look of utter helplessness. In I went. The place stank of booze, smoke and sweat. After being out in the fresh air, I wanted to get out again straight away. But I knew I couldn't. I was back in it. I would have to stay in it. Surely they must know.

And there's Ronnie, sitting in one of David's chairs: 'Hello Bobby, had a nice little outing have you? How's your mum?'

CHAPTER 11
MORESBY ROAD –
AND A TRIP TO DARTMOOR

So now the Firm are all holed up in a tiny flat with women and children as their protection. My brother David was perhaps the most terrified of all of us. His family was so caught up in it, how could he not be?

After my meeting with Butler it quickly became apparent that the police were watching us. There was a garden at the back of David's flat and the Old Bill were by now all round us. One day a copper casually knocked on the front door to ask David if his wife and family were all right, as if he were just passing. Ronnie was in the bath while this was going on. He was always in the bath at David's place as he didn't have one at home. But when David asked Ronnie what we were going to do, he just said: 'Don't worry about it.' He was so confident, so sure that they wouldn't come in if David's wife and the children were there.

There was still a lot of coming and going. The twins needed to know who'd been in the Beggar that night, who'd seen Ronnie, who was saying what to who, who to put the frighteners on. They needed information. And there were policeman in their pay who'd tell them all of that.

David had to go out for food and fags. One time he and Christine went down to the shops in Upper Clapton Road with one of their children, and passed a policeman standing outside in the street. He nodded in recognition at them, smiling and asking how they were. They just nodded and smiled back at him before going back to the flat. There were always one or two of the Firm staring at us too. Then there would always be one or two police at the shops pretending they were buying cigarettes. What would we do if they got an order to come in after us?

On the fourth or fifth night there was a knock at the front door. When that happened, we were always told to get away from it and go in the kitchen. This time it's a copper. So Christine has to open it. Ronnie and Reggie and the rest of them were all in the front room, ready for a shoot-out. Someone had a shotgun loaded and ready – there were plenty of guns. Ronnie started gesturing at Christine to get rid of him. The policeman told Christine that they'd heard there'd been a robbery in the area and was just checking up that everyone was safe. 'You all right?' he asked Christine. Christine must have been terrified but answered, 'Yes, I'm all right. Everything's fine.' It was like something from a film.

The policeman said: 'Well, we've had a report, but as long as you're OK, I guess that's it.'

Once the policeman had gone, Christine started to break down, sobbing and crying, begging David to do something, get them out of it. But David was in an impossible position. What do you tell your wife if the Kray Firm decides to come round for tea?

I really felt for David. His wife Christine was a happy, sociable girl who really loved taking care of the kids. Diane was about two and walking, and Joanne was one and still in a pushchair. Christine would not let liberties be taken and not surprisingly she was constantly on at David to discover when the Krays would be leaving. Most people have that sort of row about the in-laws at Christmas, not about having their two-room flat full of armed villains.

She didn't know at first that there'd been a shooting, although she must have had a pretty good idea after a few days of all this. David had given her some old guff about the police trying to pin it on the twins but she'd have seen through that, I'm sure. And so it went on. I heard them arguing through the thin walls of their bedroom. If David was a real man, she would say, why couldn't he just get rid of them? I felt for my brother and was impressed by Christine's courage. She wasn't afraid of them, that's for sure. That's the sort of woman she was.

David at last told Ron, 'Look, you just can't stay here.' He begged him. 'Ron, Ron, Ron, don't do this to me!' But he wouldn't listen. The Firm holed up in David's flat for the next two weeks, with people coming and going all the while. Occasionally Ronnie would send someone out to buy toys for the children, trying to make him look like he was all heart. Alfie was sent out more times to buy the drink.

Ronnie drank crates and crates of brown ale. Reggie liked a gin and tonic too. There were clouds of cigarette smoke all the time. One night Nobby Clark brought Violet Kray over with some shirts for Ron. She said she was very worried about him, and Ron told her, 'I didn't do Cornell, Mum, but they are trying to fit me up, the Old Bill.' Violet said someone had been round and smashed their windows. We found out later it was Cornell's widow, Olive. Mrs Kray was there for about an hour, and then they took her home.

Ronnie's doctor came to give him some drug or other, and gave Christine and some of the Firm some tranquillisers as well. The strange thing was Ronnie seemed to be in his element, enjoying every moment of it. There were moments of hilarity and moments of terror. We could even go out to the shops, or to visit our families. But not all together. And of course, no one was allowed do a runner.

We used to go out to pubs as well, not the Grave Maurice or Madge's, not for the first few days at least, but pubs in Stoke Newington. There was a social club in the Lebus furniture factory in Ferry Lane in Tottenham where they had boxing nights and we'd sometimes go there.

Occasionally Ronnie and Reggie would start whispering to one another about 'getting a few quid' to this or that officer in Scotland Yard or the East End nicks. It soon became clear to me that not only did the police know where the Krays were almost from the beginning but that the twins were actually passing and getting information from the Old Bill, with members of the Firm going in and out as the message boys. The campaign to keep any witnesses quiet was working. It was starting to look like they were going to get away with it.

Ronnie actually left for a couple of nights – only to come back to David's two days later, telling us that he 'felt safe here'. Presumably a police informer had told him that he was.

Meanwhile I had made my offer to Butler. Now the squeeze was really on. I was suddenly the Yard's best hope of bringing down the Krays. Me, Bobby Teale. I didn't know it yet but perhaps I was their only hope. Their demands began right after I'd first made contact.

It was clear to me that the police knew perfectly well it was Ronnie who'd gone into the Blind Beggar and done Cornell. But they did not know who the other man was – who had fired into the ceiling. If they could get to him they could get to Ronnie.

As I would hear it pretty soon it from Pogue, two witnesses to the shooting (who'd been in the Beggar when it happened) had gone into Arbour Square Police Station in Stepney and told the Old Bill exactly who had done it. They had told them it was Ronnie Kray on 12 March, three nights into the siege of Bobby's flat – and when I'd first told Butler where they all were.

Everyone knew it was Ronnie. But there was no one brave enough to say that in a statement that could be used in court. The other man in the Beggar was still a mystery. He was said to have 'scars, similar to scald marks on his face and hands'. He might have had a Scots accent. Well, I knew it was Scotch Ian Barrie. I told Pogue that. You could not mistake him.

There were plenty of pictures of Ronnie, of course. But Mr Butler needed a photograph of this other man, so Pogue told me. So what was I supposed to do – get out a camera and ask Scotch Ian to smile?

It happened like this. I saw a picture of Ian Barrie among a stack of photos belonging to Reggie on the table in David's flat. Reggie was looking through a pile of them for some reason. It was common for the twins to have a stack of prints with them wherever they were. They had suitcases full of them, taken in clubs, in pubs, with celebrities, with boxers, with the Firm. They lived for their image.

This lot of snaps had come over after some errand to Vallance Road. I think Billy Exley brought them. Poor old Billy was going backwards and forwards with the twins' washing. So I waited until Reg was out of the room and I took a full-size photo of Ian Barrie out of the stack and slid it into my jacket. It showed him standing outside the house of a mate of theirs, a bookmaker called Charlie Clark, and it had been taken recently.

Needless to say, doing this was a huge risk. But Butler had asked me to do it so I did. Remember that at this point I believed that he was going to come and rescue my family at any moment. I arranged a meeting with Pogue to hand it over by phoning a particular number from a call box. I'd got out of the flat again by saying I was going to visit my mum. Mum was getting a lot of visits. I gave the picture to Pogue at our next meeting. He just sort of grunted. 'We'll need more than this,' he said.

Certain times I would be told to phone back, or phone a different number at a special time. It was absolutely terrifying.

The actual meet would be in an unmarked car, which would pick me up in some side street. They told me to keep my head down. We would be driving around as we talked. The conversations were recorded on tape, though at times I had my suspicions that one of the police sitting in the front of the car would turn off the tape recorder at crucial moments.

Sometimes Pogue would sit next to me in the back, and other times he would be sitting in the front asking me questions. Sometimes there were even two officers sitting in the back of the car on either side of me. At no time did I ever sit in the front. Maybe they thought I was going to suddenly jump out.

On one of these meets – and I guess there were around three times when I could get out of the flat during those terrifying two weeks – I was telling Pogue how Ronnie had been trying to get my little brother into bed. I said that I was on the verge of shooting him. At this, Pogue interrupted me to ask what kind of gun I had. As soon as I started to speak the copper in the front started to fiddle with the tape. They didn't want this bit recorded.

I said I had a nine millimetre, at which Pogue said: 'Well, we need you to use a Luger.'

He then turned to the other officers and asked: 'Have we got an old Luger lying around anywhere?'

At this point I had no idea what they were really up to. Perhaps they had it in their minds to genuinely explore whether I would be willing to kill Ronnie Kray for them and so avoid the bother of bringing him to trial. Although, whether they would have had me go through with it, had I been willing, I had no idea. Alternatively, it occurred to me that they may have been testing to see whether I was a genuine gangster. I had told them that I was on the edge of the Firm and not part of their criminality. I wondered whether they believed me.

Had I said yes to that Luger then I would have shown them I was as bad as the Krays. Obviously, I said 'no'. But I have wondered to this day what was really going on when they made that offer and what would have happened had I said 'yes'.

Only one man in the Yard took me to one side and warned me against going down this path – although of course it was never spelled out in so many words. He told me I would 'be fished out of the Thames in pieces'.

And all the time I'm trying to stay calm. I knew my life was hanging by a thread. I was terrified that I was going to be exposed at any moment. And what if those stories about the Krays having police informers were true?

It didn't take me long to find out. A few days after I passed the Barrie photograph to Butler, with the twins and half the Firm still holed up in Moresby Road, I left the flat to go out with Reggie on a meet. It was pretty terrifying. Here I was trying to get information to the police about what's really going on – and I've got to look as if it's business as usual with my best friend Reggie.

Suddenly he tells me he had just got word from what he called 'his man in the Yard' that 'the Old Bill have got David's address and have the whole place under surveillance... So we will have to move.'

Well, that was one way of getting these psychotic killers out of my brother's flat. But it did not help me much. I had crossed the line. I had told the police directly that Ronnie Kray had killed Cornell. And now Reggie had told me they were getting inside information. What do I do? I had no choice. I had to play along. That's what Alfie and David were doing. Like me, they had to. Look at what Alfie did for Ron after just a few days.

As the time passed in the flat, Alfie hadn't been caught up in the events as much as David had been. Alfie was there the first couple of nights, and then he said to Ronnie he had to go back to Wendy and the boys.

Ronnie told him, 'Make sure you come back tomorrow night, and that you don't say a word to anyone.' So Alfie didn't tell Wendy the Krays had done Cornell, just that the police suspected them.

After that Alfie came over to David's place to bring drink and food, whatever they needed. So even before it ended, he was back to doing more or less what he'd always been doing. Running errands. Part of that was for the 'Away Society'.

A part of the big-hearted Kray myth was that they would do little favours for villains who'd been put away. The Krays would go round to see their families and give them some money, weekly or fortnightly, whatever they could. Alfie, David – or once or twice it was me, Bobby – would be told: 'Go round to see so-and-so's wife and give her this for herself and the kids – make sure they know where it came from.' It was all part of the propaganda.

But now Ronnie had a bigger plan – a real spectacular.

A week or so after the Cornell murder – it was 20 March 1966, as Alfie would state later at the Old Bailey trial – Ronnie and Alfie were in the Grave Maurice and Ron told him, 'We're going to give you a driver to go down to Dartmoor and visit a friend. We want you to tell him we'll get him out if we can't get a date for his release from the Home Secretary.'

Well, the friend turned out to be Frankie Mitchell. He was a legend. Alfie had never met him – none of us had as he'd been inside so much. But he'd heard of him, everybody had. He was the 'Mad Axe-Man' detained at Her Majesty's Pleasure at Dartmoor Prison with no date for release.

Alfie told me a bit about Frankie's background. He'd started his career of crime stealing bottles of milk as a kid, and wound up going to approved school. He was strong and big and caused mayhem in there, so afterwards he got taken straight to Borstal. From there he went to YP – young people's prison – and then he graduated pretty quickly to the great and gruesome Wandsworth. He ended up getting eighteen years for violence.

It was Frankie Mitchell who started the famous Wandsworth riot in 1954, after smashing a projector up into the air in the hall during a Saturday afternoon film show that had been put on for the prisoners. Afterwards he broke out of another jail and eventually got put away again, earning himself the nickname of the 'Mad Axe-Man' in the process. The newspapers called him that after he was done for threatening an elderly couple while on the run from a hospital for the criminally insane.

He was a big man, so strong he became a legend. But he had low intelligence and at heart he was like a puppy.

Ronnie had met Frankie in Wandsworth Prison and had befriended him. He could be quite sentimental like that. He promised to help him after he came out. But it looked like Frankie was never coming out.

So Ronnie had decided he had to do something about Frank Mitchell. He would start a campaign to get him released, make a noise, show what a big man he was by getting the government to do something.

Mad Teddy Smith would be the one who would write all the letters to the newspapers and the Home Office. My brothers thought the whole thing was Mad Teddy's idea to get some good propaganda after the Cornell killing. Most of London's villains thought Ronnie was out of order after the Blind Beggar incident, although they wouldn't dare say it. Perhaps Ron believed this would be a way of salvaging his reputation amongst them.

So now he wanted Alfie to go down to Dartmoor and sort of bump into Frankie Mitchell. Two of the Firm, Tommy Cowley and Wally Garelick, had already been to see Mitchell a little before he did.

Alfie couldn't quite believe what he was hearing.

'You want me to plan Frank Mitchell's escape?' he asked Ron.

'Well, yes. If we don't get him a date for a release, then you'll be the one to go down and get him out and fetch him back to London,' said Ronnie.

So it's down to Alfie to go and see Frankie and tell him what the twins have got in mind. He would go with Fat Wally Garelick, who was a minicab driver in his normal life. They would go there in his Rover 3-litre, and they were to leave that same night.

So early the next morning, 21 March, they set off. Almost immediately, they got pulled by the police on the way to Dartmoor. 'Who are you and where are you going?' they demanded. Maybe the police were watching them all along.

The police obviously CRO'd them [checked with Criminal Record Office via radio] but then they let them on their way. Maybe they wanted to see whether they were really going to Dartmoor or anywhere else. When they got to Dartmoor it was just as Alfie had always imagined it to be – mists were swirling around the moor and it was so cold you could feel the damp in the wind, even though it was March. Alfie and Wally went up to the prison door, gave their names and went upstairs into a visiting hut, with a little canteen inside, like something out of a prisoner-of-war camp. It reminded Alfie of stories about Colditz.

'He won't be long, he'll be back in a minute,' a prison officer told them. 'He's just out on the moor.'

Frank's cell was never locked – he'd been inside so long the officers trusted him to go down to the gatehouse and ride his horse for an hour, or go to the pub and have a couple of pints before coming back to the prison. He'd even got a girlfriend in one of the villages. He'd been inside for eighteen years. He had the mind of a child but the strength of Goliath.

All of a sudden Alfie and Wally heard the sound of Frank's heavy footsteps coming up the wooden stairs, more like a giant approaching than an ordinary man.

He looked at Wally and my brother, and shook Alfie's hand so hard he nearly broke it. He didn't know Alfie, and all Alfie knew of him was a photo he'd seen in the paper.

It was freezing in the hut where they were sitting. Frank was dressed in a denim jacket with nothing underneath it, a pair of jeans, no socks and a pair of boots with the laces missing. He looked like a mad ogre of a man. He kept asking Alfie to feel his bulging arm, repeatedly telling him how he did two thousand press-ups each morning to stay in trim.

'Right, do you want a nice cup of tea?' Frank asked them. They nodded yes.

From behind them, a prison officer called out: 'Would you like a cup of tea, too, Frank?'

Frank turned on him with a face like thunder. 'You know full well I don't drink tea! I'll have a glass of milk, like I always do,' he barked.

'Sorry, Frank!' said the officer, clearly petrified. Later Alfie was to hear stories of how Frank used to walk round the exercise yard with the governor of the prison tucked under his arm, while the governor shouted, 'Put me down, Frank, put me down!'

Frank then turned round and whispered to Alfie, 'Any news?"

Alfie repeated what he'd been told to say. 'Ronnie and Reggie are going to go to the Home Secretary and try to get you a date. They have got some police onside who are going to try and help from inside Scotland Yard and MPs they know who are going to help too. And if they can't get you a date, you are going to be sprung from this prison. Ronnie suggested that I do it.' That's exactly what Ronnie had told Alfie. But it wasn't going to turn out like that.

Frank's eyes lit up at what Alfie had told him.

'Tell them that once you get me out of here, I can get a machine-gun and kill anyone they want,' he said.

Alfie didn't think that was quite what Ronnie had in mind, but you never knew.

Anyway, whether he meant to or not, Frank scared the hell out of Alfie. The guards were terrified of him too, sitting well away from him. Whenever they came too near Frank would shoo them away with his hand and they'd scurry off.

Frank leaned forward and said, 'I like you Alfie.' Alfie laughed and said he liked him too. Then Frank continued: 'I want you to bust me out of here today. I want to you stop at the phone box you passed on the way here and wait there for me. I want you to take me to London now!'

Alfie said, 'All right, Frank, all right,' while trying to think quickly how on earth he was going to get out of there in one piece. What the hell was he meant to do?

Poor Alfie was truly terrified now. There was no way he and Wally were driving Frankie Mitchell off that day. Ronnie would have killed them if they'd pitched up back at the flat with him. So Wally and Alfie just looked at one another, walked straight out, down the stairs and out of the prison – and sped back to London without stopping.

CHAPTER 12
BESIDE THE SEASIDE

Those last days at Moresby Road were the most chaotic – and the most dangerous. What was this – a hostage siege or a gigantic piss-up? There'd be treks out to boozers, as if we didn't have a care in the world. At first we went to a dreadful place in Clapton filled with pensioners sipping stout. We called it the Dead Pub. Then after a few days we started going back to Madge's or the Grave Maurice, where the twins were greeted like long-lost friends. 'Where've you been Ronnie? There's all sorts of talk about you.' Well, you can imagine how it went. In the end, after two weeks, Ronnie, Reggie and the rest of the Firm finally left the flat. I think they wanted their old mum back washing their shirts. And by then they'd got word that nobody who'd been in the Blind Beggar that night was talking.

We were all pretty roughed up but grateful to be alive. Ronnie was still exulting in what he'd done – killing an unarmed man sitting on a bar stool in a pub – and now he started telling Reggie to do the same.

I'd been having my little meets with Pogue but no one from the Yard seemed to want to do anything. All they wanted was more, more information. By now Ronnie was lying low somewhere different but I knew exactly where he was.

David, meanwhile, just wanted to give his family a break. And where do they go? To Kray territory, down to Steeple Bay, the caravan site on the Thames estuary, where the twins and their mum would go down more or less every weekend that spring of 1966. A few days later I'd go down there myself. So did Alfie.

David knew the place well. It was his job to drive the Krays' mother and their old man down there. Christine wanted to go to her parents in Birmingham after the Moresby Road siege but David persuaded her it was the only place to go, crazy as that might seem. They were pretty skint and their flat was a wreck. It was easier all round just to pack their bags and get out of it. So they ended up staying down there for several weeks during the next month or so, with Alfie and me joining them, and the Kray family coming and going too.

Charlie Kray had a caravan down at Steeple with his old woman, Dolly, on the opposite side of the bay. We all liked Dolly. She was a nice woman, strict perhaps, but otherwise OK. Charlie was a right playboy. She had her hands full with him from the beginning.

There was one time Charlie and David were in the pub, and he said to them: 'I want you to do me a favour. Come with me. I want you to go round and tell my wife that we're going to Dartmoor together. Say we're going to share the driving.'

So David went round to see Dolly with him, at their gaff off the Mile End Road, and backed up his story for him. He felt a bit bad because he genuinely liked Dolly, but he didn't feel he could refuse.

As soon as they came out, David asked him, 'What's happening, Charlie?' He said, 'Nothing. I've got to go now. I'm going to see a bird…' David had been used as part of the plan. The next morning Charlie came round to the 66 Club at about eleven or twelve, and asked David to go back to Dolly with him so that it looked genuine.

David would later have good reason for mistrusting Charlie, and I mean good reason. We would all come to consider Charlie as the most cunning one out of the lot of them. There he was walking round in expensive suits with diamond and gold tie-pins, all the time telling people 'I'm the good guy.' He boasted that he was 'in entertainment', but he wasn't even in the business until Alfie and David introduced him to it.

According to David, whether it was stolen out of the bank or took off a church collection, Charlie was always the first in the queue for his money. He didn't care where it came from. Then he'd say: 'I've got to go, Dolly wants to go to the hairdressers.'

David reckoned Dolly must have lived in the hairdressers the number of times he heard Charlie say that. But underneath all his charm and swagger he was a two-faced womaniser and not to be trusted. Barbara Windsor had an affair with Charlie when we knew her. The rumours that Reggie was going out with Barbara were just put round by the twins to keep Dolly quiet.

But Charlie wasn't the reason we were heading for Essex. After that time in the flat, Ronnie seemed to want us down at the seaside all the time. Did he want our company, or did he want the kids round him as protection? He seemed pretty keen to get David's family down there.

After they all went down to Steeple Bay, Ronnie started urging David: 'Get a caravan, Dave. I know the geezer on the site, he'll get you one.' So David took Ron's advice and got a caravan, a lovely, big, beautiful brand-new one that they put right next to Ronnie's. Ronnie and Reggie came over to admire it: 'Look at that, Ronnie. We've got another caravan. Isn't it great?'

So of course it wasn't David's caravan. It was in David's name and he had to make the payments on it, but it was the twins' caravan, their possession, just like everything else.

That spring, in the evenings, everyone would all go to the caravan park clubhouse together. Christine would sit and have a chat with Mrs Kray who she thought was a really nice woman. You'd see Ronnie down there one day, but the next minute he'd be gone.

Alfie and I used to come down too. We were drawn back to the Krays', despite all that had occurred. All of us were in too deep to do otherwise. Plus of course I knew I had to carry on acting like their friend so as not to arouse any suspicions.

So there we'd all be – Ronnie, Reggie, Charlie, Mad Teddy, David and me – we'd all have a laugh, all be pissed. Everyone used to walk in and out of everyone else's caravans like next-door neighbours. One minute we'd be on our own, the next minute you'd look out of the caravan, see four cars and know that Ronnie or Reggie had arrived.

At that time Ronnie wasn't too bad. It could change minute to minute. One night he got up and said he was going for a walk. He was in one of his black moods, which he would get for no reason at all. That evening Ron came over and told us: 'See that graveyard in the woods over there? We're all going to go in there.'

'What you talking about, Ron?' I asked.

Ron answered, 'I bet you can't! We're all going in the grave-yard to see who gets scared.'

Alfie, David and I all said we didn't want to. But Ron threatened he'd give anyone who didn't 'a good hiding'.

'I'll go through it first,' he volunteered. We got to the woods, and Ron disappeared off into the graveyard, ordering us to wait a little while before we followed him.

So we gave him a minute, and then I said, 'I'll go.' Then someone else offered: 'I'll go too.'

In the end we all went together into this big graveyard. We were all laughing and making spooky noises. The Colonel had gone on ahead, of course. Ronnie was waiting for us at the other end. When we came out together, calling to him, he went mad.

'David, Alfie, Bobby! What are you doing? I wanted you to come in one at a time, not all together. You've spoilt the whole game now.'

When we got back to the caravan he sat there, sulking like a baby and refusing to talk to us. At one point he wanted us all to go back out and do it again, but this time we refused. He was muttering about how a graveyard would be a good place to hide bodies. Then there was another place nearby, an old Roman camp with gravel pits around it. That really got him going, too.

On another day Ronnie turned round to us and said: 'Come on, we're going for a lovely walk... Do us some good, have some nice fresh air.'

We walked down to where the inlets came in from the sea. The place was like a bog and you could easily sink into the sand if you didn't watch where you put your feet. We got to some creeks and I said to Ron, 'Look at that, Ron. If you stepped in there you'd be up to your neck.'

Ron said, 'Yeah, if you put a body in there it would sink to the bottom and no one would find it for thousands of years. Coo, there's some lovely places to hide people here, aren't there? Isn't it great?'

'You're not going to put us down there, are you?' Alfie asked, only half-joking. Ron's eyes just glazed over, staring into space. He didn't reply.

This kind of fantasy was starting to come on him more and more. Except it wasn't fantasy. He was quite capable of doing somebody over even when he was supposed to be on 'holiday' – even when he was supposed to be looking after his mum.

We were in the clubhouse one night when we noticed another caravan owner sitting at the bar, who we used to call 'the bully'. His family had stayed in caravans on the site for years and he behaved like he owned the place. Ronnie wasn't there but his mother was with us. We were all having a drink when Violet got up and went to the toilet, and the bully pushed by her.

About a week later we were all in the clubhouse again when Ronnie arrived. Afterwards as usual he suggested we all went back to David's caravan for a drink. We were just getting there, at about eleven o'clock, when we suddenly noticed that Ron had slipped back to the clubhouse on his own.

Minutes later Ron came in, breathless, gasping, 'Give us a brown ale. That's better...'

Everyone was smoking and we put a few records on and started drinking and enjoying ourselves again. Ronnie in particular seemed as happy as a pig, staying the night in David's caravan, on the spare bunk.

The next morning Alfie got up early to go out and get the papers. He told us when he got to the shop a feller in there said: 'That Ronnie Kray came down and did Bill [the bully] last night. Came into the clubhouse and just smashed into him... knocked him out. We had to get an ambulance and everything.'

When Alfie got back to the caravan he asked Ron about it. 'What happened, Ron? I heard they had to get an ambulance for that man last night.'

Ron shrugged. 'He was only a cunt,' he said.

Next he threatened to drown a dog whose barking was keeping his mother awake. He would have done it, too, without a second thought.

But he didn't always have the upper hand. Another time a young man on a motorbike, a straight guy, not a villain, pulled up outside the caravan. We all started admiring his bike, and when Ron mentioned he'd never been on a motorbike, the young man offered to give him a ride on it. Ronnie had no shirt on, just his trousers, but he climbed on and the guy drove off, with Ronnie grabbing him round the waist, his face white with horror.

The motorcycle rider, thinking Ronnie was enjoying himself, took him all round the camp. It was hilarious to see Ron's face. You didn't know whether to laugh or not, but the language Ron used was unrepeatable.

I remember Charlie coming round one night. It was pretty late, but then before you knew it Reggie and Ronnie had arrived too. I thought, 'Oh no,' because we were all tired, but we got up and gave them a drink.

Ronnie said: 'We need to have a talk, all right?' So Alfie, David and I said, 'Yeah, all right, Ron.'

He said he had some money, ten thousand pounds, which he wanted David to look after – to 'put it away somewhere safe'. David told Ron that he'd bury it under his caravan. We knew Ronnie had guns, too, buried all round the place. One way or another my brothers were being drawn more and more into Ron's criminal plans, whether they liked it or not.

Even David was realising by now that we just had to get out of this situation. He told me he knew he should have done this straight away after Moresby Road. I just agreed with him, longing to tell him what I was trying to do to help get us out of the Krays' grip, but scared of getting us into even more trouble if I said anything.

Alfie and David were just ordinary market traders – not career criminals. They both had young families to look after. And unlike me, they weren't going to abandon them. They'd been in trouble with the law as kids but they had always got their own money, not taken the Firm's handouts. That was the difference. The Firm, some of them had wives, but they were invisible. Reggie's bid for married bliss lasted two months. Mine hadn't lasted very much longer. Ronnie, well, you know what he was.

After no one got him for Cornell, Ronnie started getting his confidence back. You could see it. Everyone knew what he'd done but no one was saying anything. It made him feel even more in command. He really was untouchable. In the meantime his madness seemed to be getting worse.

He'd started talking to himself, just muttering: 'Yeah, right,' all the time as if he was in conversation with someone else. Or else he was constantly reminding everyone: 'I'm the governor round here. I'm the Colonel. Fuck the police, fuck the government.'

The only authority was his mum, Violet, whose disapproval did bother him. As for me, David and Alfie, the twins had no respect for us whatsoever. We were all just errand boys.

I could see my brothers wanted to get away from the madness and violence of the Krays. As much as I was trying to, perhaps – but I was on a different track. And by this time they knew so much and were so far in, they really didn't know how to escape.

Alfie and David knew that if they went missing for a few days and they went into a pub on our own manor, a car could pull up at any second and the Colonel himself could jump out. It didn't matter where you were – he'd find you. Even on the night of the World Cup final later that summer when we were watching it on TV round a friend's house – when practically everyone in Britain was glued to the telly – there was a knocking at the door with a message that he wanted to see us.

There was no hiding place from Ronnie. And I was in as deep as anyone. What I did not know then was just how much Ronnie was preying on my family. For many years I had no idea what had happened to David that spring, when he was back in London after they'd come back from Steeple Bay. One day, several decades later, he found the courage to tell me. This is his story, in his own words:

We were down the Astor Bar at about two or three o'clock one morning when Ronnie asked me if I was going home and would I give him a lift. I was tired and half-pissed myself and said I would. We were driving along when I began to realise how dangerous it was to drive after so much to drink. So I started saying to Ron: 'This looks bad, Ron. If we get pulled I'm going to be done.'

'Don't worry about it,' Ron answered.

By some miracle we managed to get to Vallance Road without being spotted. Ron said, 'You might as well stay here. You were all over the place driving back here. You'll get nicked if you don't.'

I didn't want to, but had to agree that Ron was right. I told him I was going to kip on the couch. But Ron insisted I sleep upstairs in his bed to avoid disturbing his parents Violet and Charlie, who were sleeping down-stairs, next to the kitchen. The toilet was out in the backyard so you had to make sure you used it before you went to bed or you'd wake everyone else in the house.

Knowing Ron was a pouf, I told him: 'No, I'm not like that, Ron. I don't want any of that.' Ron said, 'No, I know you're not. I promise I won't touch you. It will all be OK.'

I crept downstairs to use the toilet. I then went back up to Ron's bedroom, and climbed into his very small bed on the side next to the window. I put my head down on the pillow and went spark out.

All of a sudden I woke up and Ronnie's playing me, sucking my cock. I couldn't believe it. I thought I was dreaming. But there he was crouched over me – more and more insistent, wrestling with me in the bed, and using his weight to force me down, telling me, 'Just try it.'

I kept saying, 'No, no, Ron, get off me,' struggling against him for all I was worth, and shouting and screaming for Violet and Charlie to come and help. No one came. Ron kept telling me: 'Shut up, me mother's downstairs!' In the meantime he seemed to be becoming stronger than ever.

I knew he fancied me, but I never dreamt he would do something like this. He held me down, and forced my legs apart. At one point he put his arm round my neck in an attempt to strangle me. In the end he overpowered me. To my lasting shame, Ronnie Kray raped me.

After it was all over I sat on the bottom of the bed all night, shaking with cold and shock, while Ron slept, oblivious to everything, in a drunken stupor.

I managed to get away and ran down to the khazi to throw up. I felt sick and ill, and just wanted to be out of there. Ronnie woke up and came after me, whispering: 'Be quiet, be quiet!' I went back up to the bedroom but was awake all night after this. If I tried to leave, Ronnie would physically stop me. After two or three attempts, I gave up.

About six in the morning I had to go downstairs to use the toilet. Ron stirred then and told me: 'Don't say nothing' (to his mum and dad). They must've heard. I'm sure of it. I was screaming and shouting loud enough to wake the dead. I then threatened not just to wake his mother but also to tell her what he'd just done.

Ron said, 'You open your mouth one word about this and you know what to expect. You won't have a family any more.'

He still wouldn't let me go. So we all had tea, like nothing had happened, with Mrs Kray fussing round in the frontroom.

Ronnie was blustering, but I could see in his face that he might be remorseful – embarrassed even. He looked like he was thinking: 'What the hell did I do that for?'

Inside I was so angry I wanted to kill Ron then and there. I'd never felt like this about anybody. I knew I couldn't fight him as he was physically much larger than me, but I felt I had to get my revenge somehow. Forgetting all my fear of him, I told him I was going to go straight to the police and 'get him nicked for this'. Even though that was ridiculous, Ron looked worried and started insisting that he'd been drunk.

'Ron, you weren't that drunk,' I told him. 'You knew exactly what you were doing. I'm going to tell your mother, and make sure everyone, all the chaps and all the villains, get to hear about this.'

He got up and, with his face very close to mine, said: 'Don't you ever say a fucking word!'

If I ever said anything, I was dead, he told me. And my wife and kids. 'I will know, you see.'

And I didn't say a word. For a very long time. I didn't tell my brothers. Nor my wife. I felt too frightened and too humiliated. The first time I ever spoke about it was when I told Alfie. And that would be more than forty years after it happened.

We weren't like the rest of the Firm. We never thought we were. We were like family to the Krays. And now he'd done this, an act that changed everything. After this I avoided Ronnie as much as possible. I kept away, hiding from embarrassment and shame.

CHAPTER 13
A CLOSE SHAVE

However much they were being abused, David and Alfie found it impossible to break away. As for me, I was an informer. I had to stay on the inside. I had expected it all to be over once I'd told Tommy Butler who'd done Cornell. I'd assumed that the police would do something immediately, that the cavalry would arrive at David's flat and rescue everyone. But it didn't happen like that.

I never seriously thought for a moment to tell my brothers what I had done, what I was doing – either before I'd made that first call to Scotland Yard or afterwards. I didn't think there was going to be an afterwards.

I believed I could just about handle the strain and fear of turning informer – but if I'd told Alfie and David and they had panicked, we would all have been lost.

There was one little survival technique I had. Ronnie was always telling me I was dozy, and thought I was a bit slow. I played on it, thinking quite rightly that it might protect me. But for how long was that going to work?

After the Blind Beggar shooting, it all ran according to East End form. Everyone knew it was Ronnie who'd done it but no one would say. The barmaid said she wouldn't be able to recognise anybody. According to her, she'd run down into the cellar as soon as she saw a gun. There were people in the pub who'd talked to the police but they weren't going to make a statement. The twins had put round the frighteners. They were doing that from the moment they'd set up in David's flat.

When Cornell's widow went round to Vallance Road throwing bricks at the windows and calling them murderers, she was the only one brave enough to say it. Ron and Reg didn't do anything about it, even though it had upset their mum. No one got nicked.

So in spite of the Firm trashing David's place, in spite of my run-in with Ronnie in the flat after his move on Paul, in spite of what, although I was unaware, had happened to David, we all of us went back to business as usual – being pals with the Krays. There wasn't really a choice.

My marriage to Pat was over. Alfie and David had their wives and children, but what was I supposed to do? Well, the Firm had become my family.

After the two weeks in Moresby Road, Ronnie found a new gaff, a bungalow in Chingford into which he moved with Ian Barrie. I knew all about it. The place was owned by Charlie Clark, a bookmaker, and his wife who had twelve cats. I know they were terrified but what could they do?

And what do I do? There we are, Reggie Kray and me, both with our marriages over, both heterosexuals, both up for a party. Reggie's got a ready-made place, a flat in Manor House rented off two Jewish birds. He'd once very briefly lived there when he'd married Frances. It was about half a mile from Cedra Court.

So I moved in with Reggie.

The flat was done up very flashily and it was our party place. Reggie would tell me to go and get a couple of birds and the four of us would all sleep in the same bed. I never knew who was with whom.

Or we would get back to the flat at all different times and Reggie or I would go up the stairs like a cat, not making a sound. Most of the time it was me who would go up on my own with my gun at the ready and as soon as the coast was clear I would signal to Reggie and he would come up with the girls and so it went. I would always act like I was a lot more drunk than I really was. But in fact I generally had very little to drink. It was safer that way.

It was especially dangerous when Ronnie would come over with some of the Firm and his boy to stay the night. Ronnie would just glare straight at me. 'Go on, go,' he would say. 'Get out of it and go home!' I would find a way to ask Reggie if that's what he wanted and he would just shrug and tell me to meet him at another place later. Or he would say: 'You'd better leave and I'll see you tomorrow.' The next day Reggie would apologise for him, saying: 'I'm sorry about what happened last night but Ronnie has a lot on his mind.'

They were always arguing. Ronnie would have screaming matches with Reggie over Reggie's drinking or any trivial thing he could come up with, but it always came back to me. When Ronnie told me to drive Reggie on a meet, I knew Ronnie wanted Reggie to kill me while we were alone. Ronnie wanted his twin to prove his love and loyalty. All of us in the Firm (and as far as they were concerned, I was now well in it) would hear Ronnie telling Reggie it was his turn to do one. In other words, kill someone. It would suit Ronnie perfectly if that someone was me; he had always been jealous of my friendship with his brother.

But alongside this type of behaviour, Ronnie was also perfectly capable of being a childlike clown again – if just for a few minutes. I was with Ronnie and Cornelius 'Connie' Whitehead (another member of the Firm) one time when one of us noticed a frog stuck at the bottom of a hole in the tarmac. As we went to walk on, Ronnie got down on his knees, insisting we had to rescue it, getting slime all over his hands in the process.

Connie Whitehead stared at Ronnie in amazement.

'You're trying to save a frog?'

Ronnie just replied: 'Can you fuck off? The poor thing's going to be run over!'

And all the while I'm living with Reg I'm having my little meets with Detective Sergeant Pogue. And he and his chums are hinting to me that it might be better all round, save a lot of trouble, if I pulled out a gun that they would supply (even though I already had a gun) and put a hole in Ronnie. Whether they were just playing with me I had no idea, as I've already said, but I must have been out of my mind to have even been having such conversations.

I told them where Ronnie was, over in the bungalow with Charlie Clark and the cat lady. Ronnie liked pets but wasn't keen on cats. Weekends he might be at Steeple Bay. I also told them more about what had happened the night of the drive from Madge's. But it was pointed out to me that whatever I might have to say about the Cornell killing and the aftermath wasn't going to be enough to nick them. Butler's got absolutely no one telling him what happened that night, except me. But I wasn't in the Blind Beggar. I only heard them talking about it afterwards. That wasn't enough to get anyone put away.

And what about what had happened at David's place? What was that – kidnapping? A hostage situation? If it came to court, they would just say it was all a big family party – which in fact is exactly what the Kray's defence would say later. Butler wanted more and put the squeeze on me to get it.

Joe Pogue was Butler's man. He was my controller – everything that happened after the initial meeting with Butler was going to be through Pogue and his men. And every time I met them they wanted more. And now Reggie himself tells me he's getting word about an informer within the Firm from inside the police. So now it's really a question of how long it is before I'm exposed.

Then there came the moment I thought I had been. I was sitting next to Ronnie, who starts going on about this supposed informer. He's even got a name: 'Phillips.'

How the hell did he get hold of that? It must have come from the police. I realised at that point, if I hadn't done so already, the information I'd given to Pogue was coming right back to the Krays. Perhaps I was being incredibly naïve. The twins were always boasting about their information service. But

I had thought it was just that, boasting – propaganda to keep people frightened. I hadn't been around when there had been all those meets with coppers and envelopes of cash passed at the 66 Club.

In April sometime we went to Saffron Walden in Essex, to see Geoff Allen, Ronnie's old friend who'd got him out of trouble plenty of times before. He had a big sixteenth-century house called Hempstead Hall and seemed very wealthy. The house had a library and was full of antiques, and I remember his wife had just given birth. For the twins it was a way of getting out of London for a while. After that we stayed at some big hotel. It was supposed to be a kind of holiday.

Albert Donoghue was there, Scotch Ian Barrie, and Scotch Jack Dickson. They all scrawled false names in the register. I put my real name. I was so scared of something happening to me, I wanted people to know I had been there.

I got a message out to Pogue to say where we all were. Soon after that I could sense we were being watched. You get to know these things.

We were all at some country pub when Ronnie started going on about 'fucking Phillips' and glaring at each of us in turn. I was so terrified, I remember feeling the hairs stand up on the back of my neck.

So I did what I always did when I wanted to get a read on Ronnie – made my eyes go a little dozy as if I was drunk, and then wait for his eyes to flick over me, dismissing me as too dumb to be a threat. At that moment I glanced out of the window and saw a copper in uniform on the street. Telling Reggie I was going out to get a breath of fresh air, I slipped out and went over to the policeman, telling him quickly, 'I need you to get a message to Joe Pogue in the Yard. Tell him it is from Phillips and that information received is coming back.' All this time, I didn't know if the others in the pub had noticed me missing, let alone seen me talking to a copper. So when I got back in the pub I said to Reggie, 'A copper outside pulled me and asked me what we were doing here, and I said we were on a holiday.' Ronnie overheard and said he thought it was a good answer.

I got back to London and received a message by phoning in to the contact number. It said that I had to come to another meeting with Pogue. He was angry. 'Don't you ever, ever do that again!' he said. 'Don't ever try to contact us through that low level again.' He was mad that I had spoken to a copper in uniform.

Then I was warned again by Pogue that I was going be fished out of the Thames if I didn't take more care.

I asked the detectives whether, if they could not identify the Kray informers inside the Yard, they could not at least use them to pass misinformation to cover my back. I told them that, right now, I believed Scotland Yard was the biggest threat to my life out of any of them. It felt like no one there could care less about my safety. One of Pogue's men replied: 'Now Bobby, that's not true, we are doing everything we can to keep you safe.'

'It don't look like it to me,' I said. And it didn't.

And so it went on. Ronnie was sinking into one of his manic periods, drinking for days on end, leaving Reggie in charge. Now it was Reggie's turn to show what he was made of.

There was a time when Reggie was in the Regency Club. Cornelius Whitehead, Big Albert Donoghue and Scotch Ian Barrie were with him. There was a small-time villain called Jimmy Field who either owed money or had said something out of order about the twins in Madge's, I don't really know. Reggie took Jimmy behind some curtains. Next thing I heard shots, four of them, and then the sound of this guy screaming. His foot was practically shot off. Donoghue and Whitehead dumped him outside Homerton Hospital.

The Firm were getting shooter-happy. Another time some drunken punter came up to Pat Connolly at the door of the Starlight Club, another Kray favourite in Highbury, and said: 'You fat cunt. What do you think you are – a gangster?' And Pat shot and wounded him. Cornelius Whitehead picked up the shells. The victim was dumped in the street. I heard Pat say: 'I just shot some cunt…'

I was telling Pogue all of this. I was telling him how Reggie was the one getting a bit trigger-happy now. 'Not enough to nick the twins, though, is it?' he would say. 'Get us more, Bobby, get us something that will stick.' What the fuck did I think I was doing? It would be my turn to take a bullet next.

But if I needed any further proof that I was doing the right thing in turning informer, it was how Bobby Cannon nearly got done. Bobby was from Poplar and owed the Krays money. This particular time it was meant to be Reggie's turn to kill. I remember Ronnie kept telling Reggie that he should kill someone to prove he was just as good as Ronnie. The words he used were: 'Why don't you do one? You don't do fuck all, get something going.'

And Reggie would reply, 'Don't fucking tell me what to do.'
He would prove himself in time. As I had seen at David's flat,
there was a constantly updated list of people known as the
'dreaded list', containing the names of people that Ronnie
wanted executing. It was Reggie's turn to cross someone off.

In fact Ronnie wasn't there that day to witness the events
but several other members of the Firm were, including Albert
Donoghue, Big Pat Connolly – and me. Jack the Hat McVitie
and Connie Whitehead were sent out to find this face Cannon
and bring him to a flat off the Hackney Road. It was on the first
floor. I don't know why we went there. I think it was just somewhere close by. I knew it as the place where a girl called Blonde
Vicky lived.

So Reggie had sent Jack the Hat and Connie out to get
Cannon. I don't know what he'd done or what they thought
he'd done. It was just as if the mood took one of the twins and
the rest of the Firm followed.

When they found him they lifted him from the street. He
had no choice but to come with them. He was told to sit down.
Reggie, Albert and I went into the kitchen. Reggie had a little
silver revolver like a cowboy's gun.

Reggie put a handkerchief over the nozzle to act as a
silencer. The handkerchief was tied very tight on the barrel. He
put the gun in his pocket.

We went into the room – that is, Albert, Reggie and me.
Jack the Hat, Connie, Pat Connolly and Cannon were already
sitting there in the living room, waiting. Reggie started making
some small talk with Cannon while gesturing to me to turn up

the radio but I only turned it up slightly. 'Please Release Me' came over the airwaves. Reggie kept on nodding – louder, louder – but I would not turn it up more.

Cannon sensed what was coming. He was shaking.

I decided something had to be done to stop Reggie killing him. I could not stand by and be a witness to the murder of this man. What had he really done? Not a thing, as far as I could tell. He may have said something about the Krays they didn't like, but that's not it, you see. When the Krays wanted to do something they would put out all sorts of stories to justify some trumped-up reason for a killing.

So I just turned to Albert and came out with this line that someone was outside and we should stop Reggie from doing this.

Albert looked over to the door and could see no one. He said to me, 'Well, I'm not going to stop him because he will put me in the same chair.'

So I said, 'Well, I *am* going to stop him.'

As I walked over to Reggie it was almost too late. His eyes had already started to glaze as I leaned over to whisper in his ear that someone was outside. That was as good a line as I could think of. I remembered he was a bit deaf in one ear. I was whispering in his left ear with his right one out of my range, hoping I had the good ear.

Reggie had just started to put his hand into his pocket to pull out the gun but when he heard me whispering he stopped. He stepped away to face me to listen to what I was saying.

'Can I have a word with you?' I said.

'What for?' said Reggie.

I asked him to go to the kitchen and I told him what I'd already whispered in his ear, that I thought there was someone outside in the street. I didn't know who, just someone hanging around and not moving on. Could be the police, could be some friend of Cannon's.

Reggie was livid and started swearing. Just then Cannon twisted out of the chair and I saw his face pale as he saw the sheet someone had placed behind him to soak up his blood. Suddenly, he jumped up, burst through the rear door and ran out into the street. Reggie was cursing everyone for allowing Cannon to escape. But he was more concerned about how Ronnie was going to react. 'What the fuck will Ronnie say now?'

Jack the Hat said, 'He was so quick, we couldn't stop him.' That was a bit feeble.

I said I had heard a car revving up outside as Cannon escaped. That was a lie. Anyway it sounded good.

After that, Reggie and I and one of the others went to the Regency Club in Amhurst Road and got drunk. It was just another day on the Firm.

Not too much later, I was in a club in Soho with Alfie and his friend. There was Bobby Cannon, standing at the other end of the bar. All of a sudden the place was empty and the doors were locked, and Alfie, Micky and I were trapped inside with Bobby Cannon and some of his people, about six or eight of them.

Cannon came over and said in his hoarse, low voice: 'Go back to the twins and tell them to fucking do a better job next time.' Alfie said something like, 'No, Bobby. *You* go back and tell them.'

I wasn't so brave. I just said I didn't know what he was talking about – better job than what? What time with Reggie? I said I was not there. I'd been out of London. He told me to tell the Krays that he didn't give 'a monkey's about them', and he let us go. He didn't have a clue that in fact I had saved his life.

By now it's midsummer. The streets are hot, the city air is stuffy. It never seems to get dark. On 30 July it's the World Cup final at Wembley and everyone's going mad for it. But I've got other things on my mind. Life with Reggie in Manor House has long ago stopped being quite the non-stop party it used to be.

Ronnie's got the hump and is getting crazier by the day. When he's not telling Reggie it's his turn to kill someone – anyone – he's specifically telling Reggie to get rid of me.

So Ronnie and Reggie move together into a flat in the Lea Bridge Road. Somewhere anonymous, somewhere to lie low – the word's round that the Old Bill are still going for Ronnie over Cornell. It was a small place, just a couple of rooms on one floor above a barber's shop.

I'd been over there a few times. I'd even hidden my passport there (without telling Reggie) as a kind of place of last resort should I have to get out of the country in a hurry. That time might be coming. It would be the last place anyone would think of to find it. Now I get another summons.

I took a cab over from Mum's place. We pulled around the back alley and I told the cab driver to keep the cab running and if I didn't come out in ten minutes to get on the phone to Scotland Yard and tell Mr Tommy Butler to get here straight away.

It's funny but the cab driver seemed to know what was going on, because he said, 'I will.' I hadn't even paid him, but he seemed to totally understand. I then went up the stairs and knocked on the door. Reggie opened it and I went inside and said, 'How's things?' He mumbled something and I walked up the passageway and went to a picture hanging on the wall. I pulled it a little and my own passport slipped out from behind it. Reggie was surprised and he said: 'When did you put that there?'

'Oh, the other day – for safe-keeping,' I replied.

I then said to Reggie, 'I've got to go. I've got a cab waiting for me outside.'

He said, 'Don't go yet. Ronnie wants to see you.'

So he takes me to a little room, and I mean a room the size of a small bathroom, and inside are about six of the Firm, including Ronnie. Big Albert Donoghue closed the door behind me and stood in front so I could not move. Now Ronnie is about ten inches in front, looking straight at me.

'How is everything?' he said.

'Great,' I replied.

We're ridiculously squashed in this room, and the atmosphere is tense and charged. Someone squeezed their way out, then someone else knocked on the door and looked in and said, 'Phillips has been in touch again.' That's when everyone started to look at me. I know that the cab saved my life that day because I just said, as casually as I could manage, 'I have to go. I've got a cab waiting for me downstairs.'

I went to go past Big Albert and he didn't move, but just kept looking at Ronnie. Then Ronnie, after the longest time, nodded at him and Albert moved aside and let me out. Feeling almost lightheaded with fear, I managed to stumble up the passage, out the door, down the stairs and into the taxi and the cab driver, whoever he was, said: 'I was just ready to call the Yard.'

I knew I was living on borrowed time. I was terrified for myself, and was even more frightened for my family. Someone at Scotland Yard was feeding everything I said straight back to the Krays.

I asked Pogue the next time I saw him how the hell this could be happening. Pogue said that 'they' were trying to stop it from happening – by which he must have meant the high-ups at the Yard – but he must have known who was leaking the information. Once more he told me to be very careful.

I said, 'I will live a lot longer if you stop the leak. At least get some misinformation out. Tell a few lies. Pin it on someone else.'

I had already told the Yard about a very low-life character by the name of David Frost – or 'Frosty' or 'Jack' Frost as he was known – who had told me once about a little girl he had raped and murdered. She was twelve. He'd buried the body in Epping Forest. Actually he had boasted about it.

As he was telling me he was getting so excited, like he was reliving the whole thing. I felt sick, but I had to look like I was interested. I told the Yard all of this and also about a man that David 'Frosty' Frost said he had killed with an axe five years earlier. Now at last I could see the Yard at work. Soon after they let a leak out from them saying that it was Frosty who was 'Phillips' the spy.

And now the pressure's really on me. It's not yet public knowledge that the famous Tommy Butler is on the Blind Beggar case but the Yard really needs a result.

Where are they living? I told Pogue that. Number 471 Lea Bridge Road – a flat above a barber's shop. When's the best time to nick them? I told them that too. There was a meet planned in two nights' time.

'We're going to need to get John Alexander Barrie [alias Scotch Ian] as well,' Pogue told me. I could only agree with that. It was vital for my survival to have all of the twins' inner circle taken off the streets. All of them. And, although Alfie and David didn't know it, it was the same for my brothers.

I got word to Butler where the twins were. I told the Yard when would be the best time to hit the gaff. I described the internal layout, the exit routes. There was a little alley at the back. I told Pogue in no uncertain times that they had better get it right. Nick the twins. Nick Scotch Ian. And keep them nicked.

Or else I really was a dead man.

You know what happened. It was in the papers. In fact it was the first time that anyone in the real world knew that the famous Tommy Butler was on the case. The coppers hit the place at 1.50 a.m. on 4 August 1966. They went in with ladders and sledge-hammers in the middle of the night and rounded up everyone present. Ronnie and Scotch Ian were taken to Commercial Street Police Station, Reggie to Leyton nick with the others.

The identity parade later that morning was a farce. Ronnie refused to remove his horn-rimmed spectacles. It was all a big joke to him. They had briefs scuttling everywhere. The Blind Beggar barmaid failed to show altogether and the two witnesses who did turn up would not say anything except 'maybe' and 'I'm not sure'.

Reggie, Ronnie and Scotch Ian got out the next day, 5 August. The press were tipped off and got down there pretty quick. I think it was at Vallance Road. It was 'Read all about it, the Krays get away with it', just like always. I've seen the cuttings. I've seen the photographs – they're always being used – with that big floral wallpaper in Violet Kray's front room. They must have been laughing their heads off.

'The first we knew about [Cornell's] death was when we read about it in the newspapers,' Ronnie told the reporters. 'Mr Butler came to see me – the police gave me sausage and mash for tea. I don't know what they wanted to charge me with. It may have been murder, they didn't tell me.'

'Our mum's getting distinctly worried about all this,' Reggie said. 'And today's her birthday. So we're going to have a little drink and cheer her up.' How very nice. But no one was in a party mood. I certainly wasn't when I heard about their release that morning. But I had to keep smiling.

The next day their boasting about getting away with it appears in the papers. Tommy Butler fucks it up. It's all a big laugh.

But nobody's laughing when we're in private. Who's the bleeding grass? How did the Old Bill know when and where to turn them over? If I run they'll know it's me. So I have to go back in, to be loyal, dozy Bobby.

I was sitting down at a meet that day with the Firm and with Ronnie. Connie Whitehead looked into the room and said: 'Phillips has been in touch again!' He'd got that from some copper for sure. David 'Frosty' Frost was in the room with us. He did not bat an eyelid – though of course, he didn't know he was in the frame.

I was talking to Frosty at the time and staying in step with the conversation – but not letting Ronnie know I had heard what Connie had said. In fact I was absolutely terrified. Please God, don't let me show how frightened I am. Let them think that Frosty is the informer.

Ronnie started glaring at each one of us in the room as I glanced over to him. I kept talking as if I had nothing to fear. Reggie caught my eye and leant over to me and said quietly that he wanted me to go with him on a meet the next day. I asked him what for? 'You will see when we get there,' he said. 'Let's have a nice drink tonight. We'll go to Madge's.'

If there was a time to run it was now. But they'd know – and wherever I managed to hide, Alfie and David would get it. They wouldn't have a clue what was coming. 'Sure, Reggie,' I said. 'Let's go to Madge's.'

CHAPTER 14
A WALK IN THE WOODS

It was all about getting things done as far as Reggie was concerned. That was how he was. The way he made it seem that day, he was just asking me very nicely if I could come and give him a hand doing some small bit of business that had to be got out of the way. We'd have to do it quickly and do it quietly. Just the two of us – Reggie Kray and Bobby Teale, the best of friends just as we'd always been.

We'd had a few drinks the night before round at Madge's just as we'd agreed. Reggie had been very direct: have an early night and be round at Vallance Road at nine the next morning as we would have some running around to do, he had told me. I think that he and Ronnie had fixed it after I left the meet with David 'Frosty' Frost. In fact I'm sure of it. I think that Ronnie told Reggie it was his turn to get something going. It was time to get rid of me. Perhaps I was Phillips, perhaps not – they couldn't be sure. But either way I was getting too close to Reg and Ron wanted me out of the way. He'd leave Reggie to decide how to do it. Somewhere quiet – somewhere out of town.

It was Sunday 7 August. I got to Vallance Road a few minutes late and I started to open the front door to walk right in as we always did, but it was locked. So, I knocked. Reggie came to the door with only his trousers on and said, 'Oh, I'm sorry. I thought it was open.'

I closed the door behind me and asked Reggie, 'Should I lock it?' Reggie said, 'No, Connie Whitehead is on his way.' I followed Reggie down the narrow passage to the kitchen and his mum, Violet, asked me: 'Do you want a cup of tea?'

'Yes,' I said, 'thank you.' I sat in the kitchen and Reggie added, 'I won't be long,' and he went to finish getting dressed.

There seemed to be no one else in, or at least no one awake and up in the house. Violet Kray was fussing around, putting shirts on hangers. She did a lot of that. 'Reg,' she said, 'let me make you a nice breakfast,' and turning to me she started chatting away, saying, 'Bobby, you need some breakfast,' and 'How's Nell, your lovely mum, doing?'

'OK,' I said, as I looked over to Reggie, who had just walked back into the room, to see if I could get a read as to whether we really would be staying for breakfast.

'No Mum,' he said. 'I've got a meet to go on. We don't have time,' and out the door we went, with me going first. All the while we were looking all over the place as usual just in case anyone was going to make a hit on us.

It may sound crazy but I was never afraid of Reggie – or Ronnie – or any of the rest of the Firm. And if you think about it, you will see that if I did show any fear they would have picked up on it. Perhaps that is what it really was all about that summer morning. I think I knew that at the time.

So I just had to act like not a thing was going on. It was just the two of us. No muscle from the Firm. It was like we could sort things out with a little chat. There was a lot to sort out. Reggie strode out and walked very fast to the Jag parked outside.

I tried to get a read on whether he was carrying a gun. He didn't always carry one. When he did he would have it in his outside jacket pocket or stuffed in his waistband. I couldn't tell. Although normally I carried a gun myself (at least since I'd swapped running a holiday boat hire for being a villain), I wasn't tooled up today. I got in the car. It was a brand-new Mk II Jaguar – dark grey, with wire wheels, leather upholstery and a walnut dashboard.

'So where are we going, Reggie?' I asked casually. Reggie started the car and took off at great speed with me in the front passenger seat with the car door still not closed. He was always a bit like that. 'You'll see when we get there,' he replied. I asked him why. 'You will see when we get there,' he said again.

Why should I be frightened of Reggie Kray? Since we had first met a year earlier, Reggie had become my closest friend. He had even paid the solicitor's fee in my divorce. Ronnie was the crazy one. Ronnie was the only one to be a killer – as far as anyone knew – but it was no secret that he was leaning on his brother to do the same. I had once heard Ronnie say: 'You must do someone because when you do there is a rush like you would never believe.' It seemed to be just for the fun of it.

Ronnie hated anyone who got close to Reggie. But in his mad way it was important to Ronnie that Reggie did the killing. That he should kill me. I suppose it was to prove that he,

Ronnie, had been right about me all along – and that now Reggie thought the same.

If Ronnie had known for certain I was the spy for Scotland Yard he would have set the whole Firm to bring me in and then taken his pleasure in my slow death by torture to find out what information I had passed and to who. I am sure he suspected, but he could not be sure, especially with the misinformation about Frosty starting to surface and clouding the issue. Perhaps it was easier to just get me out of the way. And it was Reggie's turn.

I needed to work out if Reggie was on a downer or upper pill. I was getting good at reading him, but I would never let him know. So I would just jabber on to see how he responded. I would talk about the night before or something to make him think my mind was somewhere else.

We drove through north-east London. The day was cloudy, a bit chilly for August. I looked out the window and thought it might be the last time I would see ordinary people just going about their business. Going to church, waiting for the pubs to open, going out on a Sunday. I envied their lives. I noticed the people glancing at Reggie and me as we glided past, dressed to the nines in this flash car. They must have thought we were millionaires on our way to some business meeting. Instead it looked like I was going to my death.

I knew where we were heading. We were out of Hackney, out of the East End – into the neat suburbs. It was Epping Forest where we were going, right on the edge of the big city. It was where I had run away with my brothers as a boy. You could hide anything there.

All the while as we were driving my mind was whirring away frantically, trying to work out what to do. At one stage I thought I would jump from the car if Reggie slowed down. But he always drove like a lunatic. I mean a raving lunatic. So jumping was out of the question – and anyway he would just run me over. It's funny, but as we drove, I could see how the thing would play out as if it wasn't happening to me but to somebody else. It was like watching a film. It was as if I could see Reggie driving the car over me and backing up over me just to make sure I was dead.

We got to the forest. The sky was overcast. There was absolutely no one around. No families, no picnickers. When we got to a spot in the middle of the woods, Reggie stopped the car and turned to me and said, 'Get out and give me a hand.'

So I got out. Turns out Reggie did have a gun. Of course he did. He threw a bottle in the air and started shooting at it. He told me to go and look for a bag in the trees with some money in it. It was evidently a ploy to get me in front of him and make me an easy target. I ran into the trees but he was not shooting at me at first. Then he asked me to pick up the bottle and hold it as a target. I kept running. Then he's firing in my direction and he's shouting, 'Stand still!' The gun may have been a .22 because it was not very loud. Or he may have had a silencer.

I got to the other side of the car and thought I would use the car to hide behind. By now it appeared to me that Reggie was pretty high on pills.

He started screaming at me: 'I promise not to hit you! I just need target practice. You know I'm your best friend...'

He'd stopped shooting now. Perhaps he needed to reload. He couldn't see me but kept on yelling for me to come back. 'Come on out, we've got to go.' I knew then for certain that he was going to kill me.

I didn't trust him not to trick me. He started the car and let it run but I still didn't come out of hiding. Finally he shouted, 'I'm leaving!' and I heard the noise of the engine fade away. I waited about a half hour because I thought he might have driven a few feet away and walked back to wait for me to come out of the woods. When I did leave the forest, I circled around and came out at a different point on the road. My knees were shaking.

I thought I'd had it, whatever kind of escape I might have just pulled off. I knew that wouldn't be the end of it. It wasn't even a warning off. They must have known it was me. Tell me I could not still be getting away with it. My friend Reggie Kray had been sent by Ronnie to take me out to the forest and kill me. Then he couldn't shoot straight. There would be no second chance.

I thought seriously of contacting Pogue at the Yard and trying to get some sort of immediate protection. But right then I decided not to. I knew that all the information I was giving was getting back to the Krays somehow. So I realised that if this story got back to them and no one else knew about the Epping Forest episode but me and Reggie, I would have been exposed as the real 'Phillips'.

No, there was no way I could trust the police, any more than I could trust the Krays. It was the Old Bill who had put the smokescreen up about Frosty being the informer. It was their idea of justice to get Frosty under suspicion by the Krays – it was not done just to protect me. So what else were the police capable of? Offering me up for sacrifice?

First I thought I'd go to Steeple Bay in Essex to David's caravan. I knew Christine and the kids were already down there.

Ronnie had already made a move against me at Steeple Bay earlier that summer. It was one of his little impulses. The old boxer Billy Exley had been with us. Ronnie said it was a lovely day and we should go for a lovely walk. We got to a gravel pit. It was raining, grey and cloudy. Billy and I could both tell that Ronnie had something bad on his mind.

So, as Ronnie started walking down the slope, I just kept walking along the top with Billy going ahead of me. Ronnie went down into the big gravel pit and was just standing there saying to me: 'Come on down, Bobby, it's nice.'

I could see Ronnie was thinking that this was a great place to kill someone. I could practically read his mind. No one was around. I mean not a soul, apart from us. I knew Ronnie liked to get his victim in an arm lock around his neck until he passed out and then he would just use a jerking motion to break his neck. So when he shouted to me and said, 'It's beautiful down here, come on down,' I just said, 'No thanks. I've got to see someone.'

Then he shouted to Billy, standing at the top of the pit. 'Get a hold of Bobby and bring him down to me,' he yelled, then turning to me he said, 'It's nice down here,' in a very friendly tone. I was standing about a hundred feet away from Billy Exley and I could see he wasn't that keen on getting me down the slope. Billy was not in good enough health to do much. He'd already had a couple of heart attacks. I just walked, keeping a look over my shoulder, and made my way back to the relative safety of David's caravan. Luckily, Ronnie didn't try anything else on with me for the rest of our stay.

So going to Steeple Bay again looks like a very stupid idea. I was getting to the stage of total exhaustion. I couldn't think straight. In the end I didn't. I found somewhere else to go, staying in London and lying low.

I can only imagine what Reggie told Ronnie when he got back from Epping. Ron had been raving at him ever since Cornell to do one for himself. He meant kill me. And Reggie couldn't. So Ronnie sent Ronnie Hart (the Krays' cousin) and Frosty to Steeple Bay to find me – although what would happen next was pretty obvious – because they thought that's where I'd run to. I know that for a fact. They got there late that same Sunday night that Reggie came back from the forest having failed to finish the job.

Maybe it was a test of Frosty's loyalty, to help work out if he was the informant or not. Chris, David's wife, God bless her, would tell me later that they'd come down that night and searched all over the caravan – in the cupboards and under the trailer – and wanted to know when she had last seen me. They were not exactly polite about it. She told them she had not seen me for a few days. They were searching outside in the darkness calling my name: 'Bobby! Bobby!' Christine said she thought they were going to beat her up. Then they left.

But in the end it was Frosty who got it. The Yard's plan came good. When Ronnie heard again via the Yard informer that it was Frosty who was the grass, Ronnie killed him. I heard it from someone you should know. I furthermore think he was killed to send me a message. Ronnie Kray tortured him to death, poor bastard, trying to get him to tell them what he had told the police. And he'd told them nothing. He just screamed for mercy. His body was never found.

But Reggie knew it was me all along, I'm sure of that. It was just that that day in Epping he couldn't quite go through with it. He wasn't quite ready to kill me or anyone else, although he would be soon enough.

CHAPTER 15
THE SET-UP

I had no choice. I couldn't face it out any longer. I went through the request for a meeting procedure with a call from a phone box to the number I'd been given. It all happened pretty fast. This time it wasn't Pogue but a detective I think had been in the car on one of our little tape-recorded sessions. He told me to call him 'Dan'. It must have been Monday 8 August, the day after the drive to Epping with Reggie and the search for me at the caravan later that night.

I'd given Pogue and Butler the works. I'd told them what had happened the night of the Cornell shooting, about the mayhem at Moresby Road, Reggie's increasing blood-lust and Ronnie inciting him to kill. I'd told them about Bobby Cannon's escape at Blonde Vicky's and the shooting at the Regency Club. I'd given them the make on Scotch Ian Barrie, the second gunman in the Beggar. I'd even got them a photograph. I'd given them the Lea Bridge Road address and told them when to hit it. And then the great Tommy Butler had blown it.

So this new guy tells me that they have to get even more evidence on the Krays. It's going to take them at least six months to get it. Well, I'd be dead long before then. But the Yard also now has good information that I am going to be killed, he tells me. I know that, I say. They reckon it's not because the twins had found out I was the informer but because I had stopped a murder, the Bobby Cannon business.

Either way I knew too much. I was in the way. They said my two brothers, Alfie and David, were also in the same danger. All of us would have to be taken off the streets.

I asked this man from the Yard, Dan, whatever he called himself, what we should do. There were families involved, there were children. He said, 'We can't put you all into hiding as it will tip off the twins.'

When I'd begun all this back in March, I thought it would end in a matter of days. I really believed that the police would get them, roll up the Firm and we'd all be safe. We were the good guys. Now it had gone from days to weeks to months and nobody had been arrested. This same Yard man, Dan, told me: 'Say absolutely nothing to Alfie or David or they will panic. I will handle it. Leave it all to me, and don't worry, it's all under control and it will all be taken care of. Just remember, whatever happens, go along with it and don't say a word to a soul.'

In the meantime there'd been the trip to the Forest. I hadn't told the police about it (although there was a good chance they had had us all under surveillance). Only Reggie and I knew, and almost certainly Ronnie, so if anything got back about that, they would know that the informer in the Firm had to be me. Except that they knew that already, they had to.

So the Yard had to have some kind of plan to bring me in to safety. I didn't have a clue what it was until I found out the hard way. Alfie and David would find out too. They were not going to be happy about it. It happened like this.

A few weeks before, I'd been on my own having a drink in a bar in Mayfair (I think it was actually called 'The May-Fair'). It was late in June or early July. I was standing at one end of the bar. A man in his forties came up to me. I don't know if he was already in the bar or he just came in. No one else was at the bar and he came and stood next to me.

He started talking about how cold it was outside for this time of the year. He ordered a drink. I was just about ready to leave and was finishing off the last of my drink when he asked me if he could buy me another. It was a set-up.

I thought for a moment and then I said, 'Yes, OK, thanks.' I told him I was a street trader and mentioned a pitch I was looking at to buy with my two brothers in Chapel Market, Islington.

He said he was interested in making a small investment and he would think it over. I should have picked up on it straight away but I didn't. This was the start of the big move to bring us in. After we'd had another drink, he told me he was doing work for the government but he would not elaborate and said no more on the subject.

I met him several times again afterwards and even borrowed his car. He told me his name was Wallace. I asked him, 'Is that your first or last name?'

He said, 'Just call me Wallace.' And so I did. He lent me his car, a convertible Triumph TR3. I'd got it crammed with partygoers one night when the police nicked me. I had eleven people in the car and everyone ran off and I got caught. As I was trying to get away, I pushed the copper and that was that. When it came to court later the judge said it was not possible to get eleven people in a small car like that. I got done for obstructing the police and assault. It didn't help.

But Wallace wasn't put off by this little adventure, in fact quite the opposite. After the Lea Bridge Road arrest and the ID parade cock-up, after Epping, I started thinking he was as safe company as any. Maybe he could help Alfie and David as well. They still didn't have a real clue of the danger they were in.

So I was having a drink with this Wallace and he said: 'Why don't you bring your brothers over and we will have a party back at my flat?' He added, 'I like to party.'

I got a message out to the Yard to say we were all at this address and we weren't going anywhere. If they were going to bring the three of us in, they should do it now. Well, it didn't happen quite how I expected.

I knew what was happening, or thought I did. My brothers didn't have a clue and wouldn't for years to come. This was the hardest part of all of it.

I had told David and Alfie about my new friend, Wallace, and had said he might be interested in giving us a loan. So we all went down the West End one night, taking in a few pubs with Wallace, before eventually going back to his flat. It was in Dolphin Square on the Thames Embankment. We talked to him about our life as street traders and he told us working-class people like us were the 'salt of the earth'. That sort of thing.

We were all quite drunk by this stage of the evening and when we told him about the stall we wanted he said: 'I might be able to help.'

I offered to write him a receipt for the nine hundred pounds confirming that we would repay it within a month. By now it was one in the morning, so Wallace asked us if we'd like to stay the night. Alfie slept on the small sofa while David claimed the big one and I slept on the floor. Wallace was clearly gay but there were no sexual undertones – he didn't try anything and we didn't think anything about it.

Well, about seven thirty the next morning, the doorbell goes. I can't remember who opened the door, but it wasn't Wallace. He wasn't even in the flat. In marched six plain-clothes policemen – with Wallace behind them.

Wallace was blustering and claiming that he'd left in the middle of the night via the rubbish chute because we had been 'holding him hostage'. We had all woken with raging hangovers so Alfie volunteered to make tea for us all. It was funny really, at the time, the coppers drinking tea and Wallace going on about how we'd demanded money from him. What a load of nonsense! It was a joke.

The police were distinctly unamused, however. They said they were going to take us to Rochester Row Police Station. David and Alfie kept saying, 'I can't believe this,' but I was beginning to have an idea what was really happening. We were separated and put into three different cells. We were then brought in, one by one, to be interviewed. Subsequently we were charged with 'demanding money with menaces', booked by a police sergeant, and then carted off to Bow Street Magistrate's Court the next day, still looking at one another in a daze. I could see Alfie and David were wondering what the hell was going on. I wasn't sure myself.

It was barely a week since I'd told Butler where and when to hit the twins. Now the three of us were under arrest. I could not tell Alfie and David what this was really all about – but I assumed this was all part of the rescue plan that 'Dan' had promised. I believed we'd get a few months in prison, say nine months maximum, just to keep us safely out of the way while they took the Krays down.

I had been told that I was going to be brought in, but I had no idea that meeting 'Wallace' was going to be done the way it was. Who was he really? He'd been around for a little while by now in that long dangerous summer, and his flat was somewhere I felt safe, somewhere I could lie low. It was where I'd gone after the Sunday outing to Epping, the day the Firm had come looking for me at Steeple Bay.

It all got very strange very quickly. We couldn't get bail for this ridiculous 'blackmail' charge – even though it was all on the say-so of this one guy. That was confirmation to me that it was a fit-up.

At first it was quite reassuring. It was as if some hidden hand was moving to protect the three of us by getting us off the streets – just as I'd been promised. But the wives and kids were still on the outside, what about them? What about our mother? I thought about my little brother Paul and my little sister Jane. What if the Krays got their hands on them? I had risked my life and my family's on a promise from Butler and Pogue and then discovered there was someone at the Yard leaking it all back to the twins.

The idea of the three of us getting a sentence of nine months maximum, as the Yard had told me, was fading fast. So who could I really trust? I told the arresting officer from my cell to get in touch with Pogue at the Yard but I was told he would not come to talk to me. I know he got my message though because I got one back from him a bit later: 'Don't worry. I'll be in touch soon.'

Now I was afraid of the police more than the Krays. I had seen the way they worked during the time I was getting them information. They had contrived David 'Frosty' Frost's horrible end. They could be as ruthless as anyone.

And the worst thing of all was I couldn't tell Alfie and David why it was happening, why they'd been arrested. They had no clue about Phillips or Pogue, any of it. 'Dan' had told me, 'Don't say a word.' I still clung to that command – still hanging on to a fragment of trust. I was wrong about that, too.

I felt for my brothers, bewildered, betrayed, accused of something ridiculous and demeaning.

All three of us were put up at Bow Street Magistrates' Court and charged with demanding money with menaces – the formal term for blackmail. We were all remanded in custody and sent to Brixton Prison. It was 10 August. It was so crowded in the jail at that time that there were people sleeping in the corridors, and even in the chapel. We were going to be there for the next eight weeks.

We were then told we were being provided with a legal aid solicitor, only one between the three of us. The solicitor claimed that as we were all on the same charge we only needed one legal representative. Alfie questioned this, but at the time he was so convinced that the charge was going to be dismissed that he just let it go without insisting on a separate brief for each of us.

At the end of the eight weeks, our brief arrived in Brixton to tell us that our trial had been set for Number One Court at the Old Bailey. We were appalled. Number One Court was usually reserved for the worst criminals.

The trial was strange right at the start. On the first day the judge walked in and said: 'Before we begin today, a very serious allegation has been made to me in my Chambers by a reliable source that one or two members of the jury have been approached. Now in cases of blackmail, people do get approached. I am going to ask you one at a time to stand up and to tell me if you have been approached.'

One by one the jurors denied having been threatened. So the judge then instructed them to 'wipe this from your minds and continue with the trial'. We had been branded as jury nobblers, real villains. What the judge should have done after making such an allegation was to dismiss the jury and start again. There should have been a retrial on those grounds alone. But there wasn't. We were already guilty. I called our brief over to complain. But all he said was: 'Don't do anything yet.' Back in Brixton we arrived to a freezing cold dinner. It looked grim.

The next day the geezer I know as 'Wallace' is put in the witness box, and referred to as 'Mr X'. He was asked whether we had demanded money with menaces. He replied, 'No.' The prosecution then asked him whether we had tried to blackmail him. Again he said, 'No.' When he was asked why he had made the accusation against us, he finally answered: 'I was frightened.' It would be enough to put us away.

We were sent back to Brixton each night during the trial and I tried to keep as far away from Alfie and David as possible. What was I supposed to tell them?

Two weeks later we came to the judge's summing up. It was relentless. Our defence offered nothing by way of explanation or excuse, and we were found guilty. Up in the gallery I looked up to see our mother's face as she watched three of her sons sent down. David's wife Christine was also there along with Alfie's wife, Wendy.

When it came to sentencing we listened in horror to the judge's words. 'I am sending you to prison for three years. Take them down.'

The screws said: 'You two, David and Bobby Teale, in this cell. Alfie Teale in the other.'

We gripped one another's shoulders and sang 'You'll Never Walk Alone'. The screws actually clapped. It was the last Alfie would see of me and David for two years. He told me later he went back into the cell and cried his eyes out.

Alfie was taken by van that afternoon from the Old Bailey to go to Wandsworth to start his sentence. It was 4 October 1966. Because David and I were first-timers, we were sent to the less hard-line Wormwood Scrubs. After we were reunited, many years afterwards, Alfie told me what happened once he'd transferred to his new prison:

When I got to Wandsworth early that evening I was put into a cell with two black guys who were up for most of the night playing chess. The cell was flooded with moonlight so I could see them very clearly. They kept asking me to join in but I was in no mood to play anything. The next morning we came out of the cell to 'slop out'. There were no toilets in the cell so we had to use a bucket.

Almost immediately I met up with an old friend called Mickey who'd just been given five years, closely followed by an Italian face I remembered from around Holborn who told me he'd got twelve. All of a sudden, my three didn't seem so bad.

At the time, Wandsworth was the strictest prison in the country. I didn't know the rules. It turned out that if you stepped across a white line you weren't supposed to cross, the heavy mob would blow a whistle, come running across the room and start smashing into you. I did this on my first day.

Your dinner was a tin bowl of soup, with duff and custard to follow. Often by the time you got to the hot plate to collect your dinner, it was all mixed up together. Even a dog wouldn't have eaten it.

I stayed there for about a month when I was told I was being allocated to Lewes Prison. Shortly after I arrived at Lewes I was approached by an extremely well-spoken man. 'Hello, Alfred, I'm Gerry Glendenning. I know your mother and father. So lovely to see you... When you've settled in, pop down to my cell, number 61, and I'll give you a little welcome present.' I didn't know him, but curious about his strange invitation I went down a few hours later and knocked on his cell door. Gerry opened the door, lifted up the mattress and said, 'What do you care for? Brandy, Scotch, rum, vodka? You'll be right as ninepence here. Like Butlin's, it is.'

And he was right. In comparison to Wandsworth, Lewes was like a holiday camp.

But I couldn't understand why I was in a cell with a twenty-four-hour light on that was used for prisoners who were under special watch. The only reason I could possibly come up with was that it must have something to do with the twins – but just how I couldn't understand.

CHAPTER 16
DAVID'S STORY

David was sent first to Wormwood Scrubs, then to Maidstone where I myself was going to end up. And the Krays? While we were having our little 'blackmail' adventure with the law, the word was they'd flown off to Tangier in Morocco to live it up in the sun with the old villain, Billy Hill, and his wife Gipsy. They'd got out of the country on a private plane. Ronnie would have plenty of boys to entertain him there. Scotch Ian went with them. God knows what he made of it.

After a while the authorities would boot them out of the country but they still didn't get nicked. We were going somewhere less sunny. I'll let David recount in his own words what happened to him:

> After the Old Bailey verdict and sentencing, a prison officer came in and told Bobby and I that we were going to Wormwood Scrubs. I remember looking out of the prison van through the tiny windows, knowing the route through Holborn and recognising the streets I'd grown up on.

We got into the Scrubs at about seven at night. We were told to take off our clothes, put our belongings into boxes and put on the prison suits. It was very busy, with everyone jostling and being sent off in different directions. I remember looking at Bobby, as if to say 'this is awful', and he looked back at me as if to agree. It was horrible, like a bad dream I couldn't wake from.

The next day we saw the governor who allocated us jobs and gave us a release date, in two years' time, calculated on the length of time we'd been held in remand, and on condition that we behaved ourselves. After this our wives were allowed to visit us briefly. About a month into our sentence we were then told we were being transferred to Maidstone Prison.

It was the same old routine when we got to Maidstone. Our building was called 'Thanet,' a new high-security block of thirty cells, and we had light bulbs on in our rooms all night. When I protested about this and asked them to turn it off, the officers told us it was high security and asked me how long I was in for.

I replied, 'A lagging – got carpet for three years.'

The officer seemed puzzled. 'I don't know what you're doing in here then. This is for lifers...'

Christine used to come up and visit me. I'd ask my friends to write letters to her for me. Around this time Christine gave birth to our third daughter. Hearing this, some of the prisoners made some hooch in the toilets so I could celebrate.

At that time I was getting loads of messages from the twins – notes and little parcels, cigarettes, Scotch, lots of things. Then I started getting more direct messages from Ronnie. I was approached in prison by a geezer, a guy who knew the twins apparently. He warned me the Old Bill were snooping about and that if they came to me I was not to say a word about the twins, reminding me that my wife and kids were on the outside and that I'd be doing myself a favour to keep schtum.

I had at least five heavy messages sent in from Ronnie warning me not to say anything. He particularly didn't want me talking about any of the personal stuff. I knew what he meant. 'Make sure you don't say one word.' And I didn't. Not then anyway. But that was not the end of it.

We'd pick up rumours on the prison grapevine about what was going on outside – that Reggie's wife Frances Kray had attempted to gas herself in the kitchen oven at her parents' house a week or so after our arrest. Her father found her just in time.

We also heard that when Reggie and Ronnie had been thrown out of Morocco they'd come back to London but the Yard had left them alone. Then Ronnie had gone to ground again in north London. Apparently he had been involved in something to do with a corrupt copper.

There'd been an inquest on George Cornell in November, resulting in a verdict of 'murder by person or persons unknown'. So that was that. The Old Bill had given up.

Around that time, a couple of months into our sentence, Bobby started acting very oddly. Every evening around six, the prisoners were allowed a period of association where they could go into one another's cells, watch television or play pool or cards in the community room. So each night I'd go to Bobby's cell only to have him kick the door closed and tell me he wasn't in the mood to chat.

Instead he would sit practising his guitar, often without saying a word. When I asked him, 'What's the matter, aren't you coming out?' he'd just make some excuse, or say he 'didn't feel like it'. I'd go down to the association room and the others would ask me about Bobby, unable to believe that he was my brother. 'Have you had a row?' 'Don't you speak?' 'Aren't you close?'

I was as mystified as any of them, answering, 'Yes, we are close.' I just really couldn't understand what was the matter with him. Other times he was missing altogether. When I asked a warder where he was I was told he'd hurt his back, and was being taken to the general hospital for treatment. These visits to the hospital soon became a regular pattern, to the extent that I began to worry that there could be something seriously wrong with Bobby. The only times we saw one another were in the carpentry workshop, and even then he hardly talked to me. I repeatedly asked him what the problem was. But he still wouldn't tell me anything.

And David was right. I wouldn't. I was eaten up with anger. The coppers had given up on who killed Cornell and turned us brothers over. And still I couldn't say why we were all in nick. But suddenly there was something new going round the landings about the Krays. It's to do with Frank 'Mad Axe-Man' Mitchell. As I heard it, that December (1966), Mad Teddy Smith and Billy Exley had got him off an outdoor work party on Dartmoor and driven him back to London. That was the dummy run Alfie had been on in the spring. Letters in Mitchell's name started appearing in the *Daily Mirror* saying the Home Secretary must give him a release date. Mad Teddy wrote those. Then the letters stopped.

All we knew was that Frank was sprung out while David, Alfie and I were in prison. And we're all thinking at the time when we first heard about it – that's nice, at least Frankie Mitchell will be out for Christmas – the first time for years. Well, it didn't quite work out that way. David remembers how he heard more of what was going on in the outside world:

There seemed to be a new rumour about the twins every day. The big shocker was Frances's suicide. I heard about it from the guy who gave me warnings in Maidstone. He said she'd done herself in, but all the chaps were saying Reggie did it. We all knew he'd wanted to get back with her, and when she wouldn't, it made him really angry. He couldn't be seen to lose face in front of the Firm.

We had heard that Frosty was on the missing list. Then Mad Teddy had disappeared. They did Mad Teddy down the caravan, or so I heard. First thing we knew of it, he was missing. We were having a chat in my cell about it. Someone said: 'I reckon one of those twins has killed him,' and we all knew it was true. No one ever found him, although the word went round he's buried in the marshes at Steeple Bay, right where Ronnie used to talk about getting rid of a body.

But the really big story doing the rounds inside was about Jack the Hat. There was a contract on the money-man, Leslie Payne, who the twins had fallen out with big-time, which Jack and Billy Exley were supposed to carry out. I heard that Jack had gone round with a gun then bottled out on Payne's doorstep when his missus had answered the door. But Jack kept the money. So they killed him.

Word went round the landing, round the whole nick, like wildfire. I was shocked, and saddened too. Jack didn't deserve that. He wasn't a gangster, he was just a thief. A thief who liked a drink, that was all. Ronnie and Reggie took a liberty to do him, especially the way they did it.

The story went like this. The twins gave Jack the ready-eye and they went all back to Blonde Carole Skinner's for a drink. Reggie's going to shoot him when he comes in the door but the gun jams. Ronnie grabs him and starts screaming and Jack gets it from Reggie with a breadknife in the stomach. When I heard about, it to be honest, I thought, 'Thank God I'm in here.'

Jack's body vanished. There were plenty of rumours. It was in the concrete foundations of a supermarket, it was in a motorway flyover, it had been fed to animals, burned in a hospital incinerator. One story had it dumped over a railway line near Cedra Court.

Time passes. But now there's another big rumour – that there's a new copper after the Krays. I'm hearing it's Leonard Read, 'Nipper', the little terrier who got burned in the Hideaway club affair – when I was taking messages from Ronnie out of Brixton to put the frighteners on Hew McCowan.

This time he's got a team working outside the Yard. If it's true then the twins have got a problem. In autumn 1967 there were rumours about a cozzer called Mooney going round the East End talking to people about the Blind Beggar. They won't leave it alone.

Then we start hearing that the twins had been nicked. By now it's May 1968. Could it be true? I got another warning from the Krays messenger, saying that if the police did come sniffing around asking questions I was to stay schtum – to not say a thing and ask for my lawyer. That was a message from the twins.

I told him directly: 'Fuck them and their message. You've told me this about five times. I don't need you to tell me what to do.'

My cellmate, a face called Terry Millman, even offered to put the guy down the laundry chute if he didn't stop hassling me. But now it was really happening.

The rumour was true. Reggie and Ronnie really were on remand. Read was putting together the charges for a full trial. Well, he'd better not come round me, I thought. I was not going to grass. Nor would anyone in my family.

I'd already been trying to get to an open prison in order to get myself easier living conditions. It was very strict in Maidstone at the time. But each time I put an application in, the answer came back: 'Never.' I couldn't know it at the time, but the Krays and everything to do with them was more sensitive than ever at the Yard. They weren't going to risk losing sight of me.

I tried again for a transfer, expecting another knock-back. Then I was called in by the governor and told I was going to Ford Open Prison in West Sussex.

When I got to Ford I was disappointed to find there were about twenty of us in each dormitory. I'd have preferred to be back in Maidstone, back in my old cell. They allocated me a job, to break the tarmac of an old airfield opposite the prison with pickaxe handles. It was good exercise but I'd have terrible blisters by the end of each day.

Every lunchtime we would have a parade so the screws could count the number of prisoners and make sure no one had run away. First you heard your name shouted out and written on a board up in front of you. You then had to get into working party lines as instructed. They would then tell us which among us had visits, or appointments of any kind. All of a sudden one day I heard my name: 'Teale, hospital, over there.'

I didn't have a clue what they were talking about. I had nothing wrong with me and hadn't complained of anything. I asked, 'Me? What for?' and the two screws who were with me told me it was a check-up. 'What's happening? What have I done?'

They told me I had to go over to the hospital. When I asked why they wouldn't tell me, but just told me a car would be coming to pick me up. Shortly afterwards, a car pulled up at the gates driven by a screw. Once we were in the car together I asked him again: 'Where are we going?' But he just replied: 'I don't know.'

After about half an hour's drive we pulled up at the back of a police station in Littlehampton, taking the lift up quite a few floors until we reached a large room with a huge window, like a great wall of glass, where you could see the whole of the south coast spread out below.

Suddenly two plain-clothes policemen came in, full of apologies and strangely polite. 'Sorry we're late, Dave, only we got caught up in traffic on the way from London. Do you want a cup of tea and something to eat? Some fags?' One threw a packet of twenty fags down on the table. 'Do you want anything else?' They were acting like we were mates.

They were two detective sergeants – Nipper Read's men, as I later found out. Then it started:

'You know that the twins have been arrested?' one said.

'I had heard that,' I said.

At that, the screw left the room and one of the detectives told me: 'So you know the twins have been nicked and they are going to go away for a long time. What do you know about them?'

I didn't know what to say. I'd had that warning. 'Not a lot,' I answered.

The officer replied with heavy sarcasm: 'Oh, you don't, do you? And you don't know anything about the Cornell murder either, I suppose?'

'No, I don't,' I answered.

'Well, there are lots of rumours flying round, I suppose you've heard… When we asked Ronnie Kray about it, he said that all he knew was that "the Teales were involved". That's what Ronnie told my governor.'

'You've got to be joking!' I said. I couldn't believe that even Ronnie would try a stunt like that. But I still stuck to the line that I didn't know the Krays and that I had nothing to say.

He then started asking me to write a statement. He was very insistent.

'I can't do that. I've told you I've got nothing to say. I don't know what you're talking about. Leave me alone.'

Finally they agreed to take me back to the prison. Returning to my dormitory I didn't sleep a wink, worrying about what this was all about, and what was going to happen. Next day at about ten in the morning came the message that I had to be sent to the 'hospital' again.

At least this time I knew what to expect. On arrival I was given a fag and a cup of tea.

'Right, Dave,' the officer said, and pulled a load of photos from his desk drawer.

They were of me, of my wife, Christine and my children, of Alfie, Bobby, Ronnie and Reggie Kray, all going in and out of the flat in Moresby Road. We're going shopping, getting in and out of my car, going to Vallance Road, different pubs, lots of us at Steeple Bay, the caravan site. They were surveillance photos. They had clearly been taken when practically the whole Firm had been camped out at my place after the Cornell killing. I don't know what chilled me more, the memory of that time two years before or the fact the coppers knew all about it. How did they know? Why hadn't they stormed the place?

'So you don't know the twins?' he asked again.

'Well, I do know them… They used to go up my mother's club in Islington.'

'But you still don't want to make a statement?'

'No.'

At that moment, the telephone rang. Picking up the receiver, the officer answered, 'Yes, he's here. Do you want to speak to him?'

Passing the receiver across the table to me, he whispered conspiratorially: 'It's the wife!'

I felt myself starting to sweat with anxiety. 'Hello, love. You all right? Where are you?' I said.

'Hello, Dave. I'm in Albany Street Police Station. They brought me here. They've been round a few times asking about Ronnie Kray and the Cornell murder. They've taken the photos of us and the Krays, the ones that were taken down at the caravan. I had to give them to them.'

'That's all right,' I said, 'don't worry about it. Where's the kids?'

'They've got a policewoman looking after them.'

Telling Christine not to worry about a thing, I put the receiver down with a shaking hand.

'Listen, Dave,' said the officer now. 'I'll tell you what you're going to do. You and your wife are both going to make statements. You know your mother has been nicked?'

Well, I didn't know. I just sat there with my mouth open. What the hell was this? It had to be some kind of trick. It had to be just a crazy story to make me say something. Surely.

'It's true,' said the copper, 'and just to prove it, tomorrow we'll show you the court papers.'

'Nipper Read is working on all this in Tintagel,' the other policeman present told me. 'You're going to be doing a lot of bird if you don't tell us what happened on the night of 9 March 1966 when you drove Reggie Kray from Bethnal Green to Walthamstow.'

'Alfie and Bobby have made statements,' the copper continued (I found out later that Bobby in fact had yet to do so). 'I suggest you do the same. Do you realise you could be charged with harbouring a murderer? If you don't play right by us you'll be looking at twelve to fifteen years, your wife and mother could both get five, and your kids will end up in care. If you want to make a statement tomorrow morning, we will pick you up early and take you down to London. The other prisoners will be told you're to have an operation so that no one starts asking too many questions.'

There was no way out. Stuck between the twins and the police, we were now completely cornered.

I answered: 'You've got a deal.'

Early the next morning they came to pick me up. On the drive to London I asked if I could see my wife. They told me I couldn't see her yet, but that after I'd made the statement, I'd be allowed to see her.

So I'm taken from West Sussex and smuggled into an anonymous office block across the Thames from the House of Commons. It's 2 July 1968. I recognise Inspector Read from the time at the Hideaway and the McCowan business. And he recognises me. 'Hello, Dave, how are you?' He could not have been friendlier.

He was surrounded by piles of photos. He told me they'd got everything on me but he wanted me to continue giving them information. A couple of police officers took me downstairs to the canteen to have something to eat before taking me into a large room where one wall was completely covered in pictures of the twins at Vallance Road, Steeple Bay, everywhere, with all the members of the Firm. My brothers and I are in loads of them.

Just to make the point, the police showed me Ronnie's statement, claiming: 'All I know about the Cornell killing is that the Teales were involved.' I recognised his childish scrawl from the letter and cards I'd seen him write in Vallance Road, so I knew it was really his statement.

I told Read and his team what they needed to know. How the twins had moved in on the 66, how Ronnie had pursued me and used my flat as a meeting place. I told them about the night of the phone call from Madge's and how I had driven to Tapp Street with my brothers. How Reggie had got in my car and told me to 'get them off the manor', the drive to Walthamstow and the days of mayhem that had followed. Read loved it. 'That's good, David, that's great, and then what happened…?'

Nipper Read told me what he wanted to happen. 'What we want you to do is to go to Bow Street first. That is where the committal proceedings will be before the main trial. The prosecution are going to ask you some questions and you've got to tell them everything you know,' he said.

I agreed to everything.

They took me to visit my wife, and to the pub. I knew that they wanted to talk to her as well – that she was going to have to give a statement. I told her not to worry and to say what she knew. They came round the next day, by which time I'd been taken back to Ford Prison. It was 3 July 1968.

I found out what she told them, a little afterwards. She'd given them lots of family photographs of us with the Krays at Steeple Bay. She said that I'd come home that night two years earlier 'with some friends' who she recognised. Ronnie had asked 'permission' to stay (hardly) and said 'Isn't she lovely?' to the Firm when he saw her. Well, that bit was true.

She told them how there had been all sorts of comings and goings, how Alfie had not been allowed to go home on his own. How Alfie had said: 'What do they think we are… cunts?' – meaning he didn't like the way Reggie and Ronnie were dominating him.

'There were a few drinking parties held at the flat. I think Madge's daughter came to the flat one night. She was friendly with Bobby Teale,' Christine told them. It's in the statement she gave, I've seen it.

On the last night before they finally all left, Ronnie, Reggie, Ian Barrie, me and my brothers had all gone out to the pub they called the 'Dead Pub', she told them, when a policemen knocked on the door asking about a burglar being held at the flat. She had shown the policeman round. That's what Christine said anyway. And to be frank, her version might have been nearer the truth.

I had bought a caravan at Steeple Bay after all of this, Christine had said, where we'd all gone down. And I did have a car, a grey Ford, which in the end had either been stolen from outside the Regency Club or repossessed by the finance company – more likely the latter. So, as far as the coppers were thinking, all I'd said checked out.

But I could see the way Read was thinking. What sort of charges could be brought out of all of this? A defence could say it was all a great big party. Dancing, drinking, outings to pubs – all of which was true. That the police had come round to Moresby Road because of neighbours complaining about the noise. In fact, that's exactly what they would say.

CHAPTER 17
ALFIE'S STORY

While all this was going on, Alfie was still holed up in Lewes Prison. David and I could have no contact with him. He also remembered what he was hearing on the landings around the same time that the Krays got nicked:

> A lot of the Firm tried to visit me during the course of the two years that I was in Lewes Prison. I used to get called into the governor's office and told: 'You've had a couple of people try to visit you, Teale. But I'm afraid under the Home Office rules we can't allow it.'
>
> 'Why, sir, who was it?'
>
> I worked out who they were from his descriptions. One was Dickie Morgan, another was Mad Teddy, and then there was Connie Whitehead. I knew, without seeing them, why they had come. They had been sent to tell me that if anyone asked about Ronnie or Reggie, to say I didn't know anything. Reggie also sent me a couple of books. They were signed: 'Reggie and Ronnie Kray.' So I am getting the feeling someone wants to warn me off – but the books I was grateful for.

A little later I was also sent in a complete set of oil paints. To this day, no one has told me who these came from, but they did inspire me to start painting. I won a prize in a national prison art competition.

I knew, really, they could only have come from the Krays. No one else I knew could have afforded something like that. Nobody else would have bothered. Both the books and the painting actually gave me great comfort. I was missing my wife and children terribly and often cried myself to sleep in my cell at night. Then I got the news.

A friend of mine, Bob, an old con who'd done a lot of time, went on home leave in June 1968 and on his return came to see my cellmate, Georgie Mutton, and me in our cell, whispering something to Georgie so I wouldn't hear. When I asked what they were talking about, Georgie said to Bob, 'You might as well tell him'. Turning to me, Bob said, 'I'm so sorry, Alfie. Your mum and dad's been nicked – for doing Lady Hamilton's place.'

I was astonished. I knew my mum had been working as a housekeeper for a toff family for a while but I also knew there was no way she would be involved in a robbery of all things. It was only later I found out what really happened. For now I was just told that my father had been interviewed at West End Central back in March. They'd let him go but told him: 'We're not charging you, but we're charging your wife.'

Mum and Dad were then remanded until July. They'd never told me. I really felt life couldn't get any worse. But Georgie reassured me, saying, 'Don't worry, Alfie. It'll work out, I'm sure. Someone will get in touch with you.'

And sure enough, a few days after this, someone did.

I was called to see the governor. But instead of going to his office I found myself taken to a small private meeting room. 'You're allowed to smoke, Teale,' I was told by the screw.

Suddenly two coppers walked in. One of them said, 'Hello, Alf. Nipper Read sent us down from Scotland Yard.' I knew Read's name from that time with McCowan and the Hideaway. So he was back on the Krays' case. Well, he would have to try harder than last time.

'What do you want?' I asked nervously.

'Your mother's been nicked, as you probably know.' I did know. The whole prison knew.

'Is she all right?'

'Yes, Alf, don't you worry. We'll look after her for you. Here you are – twenty fags.'

I grabbed the packet of Senior Service gratefully, dreading what was coming next.

'We might as well be blunt with you, Alf,' the officer continued. 'Your mother looks like getting five to seven years. We've been told by Scotland Yard that she'll be put in Durham Jail with the likes of Myra Hindley and a few others... unless, of course, you want to help us with some information about the murder of George Cornell and a couple of other things about the twins. It's up to you. If you want to write a statement we can more or less guarantee your mother will go free.'

My instinct was not to grass, under any circum-stances. So I said to them, 'See you later, mate. You must be on drugs or something telling me all this nonsense. I do know the twins; everyone knows them. But I didn't have anything to do with Cornell or any of it.' Then I asked the screw, a huge man from Dartmoor who'd been listening to all this, to take me back to my cell.

As I stood up to go, one of the policemen said, 'Well, it's up to you. But we've got three statements written by the Firm saying that you and your brothers were the ones who did Cornell.'

This really terrified me. I couldn't believe that the twins would really try to pin this on us. But they had. It was true. I found out later that David saw the statement written by Ronnie at Tintagel House claiming that we were responsible.

I was taken through the prison gate and back to my block, and the policemen disappeared, probably off to have a drink, I remember thinking. When I got back to my cell, I told Georgie and asked for his advice. He didn't say anything immediately but later in the evening after I'd had my tea, he sat down on the bed opposite mine. I stared around the cell looking at our books, the sugar and milk on the table between us, the fruit we'd bought out of our canteen money we always shared, and waited for him to speak.

'D'you want some tobacco, Alfie?' he asked.

Georgie always had a few quid and often gave me half an ounce of tobacco when I was low.

I asked him whether he'd thought about what I'd told him.

He nodded and said, 'Let me tell you something. You want the truth? You would be a truly evil man if you allowed your mother to go away for five to seven years with that slag in Durham. Get the governor to get the coppers back down here and tell them you will help them. Because if you don't, you won't see daylight again, Alfie.'

There was another reason. I knew about the Krays being arrested in May. Everyone did. But I didn't want to say anything then because they would have stopped my home leave, which was due on 18 May. They would have put me on ice.

When I did go out that weekend, I told my parents some of it. Mum was on bail – though at the time I didn't even know she had been arrested – and said I should go the police. The Krays were in Brixton on remand but I was frightened of them and of the rest of the Firm obviously. Then one Sunday – 30 June 1968 – there was a story in the paper about a man being arrested at the British Oak pub in the Lea Bridge Road in connection with the Cornell murder. It had to be Scotch Ian Barrie, who I was especially afraid of.

So that morning I walked into the PO's office and asked, 'Can you make an arrangement for me to see the governor, please?' He looked at me, and knowing exactly what was going on, answered quietly, 'Certainly, Teale. I'll do that straight away.'

A day later, down came the cops again. 'All right, Alfie? What have you decided to do?' and there was another twenty fags on the table in front of me. Again they promised me that our mother wouldn't do a day in jail if I cooperated.

I replied, 'Could I speak to one of my brothers, please?'

So they got David on the phone from Ford – and he told me they had been to talk to him too.

When I heard that I knew the game was up. I told David, 'You might as well tell them everything you know because I'm going to. They've got Mum and I don't see what else we can do. They must know about you and Christine and the flat, all of it.'

David told me they'd got photos and everything. I hadn't seen my brothers for two and half years and I was pretty low, counting the days off until my release. And now this.

The next thing I know, I was being taken over to the remand wing, on strict instructions that I should tell other prisoners I was waiting to be taken to a prison in London. They were going to smuggle me out for a meet. I was taken to Tintagel House, a police office block on the south bank of the Thames. On 1 July 1968 I made my statement. Detective Chief Inspector Henry Mooney took it down.

I gave him a full account of the night of 9 March 1966. How I was having tea and watching television with David, Bobby and Christine, when Reggie had rung the flat in Moresby Road to invite us Teale brothers over for a drink at Madge's.

I told him how when we got there, Reggie had got into the front seat of David's car and said: 'Cornell's just been shot.' How we'd driven to the Chequers pub in Walthamstow and how, when Ronnie, having received some sort of a message, said 'He's dead,' and turned to David and said, 'We're all going to stay at your house.'

How Ronnie and 'Ian Scott' (that's what I knew Scotch Ian Barrie as) had come into the flat. How Scotch Jack Dickson and Pat Connolly had left and come back the next morning. How shotguns, one of them a repeater, appeared all of a sudden but I wasn't sure who had brought them.

I told Mooney how Bobby had been sent out to get the morning papers, which were 'full of the Cornell murder'. How I'd been allowed home to get some clothes and had a row with Wendy because I'd been out all night. And how I told her I absolutely had to go back to David's house.

I described the comings and goings over the next two weeks, how Firm members Harry 'Jew Boy' Cope and

Sammy Lederman had brought in supplies of salt beef sandwiches. How I'd been sent to pay off Reggie's furniture bill for fitting out his flat in Green Lanes at the Harrison Gibson store in Ilford.

I told him about an outing with the Krays to the drinking club at the Lebus furniture factory in Tottenham. And then how we'd gone for a drinking session in the Grave Maurice pub where Ronnie had set up the reconnaissance mission to Dartmoor with me and Fat Wally to find Frankie Mitchell.

I ended my statement by explaining that now me and my brothers wanted 'to break away from the Krays – but gradually'. Well, that was true. We wouldn't have minded breaking away pretty quick, to be honest.

CHAPTER 18
MY STORY

As for me, I was still in Maidstone Prison after David was transferred to Ford. I think they wanted to keep me tucked up extra secure. All those months when we'd been in the same nick I'd shunned his company, really hurt him, and I couldn't tell him why. By now it was summer 1968. I remember still feeling completely eaten up with anger.

I had made contact with Butler, put my life on the line for months, been through that nightmare as 'Phillips' – and then I'd been thrown to the wolves. I suppose I had brought it all on myself. In Maidstone Prison I had just withdrawn inside – I wouldn't talk to David even. I just concentrated on doing my bird, wrapped up in my own anger, but I still heard whispers from outside.

I had heard about Jack the Hat from another inmate. Christine Keeler had visited him in Maidstone and had brought him a message from the twins. That's how we all heard. I wasn't so shocked about Jack being dead. In fact I'd warned him they'd do this and he wouldn't listen. But I was sorry. He'd sort of helped me get Bobby Cannon out of it that time when Reggie was going to do him. And now Reggie had done him instead. I would have saved Jack too if I could. But I was inside. What a disgusting way they killed him. It could have been me.

I heard about Frankie Mitchell the same way, through the same guy coming into my cell for a chat. The way I heard it, Big Frank had become a liability. Albert Donoghue told David a little later that when he had visited Frank in hiding somewhere – I think it was Barking in east London – Frank had said to him: 'Go back to the twins and tell them if Ronnie doesn't come to see me straight away, I'm getting out of here, that's it.'

I heard that when Albert took the message to Ronnie, Ronnie said: 'We've got to get rid of him. We can't handle him any more. He's too much for us.'

Frank was as strong as a bullock and the twins knew the only way to get rid of him was to shoot him. So they arranged it with whoever it was who did it. Some said it was Freddie Foreman, but we thought that was all hearsay. Poor Frank didn't even have a Christmas out. They did him on Christmas Eve.

About halfway through my sentence, 'Mr. Warnings' changed his attitude towards me. It wouldn't have been perceptible to an outsider, but I felt it in my guts, a feeling that he was suddenly dangerous. I noticed he started offering to make me cups of tea, or soup, and became suspicious he might be trying to poison me.

Sometimes he'd come into my cell looking for a pencil sharpener. A lot of the cons used to give a pencil as fine a point as they could and then write a message in the space on an envelope where the stamp would go, carefully licking the stamp around the edges only so it wouldn't pull the writing off when it was removed. I saw him do this, sending messages out to the twins several times. That's how it was done. That's how things on the outside – and on the inside – got known about pretty quick. That's how I'd heard about the Krays being arrested.

Then I was told by a screw that I was being taken to the hospital wing to have some X-rays done on my back. I had previously slipped over during a carpentry workshop and did indeed have a problem – but nothing urgent right then.

I came out of my cell and changed into my clothes. I was told I was being taken for a drive, and led outside the prison to a car. I'd had enough of this sort of pantomime with Butler and Pogue. I tried a few one-liners but the coppers never said a word. So I just shut up.

I was taken to Maidstone Police Station. There's a little guy in a suit behind a desk. This was my first encounter with Nipper Read. I'd heard of him. He was a small man but with a lot of natural authority. He treated me very kindly. But I was suspicious.

How much was I supposed to tell him? There were plenty of things I needed to know first. Where's Butler? Who's the Yard informer? What the f*** happened to Pogue? What about the deal with 'Dan' and getting lifted off the streets for nine months? Can I trust this guy Read? What does he know about my previous dealings with the Yard?

I convinced myself that Read did know about me. Butler must have told him everything; shown him the surveillance photos featuring us all of us coming and going from David's flat. But in his memoirs, *The Man Who Nicked the Krays*, Read says that on 18 September 1967, a month before the McVitie murder, he had been summoned to a meeting at the Yard with the new assistant commissioner, Peter Brodie, who told him: 'Mr Read, you're going to get the Krays.' He was to report to Commander John Du Rose, head of the Murder Squad.

'My only concern was about the enemy within,' Read wrote. 'I received my first shock when I discovered the criminal intelligence files contained not one single item added to the wealth of stuff I had put in during my own Commercial Street days.' That was when he had been working the East End in the early sixties. But after that, in the aftermath of the Cornell murder – during the time when the local police and then Tommy Butler were on the case – there was nothing on file. That's what Read said anyway.

So what had Butler been doing? Was he asleep? Was he doing nothing for some reason we can only guess at? In his book, Read excuses Tommy Butler in a line I still find funny: 'The fact I was starting with an absolutely clean slate was probably just as well,' he wrote.

I found that difficult to believe. How could Nipper not know about me? But then, I'd spent a lifetime convinced that he must have. So, maybe Butler really did keep a lid on on everything I'd told him?

Read told me in that interview room at Maidstone Police Station he was very sorry about everything that had happened, but there had been a changeover, a new broom. Though he's not going to say it outright, the Krays were always poison at the Yard. Only a very brave or a very foolish copper would go after them.

The commissioner, Joe Simpson, had not wanted to know – then he'd died in office on 8 March 1968. As far as I have come to understand, Tommy Butler of Great Train Robbery fame wasn't going to get into some tangle with the untouchable twins and their mysterious protectors. So after my brothers and I were taken off the streets in August 1966, he simply gave up.

But this time the twins were under arrest, as I knew. So were those members of the Firm that mattered. Scotch Ian Barrie, the man with the scald marks, was in custody. So were Albert Donoghue, Cornelius Whitehead, Scotch Jack Dickson, Big Pat Connolly, and some more who'd been involved in the killing of Jack the Hat.

Read was confident that he and his team could build a case that would put them all away for a very long time. Would I help him? It seemed to me that Read was willing to do almost whatever it took to take down the Krays. I made my own assumptions about how much he knew about me and I wondered if he was holding back on information because he didn't trust me. But one thing was certain: it was a big ask.

The Krays were in the security block at Brixton but the members of the Firm remaining on the outside could still get me and my whole family at any time, even if I was still in prison. At one point before he was arrested, Reggie himself had tried to see me in Maidstone, but it wasn't allowed. He did send me a book, though, called *My Kingdom for a Song*. I suppose he was being ironic.

Where was the guarantee that it would work this time? There could be no guarantee – not yet. But I would make a statement. I would discover later that this was a little after Alfie and David had first been interviewed and had given theirs on the 1st and 2nd of July. So I started to say what I knew.

I told Read's men how, although I'd heard stories about them from my brothers, I'd not actually met the Krays until spring 1965 when I was working on the Isle of Wight – when David rang up to say that Reggie and some friends wanted to visit someone on the island. I told them how I'd taken them to Parkhurst then brought them home for a meal. How when my wife saw who it was, she had 'done her nut'. Those were my actual words (and she had – done her nut I mean).

I told them how our relationship had gone downhill after that, and how I'd returned to Holborn. I told them how gradually I'd met people I had known earlier in London and had done some street trading with in the West End. I told them how I'd got sucked into the Krays' circle once I was back in London, going to parties and pubs with them in the East End.

Then I told them about the night of the summons by phone to come to Madge's. I've got a copy of my statement from the archive. This is exactly what I told them back then:

Reggie came over to us and said something like: 'Get moving quick, we're going over to Walthamstow.' Everything seemed urgent. He jumped into the front passenger seat beside David who was driving. There were a lot of other people leaving the pub but I cannot say who the others were as the degree of urgency cut out any observation.

My impression was that a lot of them were from the Firm. We drove straight from Madge's to the pub at Walthamstow. In fact, I think we drank at one or two pubs in Walthamstow before going to this particular pub... While we were drinking Ronnie was concerned about cleaning himself up and was washing his hands in the sink beneath the bar. He washed his hands in Vim and was very worried about things. I think he changed and someone brought him a change of clothes there. As far as I remember there were present Ronnie, Reggie, my brothers and me, Scots Ian, Scots Jack, Big Pat. About twenty people in all. Sammy Lederman [the one-time theatrical agent who'd become a Kray errand boy] was there and served drinks from the bar...

I recall Sammy saying to Ronnie, 'Ronnie, you're a cold-blooded murderer.' Ronnie then went out with Reggie from the bar.

When they came back Reggie told a group of us that Ronnie had just been sick and said that Ronnie had seen the bullets going into the head and had explained to Reggie how all the blood had made him sick. They then went upstairs, in fact, all of us went to a room above the pub with our drinks. The radio was switched on and Ronnie made out that he wanted to hear the football results. Anyway there was a news flash about the shooting in the East End and that the person had since died.

And then it appeared that there was a carnival. Ronnie almost jumped for joy.

Then I told them about how they'd holed up in David's flat – but not about Ronnie's move on my young brother Paul or what I had done as a result, not yet. I wanted to know more about what these guys already knew about the Butler-Pogue set-up before I gave them my side.

I told them about the guns in the flat and how to begin with I thought that these had been brought in to counter the threat of reprisals from Cornell's friends, the Richardsons, rather than because the Krays were getting ready for a shoot-out with the police. What happened afterwards was harder to explain. This was my statement:

We stayed there for about two weeks when Reggie moved to a flat in Green Lanes, Manor House, in a new block of flats. It was the flat he had lived in [briefly] with his wife … I moved in with him. [It was No 6 Manor Lea, 295 Green Lanes N4.] I stayed with him there for about a couple of weeks then we moved to Cambridge. It was supposed to be a holiday. We went first to Saffron Walden where the Krays had a friend [this was the con-man and arsonist, Geoffrey Allen].

There were two cars. There was me, Frosty (an East Ender) [David Frost] and Reggie in one, and in the other car was Ronnie, Ian and I think Connie Whitehead and Scotch Jack. This friend of the Krays is a very rich

The twins being welcomed home after being found not guilty on a menaces charge. (Ron Gerelli / Express / Getty Images)

With their dear old mum Violet and their grandfather Jimmy Lee. (Ron Gerelli / Express / Getty Images)

Reggie and sweet Frances Shea on their wedding day. (Express / Getty Images)

David's caravan and the one owned by the Krays behind it.

Reggie relaxing by the
sea on holiday.

(Evening Standard / Getty Images)

Inside David's caravan. L-R: Ronnie Hart,
Frosty, Alfie, Christine and me.

Jack 'The Hat' McVitie.

(Popperfoto / Getty Images)

George Cornell. (Popperfoto / Getty Images)

The Blind Beggar where Cornell got shot.
(Popperfoto / Getty Images)

The crime scene with Cornell's blood on the floor. (Kirsty Wigglesworth / Press Association)

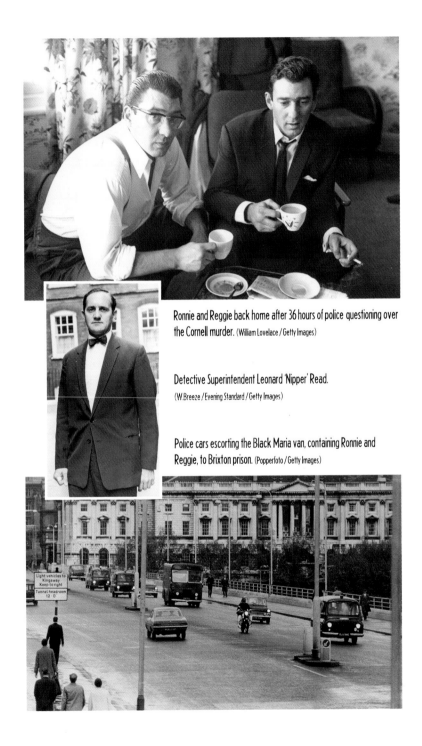

Ronnie and Reggie back home after 36 hours of police questioning over the Cornell murder. (William Lovelace / Getty Images)

Detective Superintendent Leonard 'Nipper' Read.
(W.Breeze / Evening Standard / Getty Images)

Police cars escorting the Black Maria van, containing Ronnie and Reggie, to Brixton prison. (Popperfoto / Getty Images)

Reggie was let out of prison for Ronnie's funeral. (Kent News / Pictures / Sygma / Corbis)

The haunting picture that prompted me to finally tell my family the truth. (Adrian Dennis / AFP / Getty Images)

on a charge of conspiring with the KRAYS to defraud.

199.   It has been established that CLARK had possession of a 1958 Rover 90 car No. 685 RFG at the time of the CORNELL murder but it was registered in his wife's name, she being shown as the purchaser under a hire purchase agreement with F.C. Finance Limited dated 14th December, 1965. A photograph of this car will be available if required at the trial.

Statement
349-351

200.   **Robert F. TEALE** came to see me on 24th September, 1968, when he was on home leave from prison, to give further information about the KRAYS and others. It will be recalled he gave evidence at Bow Street Court and during cross examination he was obliged to reveal that he had been in contact with police shortly after the murder of CORNELL. A further statement was taken from him, which includes the fact that he used the name 'PHILLIPS' in his dealings with Police.

352-354

201.   **Detective Sergeant POGUE**, confirms that Robert TEALE was in contact with him shortly after the CORNELL murder and used the nom-de-plume PHILLIPS. TEALE actually showed a photograph of BARRIE to this officer and a copy of this was taken and can be produced.

202.   Enquiries have been made at the B.B.C. about sound radio and T.V. broadcasts on 9th and 10th March, 1966, relative to the CORNELL shooting. Evidence was given at Bow Street Court that witnesses heard broadcasts about the shooting, although they did not specify B.B.C. programmes. **Miss Marjorie Helen MANN** of B.B.C. T.V. states there was a newsflash at 11.25 p.m. 9th March, 1966 on television about the incident. **Miss Mary Sheila FINNEY** of B.B.C. sound broadcast states there is no record of a news item on 9th March 1966 on sound of the incident.

355-356

357-359

Some of the police statements and court reports detailing my part in the downfall of the Krays. (The National Archives UK)

24.9.68.

349

STATEMENT of: Robert Frank TEALE

Age:
Occupation: Unemployed - Prisoner on Home Leave
Address: H.M. Prison Maidstone

Who Saith:

I have given evidence at Court in regard to the murder of George CORNELL and Chief Inspector MOONEY has informed me that no conversation about this case should take place now.

I remember some time after this murder being in the company of Ronald and Reginald KRAY at various places like Green Lanes and the home of Charlie CLARK in Walthamstow. I remember Ronnie saying that Reggie should kill someone to prove he was just as good as Ronnie. The words used were, "Why don't you do something, I have done one, you don't do fuck all, get something going". There was a list of people known as the "dreaded list", of people to be executed. There were about ten names on it, one being a fellow connected with Blue Films in the West End. Ronnie was egging Reggie to do a killing to show he had guts. Reggie used to say, "Don't fucking tell me what to do" and he often said he would prove himself in time.

I remember one day going to a party in a flat off Hackney Road. I think it was the flat of a girl, Blonde Vicky, but of her name I am not sure. She was friends with Ronnie HART. I went to this flat and Reggie KRAY, Albert DONAGHUE, WHITEHEAD, and Scots Pat CONNELLY were there. Perhaps Connelly was not there.

Finally reunited with my dear, dear brothers. That embrace was one I never thought would happen again.

The Krays may have come between us, but we'll never be parted again. (L-R: David, me and Alfie)

man and owns a Mercedes and has an estate agent business. We went to his house outside the village. It was large with tennis courts and everything. I can't describe where it is but could point it out if necessary. We stayed the day then came back to London.

We went to this village again on another occasion when we stayed in a hotel. Then after we had been there a couple of days we left because of trouble by us in the hotel. At the hotel there would have been about six of us – the twins, Ian, Scots Jack, myself and I think Connie. We then went on to Cambridge where we stayed in the Grand Hotel, I think it was called [it was the Garden House Hotel]. They all gave different names. I stuck to my own name.

We returned from Green Lanes and after a while they got a flat in Lea Bridge Road. During this time Ronnie went to live in a little bungalow with Ian [Barrie]. The man [Charlie Clark] and his wife who owned the place were there as well. The woman kept a lot of cats. It was in London but I can't remember where. It could be Walthamstow near a dog track, past the stadium on the right-hand side, two turnings down on the right-hand side. The guy is a bookmaker.

He was terrified of Ronnie. I used to go there with Reggie. I think the road was called Loxham [Loxham Road in Walthamstow E4]. Later Ronnie and Ian left this flat and Reggie and myself left the Green Lanes flat and went to the flat in Lea Bridge Road. It was over a barber's shop.

After a while I left them and moved away from the area. I know they were looking for me from enquiries I now know they made for me, by them I mean the Krays. I have not seen the twins or Ian [Barrie] since I left the flat.

That is what I told Nipper Read's men in early July 1968.

There were some things I didn't mention, such as the drive with Reggie to Epping Forest when he'd started shooting at me. I did tell them that they'd come looking for me at Steeple Bay, though I didn't mention where. But I certainly didn't mention how I'd taken refuge with that 'Wallace' character in Dolphin Square – though I think Nipper Read knew a lot of it already. He wanted to work on us one by one. The police could not know for sure that I hadn't somehow been able to get a message to David or Alfie – but in fact I had not.

In each of our three cases, Alfie, David and I, the police used a different form of leverage – but all the methods were equally subtle and cynical. Whatever they claimed, they were working on us to give evidence in open court.

Then they played really sneaky.

In between my little visits to Maidstone Police Station and Tintagel House they brought my mother up to have tea in the governor's office at Maidstone Prison. They told her how brave I was being, and what a hero I was. Mum looked very pleased to see me. It was all about softening me up to give evidence.

They also told me on several occasions that what I had done, what I had already given them, was so powerful they would never, ever ask me to give evidence in open court. There would be others who could do that.

That part was not true. Read was determined to do whatever it took to get the Krays. He would let criminals off, even let murderers off, as long it brought them down.

Nipper Read wanted me not only to give evidence but also to reveal in court that I was an informer. Only then might others follow. Only then would he have his case. He was asking me to gamble with my life.

When the time came I would have to face them from the witness box. And I would do so.

CHAPTER 19
BRINGING DOWN THE HOUSE OF CARDS

All of three of us had given statements. We would soon be on our way to London under heavy guard to give them again in open court at the committal proceedings, when the prosecution must produce enough evidence for a case to be made to proceed to a full trial. Of us brothers, David was up first. This is how he describes what happened:

They took me from Ford Prison to Bow Street for the committal. It was 16 July 1968. We were in a squad car driven fast in a convoy surrounded by yet more armed police. It was Covent Garden, an area I knew well from when Alfie, Bobby and I used to play there as kids, nicking flowers from the market for the altar in our church (St Joseph's). At that time, early in the morning, the market was very crowded, and I knew a lot of the porters who worked round there. The police told me to 'put this blanket over your head'. It was exciting, but also terrifying and strange. We just didn't know what to expect.

I was in the back of the car just near the Opera House when I peeped out from behind a corner of the blanket, and saw a face I recognised in the crowd – a family friend called Johnny Cracknell, a market porter known as a 'cart minder'. Johnny was directing the traffic around Bow Street as there was quite a back-up by then. I thought to myself, 'If only you knew it's me in the police car!' We then went through the big gates, into the back of the yard behind the court. The place was packed. It was overrun with police, a lot of uniform but even more in plainclothes.

I was whisked into another crowded room where we waited for about half an hour and they gave me a cup of tea. I glanced round the room. I recognised the barmaid from the Blind Beggar and also Leslie Payne. And then we went in the court. Nipper Read was there and all the other officers who'd interviewed me in Tintagel House. Read said to me before I went in: 'Just say exactly what you've been telling us, and confirm that you are prepared to go the higher court and say the same.' I would be known as 'Mr D'.

I didn't know much about what had been happening with the Krays since their arrest but I soon picked it up. They'd been nicked on holding charges – a lot of guff about stolen bearer bonds, the Mafia, dynamite and assassination plots that Read had cooked up somehow.

Then, much more to the point, Billy Exley had given evidence about the escape of Frank Mitchell. Then after Scotch Ian Barrie was nicked, the Blind Beggar barmaid said she would identify him. So that was it: Ronnie and Scotch Ian were down for the murder of George Cornell. And Reggie was charged with 'acting to impede their apprehension'. Read's told me to say what I know about that – and I was prepared to do so.

The witness box itself was surrounded by armed police, and looked like something out of Dickens. The court was so crowded it was hard at first to make out what was going on. I tried to 'front it up' the way I always used to, to act tough even if I didn't feel like it. But inside I was absolutely petrified.

Until I looked at Ron across the court, that is. Suddenly I felt a tremendous anger fill me, for all the damage Ron had done, not only to me but to all my family. I didn't have the strength to beat Ron physically in a fight, but now I did find I had the courage to tell the truth about him. As I caught his eye, I saw that he was scared too.

I was so nervous as I began to give evidence that the magistrate had to stop me and ask me to 'speak up and also speak more slowly', so that the stenographer could get everything written down. And so I made my statement.

I went through the night of the Cornell killing and the drive to Walthamstow. I told how Christine had reacted when we all got to our flat. I told them about what happened there. How, after it was over, my wife had wanted to get away and live in Birmingham where she came from, but instead we'd gone to the caravan in Steeple Bay. After that, we'd left the flat and stayed at Alfie's place in Holborn.

I remember the magistrate asking me: 'What guns were in the flat at the time?' I got some black looks from Ron across the court as I told them about the guns, and he shouted out 'Lies!' to try and drown out what I was saying.

Then Scotch Ian's brief has a go at me. If what I was saying was true, why hadn't I gone to the police straight away? I was too frightened for myself and my family, I replied. The first time I'd said anything to the police about any of it was two weeks before, on 1 July, when they had offered me and my family protection. And we needed it.

Once I started giving my evidence I tried not to look around the courtroom. It seemed to be over quite quickly. As I was led out of the court again, we passed Bobby on his way in for his turn, also surrounded by police. We were meant to be apart, no contact. I called out to him: 'Are you all right, Bob?' and he called back to me, 'I'm OK, Dave,' or something like that. That was all the conversation we were allowed. It was a very strange moment.

When I got back into the waiting room, Nipper Read and the others praised me for giving my evidence so well.

So I asked: 'Can I just pop and see the wife and kids for a while?' They said yes, taking me home and allowing me to spend some time with Christine and my daughters. It was wonderful to be able to hold my wife in my arms again, and to kiss and cuddle the children, even if it was only for a couple of hours. I still love my wife Christine; I've never stopped loving her. I dreaded the knock at the door, signalling it was time to take me back to Ford. All I could comfort myself with was the thought that it would not be long now until my release.

Alfie was on next. He told how he had first been approached by the police to give a statement two and half weeks earlier. He gave the magistrates' court a full reprise of the holing up in Moresby Road. 'Some time after that I broke my connection with Reginald and Ronald Kray,' he said. That was an understatement. Then, after David and Alfie, it was my turn.

I'd been woken before dawn and brought in a fast convoy from Maidstone Prison to Bow Street. Nipper Read was there, looking anxious, whispering encouragement. A lot more useful was a guard who told me he was the one who took men to the gallows and showed them how to do a deep breathing exercise to stop them losing control of their bowels. So he gave me the same instructions. Another told me he'd 'take a bullet for me if necessary'. I wasn't so sure about that.

I looked down the row of faces in the dock and could see no one was ready for this. Ronnie's eyes were sending a raging, killing stare at me. Just the way he looked was terrifying. The public gallery was full of the Kray fan club. I felt my legs shaking beneath me.

My voice was breaking, the adrenaline was pulsing, I just wanted to get away, run for it … but I had to find my courage. It was if all those times I'd been on the brink of discovery as Phillips were replaying in my head at once.

I told the court about the night of the drive from Madge's to Walthamstow and the arrival at the Chequers pub where Ronnie had washed his hands with Vim sink cleaner, just the way I'd given my statement in the first place. I told them how Sammy Lederman had turned round to Ronnie Kray and said: 'Ronnie, you're a cold-blooded murderer.'

I told the story of Moresby Road in a kind of matter-of-fact way without too much detail. And I explained what happened after it was over – my time on the Firm in summer 1966, my trip to Cambridge and Saffron Walden, the flats Reggie and I had shared in Green Lanes and Lea Bridge Road.

After I'd finished, Reggie's brief lays into me. He says I'm being paid to say all this. 'That's lies,' I replied.

Then Scotch Ian Barrie's barrister began his cross-examination for the defence. 'When did the witness', meaning me, 'first consider giving evidence?' That's a good question. Shall I tell the truth? Shall I tell the court I'd done so the day after Ronnie put a bullet into George Cornell's forehead in the Blind Beggar? I'm under oath, after all.

Mr Read had made it clear that it would be useful if I told the truth, the whole truth. I wasn't to worry as reporting restrictions were on for my appearance. Nipper had his own and very devious game. Well, they certainly weren't expecting what I was going to say next.

I said: 'I first considered giving evidence in this matter, just after I realised [Cornell's] murder had taken place and I did something about it then. I gave it some thought. It was obvious to me that my brothers were terrified, so to speak, so I got in touch with Scotland Yard. I was then put on to another chap, Tommy Butler, and through him a man named Joe Pogue, who is in the Flying Squad. I kept Tommy Butler up to date on everything that happened.'

So that was a bit of a shocker. There was a spy in the Firm, a grass. And what had the police done with the information? Nothing. Nipper Read seemed astounded – in public at least. Tommy Butler wasn't going to say anything and nobody bothered to ask him.

Then I explained how Butler & Co had not asked me at any stage to make a statement, an official statement that could be used to bring a prosecution, I mean. In fact I had first been asked to make a statement very recently – only two weeks ago. I told the court that I'd been in touch with the police for about six weeks or two months after the shooting, till after I'd left the flat in Green Lanes, at which point I'd stopped all contact. Of course after that time I had my little adventure in Mr X's Triumph TR3 sports car, followed by the conviction for demanding money with menaces, both of which effectively removed me from the Krays' reach.

So what the hell had I done now? I'd told the world, or as good as, that I was a grass. On the way out of the court there was all kinds of praise from Nipper Read and the Old Bill. Their lives were safe enough. I had put my head in a noose. But what mattered to me now was how the Krays and their fan club were going to react.

I was taken back to Maidstone. I could not believe how fast word got back to the nick that I was the grass. A friend who I trusted in told me: 'Bobby, watch your back, the word is out on you and you are going to be hit.'

Getting on to the cell block, my path was obstructed by a giant of a man known as 'Goldfinger' for his resemblance to the Bond villain. Behind was a crowd of other prisoners who, I could see from their stance and their expressions, all clearly knew I'd just been giving evidence against Ronnie Kray. Thank God a couple of screws were accompanying me.

I was put in solitary for my own protection. All kinds of threats were fed to me from crooked screws though the prison-cell door. I would get a banging on my cell door in the middle of the night and someone would call out 'Bobby, Bobby!' in a deep voice until I answered.

'What do you want?' I'd say, and the person would reply: 'You are a dead man and all your family are going to be poisoned. You can still stop all this if you say that the Old Bill put you up to it using your mum to make you tell lies about the Krays.'

After a few nights of this, I would block my ears as soon as I heard footsteps coming down the hallway, and I would not respond at all. I could still hear the banging on the cell door and a voice, but it happened less often and finally stopped.

Then I was shipped out of prison in the middle of the night because a gun had been smuggled in to the prison to kill me, or at least that's what I was told by the governor.

The news I was an informer had reached Maidstone even before I'd arrived back there on the afternoon of 16 July. The news had got to Brixton Prison in south London where the twins and the Firm were on remand even quicker, just as fast as it took a prison van to get back there from the Old Bailey.

It was all working out as Read had planned it, of course. Look what he wrote in his memoirs: 'Things were moving behind the scenes. On 16 July I had the biggest break of all. While I was at Bow Street dealing with the Cornell committal proceedings I received a note.'

This is what had happened. Albert Donoghue's mother had come herself to give it to Nipper Read after she had been handed it by her son in Brixton. She'd visited him earlier that afternoon. Mrs Donoghue 'pleaded with me to see her son, saying it was a matter of life and death', Read wrote. He had got down there pretty quick to see Donoghue in the prison hospital early that same evening.

The 'sullen, defiant man' he had first encountered was now very different, Read said in his memoirs. 'He came straight out and said: "It's been put to me to volunteer for the Mitchell business [confess to killing him] and, if I do, my wife and kids will be all right."'

As I would hear it later, the twins got the word to Donoghue that he should take responsibility for the Mitchell murder and that their cousin Ronnie Hart would put his hand up for the

Cornell killing, thus leaving Ian Barrie free of charges. Reggie would plead self-defence for doing Jack the Hat.

Big Albert was not happy. He wanted to make a deal with the prosecution. If the murder charge against him was dropped, in return he would tell Read the lot. Over the next three days, according to Read, Donoghue did just that. So the next day Big Albert was spirited out of Brixton to Winson Green Prison in Birmingham and his wife and family were put under guard.

It was the same with Scotch Jack Dickson. He'd tell how it happened when it got to the full trial. When they were in Brixton, the twins were leaning on him to cook up an alibi. Then he wants to change his brief, get a new one, not the twins' brief. Suddenly he gets transferred to Wandsworth and asks to see Mr Read. On 16 July he made a statement about how he'd driven Ronnie to the Blind Beggar.

It was the twins who had screwed it up this time. It seems that the twins' solicitor had shown Scotch Jack our statements, Alfie, David and mine (they were allowed to do that), and asked him, 'Why have those three brothers said all the things they must know are not true?'

But their tactic backfired. Clever old Read in turn came down heavy on Scotch Jack and got him to change sides, using our statements as a way of persuading him that the Krays' influence was crumbling and that he needed to switch sides so as to avoid being dragged down with them.

'The destabilising game was working well,' Read said in his book. 'Without naming names [we] let it be known that some of the defendants in custody were working with me and that caused something amounting to panic among the others.' Well, I wasn't one of the defendants but he'd used me to start the whole thing. I pushed over the first domino.

Nipper needed more. What was going to be a big problem was what I'd said about Butler and Pogue. A defence could rip into that. Read needed more leverage to keep us in line and to bring down the Krays would use anything that came to hand. This was where our mother's exaggerated charge of housebreaking came in useful for him. While we three brothers had been busy making our statements, our mother's case had been proceeding through the courts. Gradually we came to learn what had happened to her while we'd been inside.

CHAPTER 20
MUM AND CHRISTINE'S STORIES

When we'd first been told our mother had been arrested we all thought it was a trick. Well, it wasn't. She'd got out of the club business after the 66 folded. Alfie had set her up in that pie and mash shop. Then there was a bit of a changearound. Around Christmas 1967, with us three in prison, she'd got a job as housekeeper to a society figure, Lady Violet Hamilton. She lived in a mews close to St James's Palace at 8 Russell Court SW1. It couldn't be any posher. Lady Violet's husband was 'extra equerry to Queen Elizabeth II'. He was an elderly chap. It was all a long way from a pie shop in Upper Clapton.

Mum's references, it would turn out, had come from Lord Boothby. We'd find out later that the go-between was the former Cedra Court resident, cat-burglar and rent boy Leslie Holt. Boothby was an acquaintance of the Hamiltons and, as Mum had no qualifications for the post – all she had ever done was bring up seven children and run drinking clubs – she could hardly have got the job otherwise.

Mum and Dad had been arrested around 14 March 1968. The charges were 'housebreaking' and 'conspiracy to steal with persons unknown between 28 February and 2 March a quantity of jade, jewellery, candlesticks, china, enamel, crystal, clocks, boxes, ornaments and three paintings to the value of £25,000.' It was an enormous sum. I mean Dad, he was nearly seventy. It was ridiculous. They dropped charges against him and Mum was granted bail. The trial was scheduled for 24 July.

Mum told us afterwards all she could remember of what happened the night of the burglary. On that particular evening, Leslie Holt rang the doorbell while Charlie Kray, she found out later, was waiting outside in the street. The Hamiltons were out for the evening at some society do.

Without giving Mum a chance to say or do anything, Holt pushed past her and started stuffing a large holdall with all he could lay his hands on – silver and jade and as much jewellery as he could find. When Mum began to protest, Holt told her to: 'Shut up, sit down on the sofa, and don't say a word.'

After Leslie Holt had left, Mum contacted the Hamiltons by phone. They immediately called the police. Mum knew Holt by sight from Cedra Court and by seeing him in clubs with the Krays but was too scared to name him to the police when they turned up. She just said that she opened the door to someone, she didn't know who it was, and he had come in and ransacked the place.

Then they arrested her. They accused her of being an accomplice, of letting the burglars in willingly. She wanted to tell the truth but she was frightened both for herself and for our safety in prison if she should give any kind of a statement. Meeting Charlie Kray in a club a few weeks later, she asked him, 'What am I going to do?'

Charlie had said to her: 'Don't say nothing to no one. Reggie and Ronnie will look after the boys. They'll buy them a nice little pub when they come out of prison. They'll be well set up, don't worry. Just don't you say anything and it will all be taken care of.'

But it wasn't taken care of. When the Hamiltons' stuff was fenced, the Krays got the money. Yet still she wouldn't give evidence against them.

It got even stranger after that. On the date her trial was due, 24 July 1968, three weeks after we'd given our statements to Nipper Read, her court appearance was suddenly postponed until November to be heard at the Central Court at the Old Bailey. Why do you think that was?

On that very same day that the trial had been due, she gave a statement that had nothing to do with Lady Violet Hamilton's ornaments. And guess who she's giving it to? Nipper Read. I've got a copy of it from the archives.

Read wanted to know all about our relationship with the Krays (who she calls 'the Craigs' – that's Mum, all right). Well, they didn't get much from her. Charlie, Ronnie and Reggie Kray had all been members of the 66 Club and had been 'extremely well-behaved'. There was 'never any trouble'. They liked her three sons, Alf, Dave and Bobby, and 'promised that they would look after them'.

She and her husband had moved to 30 Cedra Court, Cazenove Road, Mum said. All three Kray brothers had visited Cedra

Court and when Reggie took a liking to the flats, our dad had introduced him to the letting agent. Reggie had moved into a flat in the block. She and our dad had never visited David's flat at Moresby Road, even though it was nearby, she said, and they had no knowledge of who was there.

Not long after our arrest in autumn 1966, Mum said, one of us had said he expected the Krays would help financially with our legal defence but they had not. According to her, I had said: 'They must take us for right mugs. We've never had anything off them,' or words to that effect. On subsequent visits to see us in prison, we had said that when we came out, we 'didn't want anything to do with the Krays'. She was right about that.

Mum told Read that Alfie had said, after learning of the Krays' arrest: 'If I'm asked about them I shall tell the truth.' When she had told me about Alfie on a visit to prison, I also said: 'I will make a clean breast of it and tell the truth.'

But David, when told in turn of my decision, said: 'You can't believe all these things being said about them [the Krays], Mum.' Mum said: 'But you can only tell the truth.' David replied: 'All right, Mum, I will, I was only kidding.'

As all this was going on with Mum behind the scenes, her sons were all still in prison, coming to the end of our sentences – and fearing what would happen once word got round we'd been giving evidence against the Krays. Alfie remembers what happened to him:

When Mum was telling Read all this, I'm in Lewes. Just before lights out at nine, we were all engulfed in choking black smoke. Someone had set light to the prison. The fire was so serious that Jim Callaghan, the Home Secretary at the time, had to come down to oversee the transfer of over three hundred prisoners.

I was safe because I was in the remand centre, which wasn't touched. But I couldn't help worrying that perhaps the twins had got word that I was working with the police and had planned the fire deliberately.

Two days before my release date I was told to get ready for a transfer. When I went down to the reception they told me to put my own clothes on. I asked, 'Why? Am I going home early?' The prison officers said they didn't know. I was taken in what looked like a minicab with two prison officers and a driver. Again I asked, 'Excuse me, can you tell me where we're going?' And again I was just told, 'Sorry, we can't say anything.'

Then all of a sudden we pulled up outside what looked like a castle – it was Canterbury Prison. I wasn't there long. After two days an officer came into my cell and I was told, 'You're being released.'

I knew it was coming. I remember the night before hanging my proper clothes, my jacket and trousers, on a hanger I borrowed from a screw, just so that I wouldn't look too down-at-heel as I walked out. I was freezing that night as I then had only a blanket to curl up in, but rather that than looking like a tramp on my release.

The next morning I signed a piece of paper to get my things back. I noticed they didn't give me a travel pass and asked how I was going to get back to London. But the prison officer told me, 'You don't need to worry about that.' I guessed then that somebody was going to pick me up. Then they opened a little gate in the huge prison door and I stepped through to freedom. It was 13 September 1968.

Minutes later a car pulled up. Two men got out and walked over to meet me. 'Hello, Alf! All right? Nice to be out?' They sat me in the back of the car. I asked them where they were taking me and one of them said, 'The first thing we are going to do is get you a nice breakfast.'

So they took me a caff where I ordered eggs, bacon, sausages and a few tomatoes, mushrooms, toast, Marmite, the lot. Nothing ever tasted so good. I asked if they were dropping me home, but they said we had to go to Tintagel House again.

They then took me to London. Nipper could not have been more reassuring. 'Hello, Alfred, all right are you? Don't you worry about a thing. David and Bobby are fine. It won't be long until they are released. Everything is going to be all right, I promise you.'

Then I started talking. This time it was about my trip to Dartmoor to 'bump into' Frank Mitchell. I remembered Ronnie telling me in the Grave Maurice that he wanted us to pretend to be a pop group and take guitars with us. As soon as Nipper heard about Mitchell, he said: 'This is wonderful!' In the end I gave the full statement to Henry Mooney.

I told him about the orders given by Ronnie to go and see a 'friend' in Dartmoor. I described the drive with Wally Garelick – how we'd gone first that night to Stamford Hill to collect two girls to come with us. One needed to get a baby-sitter first. Only on the way down had Wally had told me who the 'friend' actually was. That's what I told Mooney, although of course I already knew. At the prison, Wally produced the necessary visiting orders, which were in false names. The girls stayed in the car. When we met Frank he had said: 'Wally, you'll have to get me out of here – I can't do no more bird.' There had been talk about how fast Frank could run and over what distance.

I told Mooney that I was convinced that Ronnie, Reggie and Charlie Kray were intending to spring Mitchell, and I signed a statement to that effect.

Nipper was jumping with joy. 'This is absolutely fantastic, Alfie. Just what I needed!' At the end of the interview he told me: 'Right, Alfie. You go home now. You, and David and Chrissie, have each got a police officer looking after you. They'll keep you safe.'

So the two cops took me home at last. One of them said he was going over to the Section House and I gave the other a couple of blankets and a quilt and told him he could sleep on the couch. The protection officers changed all the time. All the officers were armed and had a direct phone to the Yard in their squad car.

David was also going home. He told me how it happened:

I got picked up by a policeman outside the prison on the day of my release from Ford. Christine was with him. It felt strange to be free but even odder to be kissing and cuddling Christine in front of this man.

I asked where the kids were, and Christine said they were being looked after by her mother. So the copper, his name was Dick De Lillo, said he'd got a horse to back and suggested we all go to the races. So it was that Christine and I found ourselves at Sandown Park racetrack. We didn't get back until the evening and there wasn't much time to talk about anything intimate with Dick around us all the time. Christine, too, had a police-woman with her so it was virtually impossible for us to be natural with one another. I knew why they were taking so much interest. Was I free or wasn't I?

We were given twenty-four-hour protection. They used to come everywhere with Alfie and me after that – boozing, street trading, the lot. We tried to pick up as 'normal' a life as possible. The police used to joke with us, telling us they shouldn't do it and that if Nipper Read found out they'd get the sack.

But although we laughed about it, there was a real danger that either of us could have got a bullet in the back. But there was nothing we could do. We couldn't leave our wives and children.

But the joy of David's homecoming was quickly turned sour by a cruel revelation:

Over the next couple of weeks Christine and I gradually started to talk about all that had happened to her during my time in prison. Of me, there wasn't much to say. She told me about Charlie Kray coming round and bringing Big Pat Connolly and that at first it had cheered her and the kids up to see someone while I was banged up. She said they'd just have a cup of tea, he'd give her some money and then go. But I felt there was something wrong. I remembered what Charlie was like when we used to go out together in the past. I'd covered up for him lots of times, saying he'd slept on the sofa in the club when he'd really been with Barbara Windsor or Christine Keeler. Charlie was always with some woman or another, it was the way he was.

I asked in particular about an occasion when she'd come to visit me and seemed really upset. I'd assumed it must have been due to the stress of it all, but it had bothered me afterwards and I wanted to know more. Christine immediately started to cry, saying she didn't want to tell me.

Out it came, through her sobs. Charlie had started giving her money, and she'd been grateful. He'd said he wanted to help in any way he could. This went on for a long time before he started making the odd remark, saying what a nice figure she had and generally starting to come on to her.

He'd come round one day with Big Pat and given her a ten-pound note. He said, 'I might pop back later.' He did come back, but this time Pat left and went home. Charlie then started touching her and following her when she went into the kitchen. Eventually he began to force her. Christine screamed and kicked and Charlie said, 'What do you expect after I came round and gave you money?'

They struggled until Charlie eventually forced himself on her. Charlie Kray then raped my wife.

I felt so angry I wanted to go straight out and kill him. I was also so confused by my feelings that I started questioning Christine, asking her repeatedly whether she'd encouraged him. Did she really push him off? Why hadn't she told me before?

But Christine was so obviously distressed that I could see she was telling me the truth. She said she had felt ill and depressed ever since – but she hadn't known how to tell me.

She said she didn't want to go to the police because she was too ashamed. When she said that I knew exactly how she felt. I'd been through the same experience, of being raped by Ronnie, myself. Could I tell her that?

I could not. I already felt too humiliated. I felt she'd never think of me as a man ever again. In the end I never told her, although now I wish I had.

Things stayed very difficult between us. In the weeks and months following my release from prison and the lead-up to the trial, Christine was drinking more than she'd ever done before. I warned her several times but she didn't seem able to stop. She was also visiting the doctor frequently, getting pills to wake her up in the morning and pills to help her sleep at night.

She was pregnant when the Firm all came to camp out at our flat. She gave birth to our youngest daughter while I was in prison. And then to be raped by Charlie. What happened was tough on everyone, but it was tougher on Christine than any of us.

Charlie Kray was not as violent as his brothers – but he was the jackal of the family. I wanted to go and front him up straight away but there was nothing I could do. Not then anyway. My brothers and I were about to go and face the whole lot of them at the Old Bailey.

CHAPTER 21
SECRETS AND LIES

As for me, my own release date was getting near too. I've done my number at Bow Street and everyone knows I'm a grass. Am I safer in prison or outside? And I've got to go through the whole thing again at the full trial that's coming down the track like a train. If I can stay alive that long.

My life was in Nipper Read's hands. But could I still trust him? I guessed he was never telling me the full truth and was keeping things back from me. In one of our talks at Tintagel House, Nipper told me about the changeover at the Yard. When he'd gone to look for my files he found that 'they had disappeared'. That's what he said in his memoirs – and further that he was not aware of there being an informer in the Firm until the Old Bailey trial, which was in January 1969.

In fact he knew there was an informer from what I said at the committal six months before. Either that or he didn't believe me. That was a matter of official record. I had said it out loud from the witness box in Bow Street when I was being cross-examined by Scotch Ian's brief.

There were other puzzles too. Our mother's court appearance on a wrongful charge of housebreaking had been mysteriously postponed. And whatever Read might say, I knew that evidence from March 1966 did exist – surveillance photographs of Moresby Road, of the comings and goings at the flat. I saw them. David and Bobby saw them. Walls covered in them at Tintagel House. That was Butler's operation, when I was meeting Pogue. And I had actually got a photograph of Ian Barrie for Butler at the time. I was asked for it. I gave it to Pogue. I saw it blown up as a mug-shot at Tintagel.

Whenever I asked where Butler was, I was told he was sick, or he had retired. In fact I found out later he had managed to get his retirement postponed, aged fifty-five, and in 1968 he was in pursuit of the last Great Train Robbers still on the run. I was asked to make another statement. I did so willingly.

I think they wanted as little as possible to emerge about how Butler had cocked up the Cornell investigation. Especially how they'd left the Krays free to kill again. Not just once but lots of times. Tommy Butler was supposed to be the most renowned head of the Flying Squad in its history. I think they wanted nothing said about Butler and the Krays at all – and the Yard has kept the same line ever since.

I was allowed out for a weekend on pre-release home leave. Around that time I had a little chat with Henry Mooney, Read's deputy. I've got a note of what he said from the file. It's pretty terse but it shows the way my case was playing in Read's mind as he was putting together his part of the big Old Bailey prosecution:

Robert Teale came to see me on 24 September [1968] on home leave from prison. It will be recalled he gave evidence at the Bow Street committal during cross examination that he was obliged to reveal he was in contact with police shortly after the death of Cornell. A further statement has been taken from him that he used the name 'Phillips'. DS Pogue confirms the story. A copy of a photo of Barrie was taken and this can be produced.

So Read's man knew it was me who'd got the photograph of Scotch Ian. They even had a 'copy' of it. So why, I ask again, did Read insist there was 'nothing on file'?

A few days later it was the end of my sentence at Maidstone. I was all ready with my suit and my few belongings on my way to the prison gate when I was stopped by two men. The fear of 'the gate re-arrest', as any con will tell you, is terrible, but apparently these men just wanted to take me back to Tintagel for further questioning. My nerves were on edge in fear of yet another false arrest. I just couldn't trust them any more after all that had happened. We had to change cars three times in case anyone was following us before arriving at Tintagel.

I'd already told them at length about the chaotic goings-on after George Cornell had been shot. That was down to Ronnie. Now they wanted to know more about the time between the end of the Moresby Road siege and our removal from the streets. They wanted to know about me and Reggie.

I didn't know it but they'd charged Reggie the week before, with killing Jack the Hat, even though no body had been found.

Now it was all about Reggie – my time with him, what he was thinking, what he was capable of. So on 29 September I gave a statement to Henry Mooney in which I explained how Ronnie had been urging Reggie to kill someone after the Cornell murder. He would say: 'Why don't you do one, you don't do fuck all, get something going.' I also told him about the twins' 'dreaded list', and about the time in Blonde Vicky's flat off the Hackney Road when Reggie, Albert Donoghue and Big Pat Connolly were there, when Jack McVitie and Connie White-head had turned up with Bobby Cannon – and how Reggie was all set to kill him.

I also told Mooney all about the shooting at the Starlight Club and how Reggie had shot Jimmy Field at the Regency. It was all about Reggie – my best friend Reggie Kray who would have done for me in Epping Forest if he could have shot straight.

It was all good stuff but what I had to offer was not going to put the Krays away. I could also tell that what Read was dreading was another Yard cock-up. I repeated in this new state-ment what I'd said in open court at Bow Street about being the informer. And I added this bit, which I hadn't said in court: 'I kept in touch with the police after the Cornell murder. The offi-cer I dealt with was Pogue. I used the name of Phillips. I was arrested on 9th August 1966.'

Read and Mooney believed me, I'm sure, but at this stage they really did seem not to know too much. And so I was baffled. How come they didn't seem to know anything about Butler's operation given that I knew they'd seen all those surveillance photographs? Anyway they went off to ask Detective Sergeant Pogue and get some more out of him. I've got what he told them from the archive, dated 8 October 1968.

He told them that in spring 1966 he had been engaged under Detective Superintendent Axon of H Division (Whitechapel) in the inquiry into the killing of George Cornell in the Blind Beggar. He had 'met and interviewed a large number of people,' so he said, and 'one of them was Robert Teale who had introduced himself as "Bobby Phillips".'

According to Pogue's statement I had 'offered to supply information concerning Reginald and Ronald Kray with whom [I] was at that time living at a house in the Clapton E5 area [David and Christine's flat],' he said. Then he said this:

> [Phillips] stated that he had heard Ronald and Reginald Kray talk about the shooting of George Cornell and Ronald Kray had boasted about the way he had shot him in the public house... another man known as 'Scotch Ian' was in the Blind Beggar that night when the shooting took place. He then promised that, although he was not able to give evidence of the actual shooting, he would glean as much information as he could regarding the identity of 'Scotch Ian' and the movements of the Kray twins.

At the time that must have been gold dust. Remember, this was when nobody was saying anything to the police – especially about the identity of the second gunman in the Blind Beggar.

And here it had all been on a plate for Scotland Yard in spring 1966! Pogue went on:

It was arranged that I would meet him [me, a.k.a. 'Phillips'] daily at a particular place in the Clapton area. If he failed to turn up, the meeting stood for the same time the following day and so on. It was quite obvious from Phillips's behaviour that he was terrified of the Kray twins and he admitted this, stating he had difficulty in getting away from them without being missed.

During the following weeks I met Phillips who passed on information that the Kray twins and Ian had stayed immediately after the shooting of Cornell at his brother David's flat before moving to the house in the Clapton area. He also stated that they paid visits to a woman publican's premises with whom they were friendly, she having a pub in the Bethnal Green area. The pub was known as the 'Widow's Pub' [Madge's].

Further information given by Phillips was that the Kray twins had visited a man named Geoffrey Allen who lived in the Saffron Walden area in Essex and had stayed with him for some days and during this time had visited the Saffron Walden Hotel and a number of hotels in the Cambridge area. This information was verified by myself after a visit to Saffron Walden and Cambridge.

During this time Phillips was endeavouring to establish the identity of 'Scotch Ian' and after some weeks he managed to get to me a photograph of 'Scotch Ian' but still no identity was made. However, later this man was identified as John Barrie.

Although Phillips was unwilling at that time to give evidence [to be used in court] he stated he would [do so] if police were able to secure the arrest of the Kray twins and 'Scotch Ian'.

Some weeks after meeting Phillips regularly, he failed to show up at the meeting place and I never saw him again or heard from him.

This statement confirmed that everything I'd said was true. I had met Butler's man *while* the Firm had been holed up in Clapton E5. The great detective had presumably set up a surveillance operation as a result. Then I'd risked everything to get a picture that would identify Scotch Ian.

Pogue had even tailed us to East Anglia on our 'holiday' with the arsonist Geoffrey Allen – when, terrified for my life, I'd made my bid to get a message back to the Yard saying they had a grass on their side who was feeding the name 'Phillips' back to the Firm.

And Pogue was absolutely right when he said that, although I was unwilling at that time to give evidence for use in court, I would do so if I knew the twins and Scotch Ian had been arrested. He could have added: 'and stayed arrested'.

This was the same thing that Read had been gambling on all that summer when he'd made his move to arrest the twins first – and then used me to persuade the faint-hearts to come forward once they'd been nicked to give statements that could bring them to trial. And they *had* come forward, once I'd been detonated like a bomb in the committal proceedings.

Read had been adding to his collection. After Albert Donoghue, Nipper had got Scotch Jack Dickson to come over. He made a statement on 24 September in Brixton saying how he had driven Ronnie and Scotch Ian to the Blind Beggar on the night Cornell was shot. On the return journey to the Widow's pub in Tapp Street, Ronnie had said: 'I hope the bastard is dead.' That's what I told Pogue Ronnie had said in the Chequers pub in Walthamstow at one of our meets two and a half years before.

Ronnie Hart came over to Read's side on 2 September – and pretty soon he was telling what he knew about the butchering of Jack the Hat in Blonde Carole's flat, which was a lot. And that's what they charged Reggie with on 19 September, after which they'd come back to me looking for more stuff on Reggie. And I'd given it to them, lots of it.

Although of course I knew the Krays could still walk. Just like they'd done before when they walked out of the nick when Butler had screwed up the identity parade in August 1966. After that Butler had just given up and I'd been hung out to dry. Maybe Read was made of tougher stuff.

He was going to have to be. What would a clever brief make of what I'd said? They might say that the police had planted me deliberately. That I was put into the Firm to urge Reggie to kill. Whatever I said, it was going to be acutely embarrassing for the Yard – especially for the reputation of the great Tommy Butler.

Well, history knows quite a lot about the rest. By the end of October, the committal proceedings had been concluded for murder in the cases of George Cornell and, missing bodies or not, Jack McVitie and Frank Mitchell. The trial date was set to begin on 8 January 1969 at the Old Bailey.

But there was another trial to get out of the way first – the trial of our mother, Ellen Teale.

On 28 November 1968 Mum appeared at the Old Bailey. It was over very quickly. She'd had been told to plead guilty by Nipper Read because she 'let the thieves in' and had no proof that she was not involved in it. As far as we, her sons, were concerned, she was made to plead guilty but we had been re-assured she would not go to prison, as long as we told all we knew about the Krays in the full-scale trial that was now just a few weeks away.

Alfie was with her that day, though he had to stay in a private room with two of Read's men during the proceedings. He was not allowed to go in the court because of being a witness at the forthcoming Kray trial.

He told the policemen, 'If my mum gets one day in prison then I'm going to make the Kray trial look like a parking fine.' They looked really worried for a moment then reassured him, 'Don't you worry, Alfie. It's all been arranged.'

And yet Mum was now pleading guilty to stealing £25,000. She got two years, suspended for three, for housebreaking and larceny. She passed out in the dock – partly from shock, and partly from overwhelming relief that she wasn't going to prison. Nipper Read had come good. Half an hour later Read himself came rushing through the door to see Alfie. 'Are you all right? I heard you were a bit upset. Don't worry. Everything's being taken care of.'

So it's the end of 1968 – what a year. And it's Christmas. Usually it would be the time when my brothers would go out and work the streets, bringing home about five times as much as usual. But having just come out of prison and not having two bob between us we were all flat broke. Not only that but with the prospect of having to give evidence against the Krays in January, life could not have been more bleak.

Alfie, Wendy and the kids had moved by then from Millman Street to Bramber Court, a block of flats in Cromer Street, still in Holborn. The police got David a flat above them so that they could have them all in the same block. They were in and out of one another's flats all the time, as were the police bodyguards. They were never physically threatened, so they told me later, although they got a few dodgy looks once or twice in the pub. They also had the opposite treatment, with complete strangers coming up and shaking them by the hand, telling them how brave they were being.

So Alfie and David and their families were under some sort of protection. Meanwhile I was taken out of London and installed in an anonymous safe house in Ipswich, Suffolk. It was a flat on a top floor somewhere in the city. It had its own private entrance, one main bedroom and a small bedroom and a living room looking out at the main road. I had the big bedroom and the coppers who were with me had the small bedroom. But only one would stay overnight.

Some extra security men drove me there but they only stayed if I wanted them to. I had a girlfriend at the time who lived near my mother on Clerkenwell Road. Chris, one of the security men, would drive her home after coming out to visit me.

Now all we had to do was wait until the Krays' trial started.

CHAPTER 22
INTO THE LIONS' DEN

All of us Teale boys were out of prison, living under police protection. Alfie and David in Holborn, me in Ipswich. The start of the big trial was just a few days away. Then in the first days of January 1969, David was called to Tintagel House for a last-minute briefing. While he was there, he had something very personal to say:

> I talked to Nipper Read and another officer called Frank Cater. I told them how Ronnie Kray had forcibly raped me at Vallance Road in the summer of 1966. It wasn't easy. I stopped and stumbled several times. As soon as they realised what I was saying, they asked me to 'put it all down in a statement'.
>
> A week later they told me they would keep my statement safely, but that they had so much on the Krays already they would not need to use it in open court. But they would if the other charges failed. Meanwhile I was not to mention Ronnie's sexuality. I was OK with this, as at the time I wouldn't even have wanted what I'd told

them about being raped to be printed on a toilet roll, let alone a national newspaper.

They said not to worry, that the Krays were 'not going to see daylight' for a very long time. Maybe so.

The time had come. The opening of the full trial was just a few days away. The newspapers were full of it. The order of witnesses was going to be Alfie, David, his wife Christine, and then me. They were keeping me until last. The defence meanwhile had clearly spent a lot of time finding out what we might say, what we might know, all about our mum, our background and so on. We were all of us going to be put through the mincer. Alfie was up first. He recalls:

The atmosphere was electric, like that on the morning of a wedding, or perhaps I should say a funeral. We all had to get up at the crack of dawn to get dressed and prepare ourselves psychologically for what was coming. It was Tuesday 14 January 1969.

David and I were not allowed to see one another, or speak, and were taken under separate guard to the Old Bailey with another extra police car behind us.

I don't care who you are, if you find yourself standing in the solicitors' office in the Old Bailey, waiting to give evidence against thirteen of the country's most notorious villains, you're going to be afraid. Nipper Read said he had another thirty charges he could have used against the Krays, if the ones already filed hadn't been enough.

Maybe he had, but the twins had got off before and they could get off again.

I'd been told by Nipper the day before the trial not to make myself look smart. He didn't want the jury looking at me and thinking that I looked the part of a young gangster. But then I thought: 'I can't do that.' So in the end I wore a silver grey mohair suit, which was absolutely fabulous, made by Paul, my tailor from Berwick Street.

I was kept in another room to David, being minded by about six armed policeman with revolvers, and a few plain-clothes as well. By this time we all knew one another quite well. They were trying to encourage me not to feel nervous, but I was. Dick De Lillo, one of Read's team, had his car nearby so we went for a quick drink to stiffen my nerves.

The police gave me a talk about what the courtroom would look like, where the Krays and the other defendants would be sitting. In fact it was the same Court Number One where we'd been tried two years before. I was told: 'Take no notice of any of them. Whatever they say, whatever they do, ignore them. Tell the complete truth. Don't add anything on or you could get found out.'

We didn't have to add anything on. We knew more than enough already. So I walked in and there they were, the Krays and all the rest of the gang, looking at me from across the court.

I felt terrified as I walked into the witness box. Even though I knew I had the protection of the police, meeting the eyes of the men sitting in a line in the well of the court, about twelve feet away from me, guarded by an officer at either end, was daunting. And every single one had his eyes fixed on me.

Then it began: 'Who was in your car? Was Reggie there? What did he say? Did he say he'd shot Cornell? Did he tell you Cornell was dead?' I answered as best I could. And then the defence started, trying to trip me up.

I'd been called as 'Mr A'. Ronnie's defending counsel, Mr John Platts-Mills, let rip in cross-examination with an attack on me as to why I might want to conceal my identity. It could not be on account of fear of his peaceable, law-abiding client. It could not be to protect my children. I'd said that my youngest had been told when I was in prison that I'd been away in the army.

Then Platts-Mills starts really sneering.

'Your way of life is the most sordid known to British crime,' he said to me.

'You seem to think so.'

'Are you homosexual yourself?'

'No.'

'Any tendencies that way?'

'None at all,' I replied.

'You seek out older men who have respectable positions in life and have homosexual tendencies. Then you blackmail them,' he said.

Then he lists off every juvenile misdemeanour and adult crime on my form sheet. I get a lot of questions about Tapp Street and just where and at what time David had supposedly stopped his grey Ford to be met by Reggie saying: 'Get us off the manor!'

The defence claimed that Ronnie had never been in the Blind Beggar. There had been no siege of Moresby Road. There might have been a party there, which Ronnie had attended much later, but that was all.

It turned into the second day of questions. It's all in the trial transcript:

'Do you remember singing and dancing?' he asked me.

'No, I remember drinks there – nearly every night there was drink,' I answered.

'And some girls, people's wives and so on?'

'I don't remember no people's wives.'

'Dancing going on?'

'No, there was a record player.'

'Do you remember one of the songs?'

'I should imagine it was all modern records.'

'You and your brothers sing very well, do you not?'

'No, we sing.'

'And you sing together?'

'Now and again.'

'One of your favourites is "Zorba the Greek"?'

'You cannot sing that, it is music, there are no lyrics to it.'

'The neighbours sent for the police that night

because of the row you were making, singing "Zorba the Greek".'

'What night was that?'

'About a week to ten days after the night when Cornell was killed… and the uniformed police came in and carried the protest of the neighbours.'

'Well, I cannot remember it.'

'You mean it is the kind of thing that could happen any night at David's?'

'No.'

'The impression you sought to give yesterday was that David's flat was used as a hide-out for a week?

'Yes.'

'And I suggest, the only occasion Ronald came was either at the end of that week or at a later stage when there was quite a noisy party, far from being a discreet hiding place…'

Well, they were wrong. Then they opened up on me about Bobby. They clearly knew a lot.

'If Bobby had a meeting with Chief Superintendent Thomas Butler before September 1966, he managed to conceal that from you?' I was asked.

'He did.'

'And neither Chief Superintendent Butler nor anybody else came to ask you any questions?'

'Nothing at all,' I said. They were trying to make out that that me and my brothers were good friends of the twins. We had no reason whatsoever to fear them. We were saying all of these lies because of police pressure or because we were being paid to say them.

'You were on extremely friendly terms with the Kray family until June of 1968, were you not?' Platts-Mills asked me.

'I suppose we had to be friendly.'

'We had to be friendly... I suggest... is simply a vicious addition to your evidence to try and blacken the people in the box,' he said. Then he opened a new line.

'The [Krays] were great people for going to a caravan... Mother Kray had a big caravan on a site?'

'Yes, she did.'

'Where?'

'A place called Steeple,' I said.

'And you went frequently to the caravan at weekends with or near the Krays on the same site?'

'No, I went with my wife and children.'

'You have, have you not, been yourself a party to the taking of a number of photos showing you and the Kray families in very happy domestic friendship? [the pictures the police took from Christine] ... That was all under compulsion, was it?'

'Well, up to a certain point, yes.'

Then the defence got to our mum.

'Your mother is Ellen, is she not?' he asked me. 'At about the time you first gave a statement to the police, June [sic] of 1968, had your mother been arrested?'

'Yes, she had.'

'[She worked at] a house of titled people?'

'Yes.'

'I think ennobled people?'

'Yes.'

'Was there £25,000 worth of jade involved?'

'I don't know how much was involved,' I replied.

'Mother was alleged, as housekeeper to this house, to have opened the doors and let the burglar in?'

'That was what they said.'

'And Dad, so it was suggested, was the burglar…'

'Well, why wasn't he arrested?'

'I am going to ask you that in a moment. Is this the bargain that was made with you: you help to put the twins inside, Dad will be let off [and] Mum will plead guilty and get off with virtually nothing?'

'No, it was not.'

And then it was over. No more attacks on my character. All I did was to tell it exactly how it was. Nipper Read came rushing up to me, and I asked him: 'Was I all right?' Placing his hands on my shoulders he stood back and told me, 'Alfie, you were absolutely brilliant! You didn't let them get away with anything.'

So that was Alfie, first Teale brother to go into the lions' den. Then it was David's turn:

It was the second day for us at the Old Bailey, Wednesday, 15 January 1969. I don't think I've ever been so scared before in my life. I had a couple of stiff drinks before we went in. It started even before we'd got into the main court.

The police put us in the same room as Scotch Jack [Dickson] when we were both waiting to give evidence. Jack came over and shook my hand, telling me: 'You're doing the right thing.' But I didn't trust him, I never had, as I knew he was a Jekyll [Jekyll and Hyde – snide]. I gave him some fags. He'd run out as he was smoking like a train, he was so petrified. We both were. He kept asking Nipper's men for more.

The time had come. I crept into the court like a little weasel, hearing Ron and Reggie and others all hissing at me as I entered. I kept remembering what Ronnie had said to me when I'd said I was worried about my wife and kids: 'Dead men can't speak.'

I didn't know then and still don't, whether Ronnie meant Cornell was dead and couldn't speak, or did he mean if I said anything either about the murder or the night he'd raped me that I would be dead too? He kept spitting 'Liar!' at me each time I spoke, hissing and glaring at me in an attempt to put me off. So I looked straight at him and said: 'You know the truth, Ron,' referring both to Cornell and the rape that as far as he was concerned, only he and I knew about.

I went through the story of the night of the Cornell murder and the Firm coming back to the flat. When I said that Reginald Kray had passed a gun to Cornelius

Whitehead, Ronnie shouted out, 'You fucking liar!' and had to be restrained. I just answered: 'Ron, the truth hurts…'

It wasn't over. I had to go back in the afternoon. During the lunch-break I started to worry more and more, feeling I was betraying my family as well as the code I'd always lived by, never to grass. Even with police protection I wondered whether my wife and children would ever be safe. Christine's up after me being grilled by the defence about dancing and drinking in her flat and complaining neighbours – how could this possibly be gangsters lying low?

Platts-Mills went on and on about the Steeple Bay caravan where our family seaside parties showed how little she, we or anyone else had to fear from the twins. He seemed to know a lot. My Christine kept her dignity and answered bravely to everything.

I didn't know if I was doing the right, or the wrong thing. We had the police on one side of us, and the Krays on the other. There was no way out. We knew we were already on the Krays' death-list whether or not we gave evidence, whether or not we were on the streets, at home, in Southend or on the moon.

If I was charged and convicted by the police for aiding and abetting the murder of Cornell, I was looking at twelve to fifteen years in prison – while my wife got three for harbouring a murderer. In the meantime, on a totally separate charge, our mum had only just escaped the prospect of doing five in the company of Myra Hindley.

Alfie and David had done their stuff in the witness box. Then it was my turn. I gave most of my testimony on Thursday 16 January. First I got asked by the prosecution some simple stuff about the night Cornell got shot and what happened afterwards, the stuff I'd already given at the committal. I was asked about how Reggie and I had lived together in Green Lanes, about Charlie Clark's place in Walthamstow and about the flat in Lea Bridge Road. Nobody asked me how it came to be raided.

Then it was the defence's turn. Platts-Mills tried on me what he'd done on Alfie. Why was I hiding my identity as 'Mr B?' I wasn't hiding, not any more. I gave it right at the start as clear as day. 'My name is Robert Frank Teale.'

Was it true I'd been under constant police surveillance since release from prison? It was. And why might that be?

'For my personal security,' I replied. Then I get the same treatment as my brothers, with the full CRO given to the court. It's the usual list of youthful crimes and misdemeanours, and he's luxuriating in the blackmail conviction. How can I say I'm not lying under oath when I pleaded not guilty under oath to that fit-up at the Bailey and got convicted by a jury? I had to bite my tongue not to let it all come out.

Then there's a lot of stuff about the drive from Madge's, what really happened in the Chequers, what Sammy Lederman had said, whether I could tell Nobby Clark from Ronnie Clark, whether we'd been to any other pub or flats before going to

David's. The defence was trying to trip me up. The judge got cross with Platts-Mills' pantomime.

Then I get cross-examined about what I'd said about how Reggie and I had lived together in Green Lanes, the trip to Saffron Walden and Cambridge, with the implication that I'm making it all up. That I couldn't remember the details, I was confusing one thing with another.

Then came something that the defence brief was not going to sneer quite so much about.

'Do you not agree that if by any chance you had applied your mind to this question three years ago just after it happened, made some statement, written it down, thought about it carefully, then it would have been much easier for you to work out the details?' Platts-Mills asked me.

'I did do something about it three years ago,' I said coolly.

'What do you suggest you did?'

'I got in touch with Scotland Yard and I assisted them in their enquiries.'

'You got in touch with Scotland Yard?'

'Yes – just after the Cornell murder.'

'Was that in March 1966?'

'Yes.'

'With whom did you get in touch?'

'I think it was Tommy Butler.'

'Tommy Butler was then chief of the CID, was he not, at Scotland Yard? How did you contact him?'

'By phone.'

'You actually met him?'

'I met him on one occasion, yes.'

'This is Mr Tommy Butler, a man of enormous distinction, who has just retired from a leading position at Scotland Yard?'

'This is true, yes.'

'And it is your story that he did not take any statement from you whatsoever?'

'Yes.'

'So as far as you know he made no investigations whatsoever?'

The judge intervened at that point: 'How can he possibly answer what he does not know?' The defence replied: 'I was going to suggest to him that he had not really met Tommy Butler.'

'Did you meet some other distinguished police officers?' the defence continued.

'I met one man who I used to explain one or two things to.'

'What sort of things?'

'Look. A murder had taken place,' I said. 'I found myself in a position where I was in possession of a certain amount of information which I felt could help bring these men to justice. I got in touch with Scotland Yard. I met one or two other people who I was in contact with most of the time.'

'Did you get money for that?'

'Not a penny. I didn't expect any.'

'What were you doing it for?

'Because it was obvious to me that these people were then running around like animals and because I happen to know that they were going to kill a number of people in the area, someone had to do something.'

'Is it not the fact that you did not make a statement to anyone about the supposed knowledge of yours until July 1968, two years after the event? Why was that?'

'It would have put my family in jeopardy. Yes. Well, isn't it obvious, a man walks into a pub and shoots a man in cold-blooded murder, am I going to make a statement and wind up dead myself, or my family?'

'Why would your family be in jeopardy?'

'I knew a murder had taken place. I knew they had a list of people they were going to do.'

'Going back to the time after the shooting, you have told us that you communicated with Scotland Yard, and spoke to Tommy Butler. Did you speak to any other officers?'

'Yes, Joe Pogue.'

'Did you tell him about the Cornell shooting?'

'I explained what position I was in. I explained there were going to be some killings.'

'This was about the Cornell killing which had already taken place?'

'Well, I just briefed him on the details that occurred as far as we were concerned. I said my brothers are terrified, they have wives and children. If I am fool enough to get trapped by these animals, then it is my fault.'

'What did you call yourself speaking to this police officer?'

'I called myself Phillips.'

And that was the end of my testimony. There was plenty more I could have said.

There were no reporting restrictions this time. The press picked it up. 'Robert Teale caused a stir when he revealed himself to have been a police spy. He was asked how many times he had seen the police and what information he had given them,' so one paper reported. Well, there was quite a stir. The paper went on to recount everything I had said in court.

There it was, this time, for the whole world to see. 'Police Spy in the Firm' was the headline. I was described as a 'brown-haired youth in a suede jacket'. But what the journalists were *not* asking was why Butler had given up on the Krays and left them free to kill again. Not that the Yard was going to tell them or anyone else – and still do not want to say after fifty years.

Billy Exley was in the witness box next, the old boxer who'd been with me at Steeple Bay. He was very ill with heart trouble. He talked about staying at Moresby Road and how Ronnie had said about Cornell: 'Fuck him. I'm glad he's dead.'

He'd been ordered to get 'underclothes and suits', he said, when we were all in David's flat and then take the twins' washing backwards and forwards to their mum in Vallance Road. Somebody had to do it. Christine wasn't going to wash the Krays' shirts. So old Violet Kray did it, with Billy as the delivery boy.

Detective Chief Inspector Henry Mooney was on after that. He got it hard from the defence. They were doing the old trick of discrediting the police evidence (and I wish some of my briefs had been as good, I'll admit), with me and Butler as the weakest links.

'Have you any knowledge of the communication between Robert Teale and Chief Superintendent Butler?' Platts-Mills asked him.

'I have,' said Mooney. But he had never asked anything of Mr Butler directly about the matter during his own investigation, he further admitted. And just why was that? The defence didn't press him further, but I would have liked to.

What about there being guns in the flat in, where was it, Moresby Road? Wouldn't this have provided vital forensic evidence if the police had acted – if indeed there was any truth in the story? Platt-Mills asked Mooney.

We were all liars, was the implication, especially me with my absurd story about meeting the famous Tommy Butler. We were just making it all up. Mooney did not really know what to say. The police looked like either fools or liars or both, the way they'd reacted to the information that half the Firm were holed up in a flat in Clapton. But the police and prosecution could always produce Pogue to prove that I had been telling the truth.

So Detective Sergeant Pogue was called. It wasn't part of Read's big plan. His appearance in court could aid the prosecution in confirming what I said. Or it might do the very opposite by making the whole investigation look like a shambles from the beginning. On the stand Pogue gave the briefest confirmation of the existence of 'Bob Phillips' – me.

Under cross-examination he confirmed the meeting of 'Phillips' with Tommy Butler at Hackney greyhound stadium – but of our meets after that he said he had only made rough notes without dates.

'Robert Teale had never volunteered a written statement,' he said. And I hadn't. I had never trusted Butler enough to be sure that he could get the Krays and put them behind bars. And I had been right.

Nobody pressed Pogue further. Maybe it suited both defence and prosecution that the story of Phillips the informer should just go away. I was like the man who never was.

Nipper Read himself would be on the stand the following day. He was going to be in trouble. This is what he said in his memoirs: 'On day eight of the trial, Platts-Mills questioned me directly about [the informer]. I was at a distinct disadvantage. Now the gaping hole in the Yard's file was exposed. He put to me the names of a number of people who had been seen after Cornell's murder and long before I took over the inquiry. I was obliged to answer that there were no notes of [such meetings] or interviews.'

So what the hell had it been all about? The trial transcript doesn't help much.

Platts-Mills asked questions about the surveillance of the twins and the story about Violet Kray bringing tea on trays to the police watching outside Vallance Road, making it all sound ridiculous. Read couldn't comment. He had not been involved. That was Butler's or the local police's operation. It was all before his time.

Much more to the point was the matter of somebody actually coming forward to tell the police that there were guns in some flat in March 1966, as the defence put it. 'Is it really conceivable that the police did not act? Isn't that because the informer and the information [he allegedly gave] was utterly worthless?' so Platts-Mills asked Nipper Read.

He meant me, of course. Read didn't have an answer. He hadn't been involved back then, he kept saying.

Did Inspector Butler ever go to David Teale's flat? 'Not to my knowledge,' said Read. 'I wasn't concerned with the case.'

Ronnie's brief reeled off a list of members of the Firm whose names this 'Bobby Teale' might have revealed – Sammy Lederman, Nobby Clark, Billy Exley, Harry 'Jew Boy' Cope, Big Pat Connolly, John Dickson. Was there any record of them?

'No,' said Read.

'Of course that means, doesn't it,' said Platts-Mills, 'that Mr Bobby Teale did not mention any of their names?'

'He certainly did not speak to me about it in 1966,' said Read.

The defence were very well informed. I could tell they'd spent a lot of time working out lots of things about me and my brothers: 'The Teales at one time shared lodging with Mr McCowan?' asked Platts-Mills. 'Not to my knowledge,' said Read. 'Mr Hew McCowan [who was] the principle witness in the 1965 case of my client…?' It was all going round and round in circles. Read clearly wanted as little said about me and Butler as possible. Having used me to get the other Firm members to come over, he now wanted to keep me right out of the way. Everybody did.

After Cornell, the court got on to Jack the Hat, in which we Teale brothers had not played any part. We'd all been inside, although I'd given Read my accounts of how Ronnie kept urging Reggie to kill, just as I'd been telling Pogue and Butler fifteen months before Jack got it.

Then Ronnie made his own speech from the dock. There was no gang – all that stuff about the 'Firm' was an invention by the prosecution. 'All we have is our drinking friends we go out with in the evening,' Ron said. Mr Read had had it in for him since the McCowan case, he said. The police had bought all their evidence – including ours.

Ronnie had never spent any night at David's flat. It was all lies by the Teales about any murders. Our mum was on a £25,000 jewel robbery conviction, said Ronnie. 'She got a suspended sentence. The tale goes round that they [the Teales] are giving evidence against us so that their mother would get off that charge,' he said.

We'd have done anything to keep our mum out of prison, of course we would. But that was not why we were doing this. The Krays had to be stopped. And we'd stopped them. But at what cost to ourselves?

This time the jury had not been nobbled. History knows the rest. The twins got life imprisonment, with a non-parole period of thirty years for the murders of Cornell and McVitie, the longest sentences ever passed at the Central Criminal Court for murder. Charlie got ten years. Ian Barrie got twenty.

The Mitchell trial followed just over a month later. There was a different judge and a different jury. Albert Donoghue gave evidence for the prosecution. And Alfie gave evidence about his day out to Dartmoor. Platts-Mills could not resist reminding him of the evidence he had given in the previous trial, telling everyone that he'd told the court in the Cornell case that Ronnie Kray had gone into hiding at David's flat on 10 March 1966. Alfie had told the police in his statement that the Dartmoor episode was in May. But the prison visitors book showed the visit of a 'Mr Walker' on 21 March.

Was Alfie Teale – Mr Walker?

Alfie had to admit that he was.

And was it March when he had made this visit, or was it May as he had told the police? Did the witness lie like this about everything?

'Are you now telling the jury that when he [Ronnie] was in deep hiding with you and your brother because of the killing … in the Blind Beggar, he was drinking with his brother and lots of other friends in the Grave Maurice within ten days?' Platts-Mills asked Alfie.

'Yes,' he said.

'It is just stuff and nonsense, isn't it?'

'No, it is not nonsense,' Alfie told him.

I suppose it was beyond Alfie – it might be beyond anyone – to explain what had really happened in those two weeks. How could you explain the madness of that fortnight, the sense of invincibility that the twins had at that time? It was as if they could do anything they liked. And then Alfie said it out loud: 'I didn't get Ronnie Kray out of deep hiding. You couldn't tell Ronnie Kray what to do.'

Alfie was right, of course. That is what it was all about. The rule of fear. But we had, each one of us, found our courage. We had faced the Krays and told the truth.

CHAPTER 23
THE DEAL

At the end of the Mitchell trial, on 16 May 1969, everyone was acquitted except Reggie, who got five years to run concurrently with the McVitie sentence for aiding the Axe-Man's escape.

It was over. But it was certainly not over for us. I dropped out of sight again. I was good at that. I didn't go back to the Isle of Wight or anything like that. My marriage was long over – Reggie Kray had made sure it was. David and Alfie still had families, though. They weren't going to do a runner. The Krays lodged an appeal. Nothing was over till it was really over. David recalled what it was like for him:

After the trial, Alfie, Christine and I were all given police protection, two men for us, and a woman to protect my wife. Bobby had two to himself, as he was considered to be at higher risk. I knew why after what he'd said in court. I knew he'd been a grass since that day in the committal proceedings the summer before when Scotch Ian's brief asked him when he'd 'first considered giving evidence'. And he'd told them. What I didn't know was that it was Bobby who'd triggered the raid on Lea Bridge Road and how we'd walked into the trap with that Wallace geezer.

We didn't see him more than once or twice following the trial. But at this stage, we weren't too worried. Bobby had always done his own thing, and it wasn't at all unusual for him to disappear for several weeks at a time without saying anything. We were used to him vanishing. And I could see why he'd want to.

It was a strange time for us. We knew we'd done what no one in the underworld ever does – break the code never to grass up our friends. We'd done so under the utmost pressure but that made no difference.

What I did in giving evidence against the Krays had to be done. I'm not a grass, although I did feel like one at the time. I always think it was Ronnie himself who put me there. It was very frightening standing there in court looking at them. They thought they could walk on water. But you can't let someone go round killing and torturing people without trying to do something to stop them.

We knew we had no choice, and I wasn't prepared to live the rest of my life looking over my shoulder. You can't live your life being frightened all the time, and it wasn't in my nature to skulk around the place being scared.

The big problem for Alfie and me was that we couldn't get work. We couldn't go and get a job in Marks and Spencer, so we went back to doing what we'd always done, street trading, often with police at our side, trying to look the other way. When the police came with us, they used to have their daily wages out of it as well. Give them a fiver or ten quid, and they'd take it all right.

Alfie felt exactly the same. He says:

It wasn't like when a witness gets given a new identity and plenty of money. You just had to take your chances. So after a while I had to tell the police that David and I were going to go back out street trading.

I'd been doing that since I was nine years old, starting with rain hats for sixpence and working my way up, looking out for my uncle George who was selling brooches for two shillings and sixpence, half a crown. David used to look over to me and shout, 'Alfie, up for your life,' which meant the coppers were coming, or 'Alfie, slow up,' which meant I could serve the customers but that there was a policeman further up the street. If he said, 'Up for your life,' I'd pack everything up quickly and run into Oxford Street Marks and Spencers.

Once we were up in court in front of a judge who pointed out: 'These people pay their rent for working – look what they've paid over their last offences – two and six, five shillings, ten shillings, and two and six again.' Once I even asked a police officer to lend me half a crown to pay my fine, which he did. 'All right,' he said, 'don't forget to pay me back tomorrow.'

Our days of excitement – and terror – in running with the Krays were over. There were new temptations – like selling our story to a newspaper. I'd gone well to ground by now but the papers knew where to find my brothers. David got an offer.

Dick De Lillo, the policeman David had talked to, the one who knew about his statement saying Ronnie had raped him, told him a man named George Martin from the *Daily Mirror* wanted to talk to him. This was just a few weeks after the end of the trial.

So David went up to the *Mirror*'s offices in Holborn and met him. Martin talked to him and then asked him to come in again to meet their chief crime reporter, Norman Lucas, who had broken the Boothby story in 1964 – thus fatally compromising the police investigation. He told David he could make a lot of money if he chose to sell his story, giving the intimate details of our lives with the Krays. But in the end David decided not to, or at least for the time being.

That might have been just as well. Something big was going down.

Have you wondered why, having given evidence against the Krays, David and Alfie didn't have to do like I did, and get out of the country afterwards? Even the villains round here and up in the West End didn't frighten them. They would drink in villains' pubs and clubs round Charing Cross and Gray's Inn Road and never feared any reprisals. Occasionally, in the months and years after the trial when Alfie or David were recognised they might be asked: 'Would you mind drinking up and getting out?' Some people even thought they must either be mad, or worse than the Krays themselves. But generally they didn't get bothered.

The reason why they didn't have to run out was because they did a deal with the Krays.

The only people who knew about this were David and Alfie. I had no idea till years afterwards.

There had been a deal. It was like a miracle. It could have made all the difference to how my life would have turned out, but *I didn't know*. David tells how it happened:

One day, about two months after the trial, Alfie and I were having a drink, along with Dick De Lillo and another policeman, outside a pub called The Queen's Larder in Queen's Square, Holborn, when a geezer pulled up in a car. I thought he was asking for directions and walked over.

I recognised Patsy O'Mara in the passenger seat. He was a bookmaker and very good friend of Freddie Foreman and the South London Firm. He was a money-getter, a lovely man who was liked by everyone. The man driving I didn't know. Patsy wound down the window and called me over and, while Alfie stayed drinking outside the pub with the two coppers, Patsy said to me: 'I've got a message for you from the Colonel.'

My heart was in my mouth. 'Tell me,' I said.

Patsy answered: 'If you don't say anything, about Ronnie, or his family, about anything personal, anything private and you know what he means, nothing to the press or in print, he will let sleeping dogs lie, and leave you and yours alone too.'

It was true we knew a lot about the Krays on a personal level, the sort of stuff the papers would have loved. As Ronnie's driver I'd been everywhere with him, often on 'meets' that no one else ever knew about. But I knew what this was about.

When I was raped by Ronnie in Vallance Road I promised him that one day I'd tell everyone what he'd done. Back then I'd been hysterical. I was an acute danger to myself. But I'd said nothing. I didn't tell Alfie. I didn't tell Christine. As time went on I suppose I'd become even more of a liability. So all I could think of right then was to tell Patsy O'Mara, 'I've got to talk to Alfie,' who was by this time already walking over to join us.

Still I didn't tell Alfie what had happened in Vallance Road. Nor what Charlie Kray had done to Christine. How could I in that moment? Alfie and I told one another most things but that was just too humiliating for me as a man. Not only that I'd been raped, but that I hadn't been able to look after my own wife. I felt too embarrassed and too ashamed even to confide in my own brother.

But Alfie knew there were loads of things that Ronnie wanted kept quiet. As far as Alfie was concerned, the deal was about not giving away any of the other personal stuff we knew, like the rent boys Ronnie ordered him to get – or using my family, my children, to protect himself when he'd just done Cornell. That was hardly the act of an East End hard man.

'Tell my brother what you've just told me,' I said to Patsy.

And so he did. After he'd told Alfie, we looked at one another in desperation. Both frightened, we started to walk away from the car to discuss his offer. But as we did so, Patsy called us back, saying:

'No, Ronnie wants to know now. It's a one-time offer only.'

We stood a short distance away from the car, turning our backs as we talked. Alfie came up with the solution. Walking back to the car, Alfie told him: 'We'll do a deal on one condition only. We are going to lodge a letter with a solicitor setting down everything we know, including this meeting. And if any one of my brothers, or any member of our family, is harmed, that letter will go straight to the police, and to the press.' (We did write this all out afterwards, although we never actually lodged it with a solicitor in the end, thinking that Ronnie and the Firm would never know whether we had or not.)

Patsy then put his hand out of the window and said: 'This is the hand of Ronnie Kray… If you say nothing to the papers, you'll be safe.'

I hesitated for a moment. Alfie and I went to walk away to discuss the offer further, but Patsy said again: 'No, this is a one-time offer… The Colonel says he must have an answer straight away.'

'It's a deal.'

We then went back to the two policemen without saying anything about what had happened.

We wanted to tell Bobby about the meeting. But as he'd been missing for eight weeks by this time and we had no idea where he was, there was nothing we could do.

So why was Ronnie being so beneficent all of a sudden? It must have been the police who tipped off the *Mirror* to my story – apart from Ronnie and me, they were the only ones who knew. And in the way of these things, that must have reached Ronnie.

It had not come out in court. Before I gave evidence I'd been told not to say a word about Ronnie's sexuality. I was longing to talk about the rape but it just didn't seem right. Anyway I felt ashamed about being raped by Ronnie.

Christine and I were still young with three daughters and we wanted to have another go at our lives, to start again without the shadow of all that had happened before. In any case, I was frightened of talking to anyone about it, let alone seeing it in the newspapers. I knew when the police told me that Norman Lucas at the *Mirror* wanted to talk to me, that the Old Bill hoped to make some money out of it too. It could get very messy.

And then a few weeks later we got the message from the Colonel, and making a deal to stay quiet seemed like the right thing to do. Knowing the Colonel, it could have been a trap, to make us think everything was OK at first, and then to do us when we were least expecting it. But as time went on, we started to realise we really were safe after all. And we're still here to tell the tale.

I want to say this. When Ronnie raped me he did more than damage just me, he divided me from my wife. I wanted to tell her, and needed to tell her in many ways. But it was so horrible, and so humiliating, especially for a young man to have to admit to the woman he loved – and still loves. I just couldn't bring myself to do it. As time went on it got less and less likely I'd ever get the courage to say anything.

In the meantime Christine must have sensed I was holding something back. It became very difficult between us. In the end Christine never found out.

I still feel so embarrassed and very angry and yet I couldn't say anything to her. How I've acted for so long as if everything was all right, I don't know. I've been such a good actor all my life... telling people I didn't have my glasses when I was asked to read or write anything.

I didn't know about Charlie Kray raping my wife when I was in prison. I only found out what that jackal, that snake, Charlie had done when I came out in 1968. Charlie used to prey on the wives of men in prison, going round and giving them money, pretending to be concerned and then assaulting them. When Christine said she'd go to the police, he turned round and told her: 'What did you expect to happen? I'd given you money, hadn't I?'

She said she would have stabbed him there and then if she'd had a knife.

Christine was never right after that, starting to drink more and more. Eventually she became dependent on Valium. I tried to help her and stopped drinking myself for a while. We went to live in Holland and started up an antiques business, but even though she was off the drink she remained very depressed. One day I went out on the booze by myself. Christine called our daughter up in London and said to her: 'Look after your father.' Then she took her own life.

CHAPTER 24
SLIPPING AWAY

Alfie and David had made their deal with the Colonel. But I didn't know. As far as my brothers were concerned I had dropped out of sight just as I had often done before. But I had told the world that I was the informer. Where was I going to run to?

I had police bodyguards day and night. I was beginning to think I had more to fear from Scotland Yard than I did from Ronnie. When it had been suggested to me three years before that I could shoot Ronnie (when he was with my kid brother Paul in Moresby Road), I realised that when pushed into a corner they could be as calculating as the Krays.

I remember when it came to trial how both the Krays made eye contact with me – accusing me of being 'full of lies'. I could feel their hatred blazing at me across the courtroom.

After the big trial, the bodyguards used to take me shopping occasionally to buy a suit or a shirt. On one occasion I gave them the slip and went to Paris for a few days by myself. But when they told me they wanted me to go to Northern Ireland and do some undercover stuff then I got really scared. I could be found dead at any time and the long hand of the Krays would be blamed. The Yard would say that I told them I didn't want them to guard me any more and no one could say anything different and that would be that. That's how I felt at the time. Another cop I sort of trusted warned me not to go. I turned the offer down.

Within forty-eight hours, my bodyguards (two men armed with guns) were taken away. There was no witness protection scheme, no ready-made new life in Australia or anything like that. I had no leverage. I'd already done what they wanted. My usefulness was over.

Suddenly I knew what to do. Call it instinct, sixth sense, whatever – I just knew. When I had first made that call from the phone booth to Scotland Yard it had felt the same way, as if I was under some kind of guiding force that was telling me that no matter what happens in the end, you have to do this right now. And now I knew it was time to run.

I'd been told by my guards, for my own good and the good of my family, that I would have to disappear for at least five years. How do you do that? How do you explain to the people you're leaving behind? I thought it much better just to slip away, not tell Alfie and David what had really happened. But I had to see our mother.

As I was getting my tent and sleeping bag I went to my lovely mum and she put her arms out to give me a hug. I told her I wasn't leaving just yet, and asked my brother Paul to come with me, although of course I knew that was impossible. Paul was ready to come. He was eating at the table in Mum's kitchen and he said to me, 'I won't be long,' and I said, 'OK,' but then I just slipped out of the door. That was the last time I saw our mother.

I got to Victoria Station with the crowds of commuters going to their offices. What did they know about anything? And then I just walked around and around, thinking, I can't do this. I heard a voice in my head saying, go! Go! You've got to get out of here. Leave now while you've still got a chance! I went to the ticket window and asked for a ticket for the Dover-Calais boat-train and was told it would be leaving in about forty-five minutes.

I lugged my stuff on to the train and sat and waited. I was starting to cry and I could see my mum in my mind's eye with her arms out and I started to cry even more. Several times I nearly rushed for the door to get off the train, but I just sat there, kind of paralysed. Two elderly ladies looked at me sympathetically but could not look me in the eye. They looked as sad as I was feeling, as if they wanted to say, 'There, there, it's all right, whatever it is.'

They hadn't a clue. And nor did I. I knew what I was running from but not where I was going.

The train started to move out of the station. As I looked out of the window, London passing away behind me, I just kept crying even more. The pain was like a bullet in the heart. I have lived with it for forty-five years – deeply missing my loving mum and dad, my best friends and brothers, Alfie, David, George and Paul and my loving sisters Jane and Eileen. I never stopped loving all of you and never will. And I could only hope that each one of you would have as much love in your hearts for others as I have for you. But I had to leave you all without any more explanations. I had to hurt you to save you from greater hurt.

When I got to Dover there was no one at the customs post so I walked on through. I was almost at the boat when a passport control man came running after me, totally out of breath and all apologetic. I was thinking somehow I was going to be held, but when he looked at my passport he just said, 'Are you going to France on business or pleasure?'

'A holiday,' I replied.

'OK,' he said, and stamped my passport, adding 'Have a good trip.' With a sigh of relief I kept going and got on the ferry and started to feel a sense of freedom. Then it occurred to me the customs guy had not written anything down so the Yard may not know that I had left the country. I was wrong about that.

I crossed the Channel from Dover. I was heading for Gibraltar, only because I heard John Lennon had married Yoko there and I thought it would be a good place to disappear among the hippies sleeping on the beach. I got a job on a construction site driving a concrete mixer. It was here that I met my second wife, Eileen, a Canadian nurse, who was living with her friend in the tent next to mine. Eileen and I would eventually have three children.

But even in Gibraltar, I couldn't leave my past behind. One day a guy in a suit, obviously carrying a gun, turns up on the beach claiming to have won a weekend in the sun on some competition. When you've been around the Old Bill for as long as I have you begin to get a smell for them. But I was surrounded by so many people it was hard for him to get close to me. But one day he started asking me lots of questions about what I intended to do. While in prison I'd taught myself classical Spanish guitar. I told him I was going to go on into Africa to give guitar lessons. He persisted in questioning me. It was all very clumsy.

So when he finally left a few days later I told him, 'If you see anyone you think I might know, please give them my regards.'

The copper looked straight back into my eyes, his voice dropped and he said, 'I will, Bobby, I will.'

EPILOGUE
FORTY YEARS ON

It was a day like any other. I was working with my son, Jason, in a green and beautiful place in British Columbia, western Canada.

We'd come up to work on renovating a house on this lovely island of pine woods and sandy beaches, a half-hour boat-ride from Vancouver. I had been in the construction business for years. Along the way I'd made money and lost money, raised three kids, lost one wife and found another. Jason was making his own business for the future. Right now I could not help thinking about the past. It had been this way for a while.

I was thousands of miles away from the city where I had been born. All I'd kept of my old life was my name. Robert Frank Teale. Friends at home in Utah call me 'Bobby'.

I'd never gone back, never made contact with the people I'd left behind – my parents, my brothers and sisters, my first wife, my daughter, the two brothers closest to me in age. How could I have done that? I'd often asked myself this question, usually at around four in the morning on those nights when sleep just wouldn't come.

The ache to know what had become of them had eased a bit with time – but it had never gone away.

Were they even still alive? My beautiful mother – I remember the way she used to look when I was young, dressed in furs and diamonds when Dad had money, but always glamorous even when we barely had enough to eat. The smell of her perfume, bending over to kiss me goodnight, the warmth of her arms around me, I hadn't ever forgotten. But a tightening in my chest always warned me when I was getting over-emotional.

The kids were by my second wife, Eileen. We had married in January 1970 and over the next few years we had three children, a girl and two boys. There had been good times and there had been bad times. Eileen and I had lived in Canada, first in Edmonton, Alberta, and then in British Columbia. I had started to hit the booze hard and was doing two packs of Rothmans a day. It would be too easy to blame what had happened to me in London for my drinking. Perhaps it was just me.

Almost from the beginning, I would tell Eileen that I was somehow going to see my family again. I would get back to England when the time was right. It was never right. When I had money, it seemed just a question of getting on a plane. Then I had no money. 'Wait until the kids are older,' she said. Then it was 'Wait until they are out of school.' Ten years turned into twenty and then thirty and I began to think I might die without ever seeing my family again.

But it wasn't really Eileen who was stopping me. I think it was me all along who just could not go through with it. It was fear. And fear of facing my brothers, Alfie and David, who I thought would blame me. As each year passed, I felt an ever-deeper need to tell the truth before I died.

Eileen and I drifted apart. Sometimes I wondered whether something had happened to my heart. That having blocked off my emotions for so long, I no longer knew what I really felt. Anyhow, there were no storms, just a gradual acceptance that our marriage no longer worked. We stayed friendly. Thank God, the kids didn't give up on me. I'd lost enough family already.

When the kids were old enough, I told them a bit of the story too. There'd been that time a few Christmases back when I'd seen that photograph of Reggie Kray's funeral and got, shall we say, a bit emotional about it. Gradually I filled in the gaps in their knowledge. I told them how, as a young man, I'd been involved with some very dangerous people. How I had got away, left England, and how I was the cause of my two brothers going to prison. How I felt guilt and shame and anger – and yet felt a sense of pride in what I had done, the very thing that meant I had to leave my old life behind.

There had been a moment when with all the new power of the internet I had searched the London phone book looking for my brother Alfie's number. (The A. Teale at the top of the list turned out later to be the right one.) But I was too scared to try and contact him.

Then I'd found Dawne – on the internet – and we spent one hundred and fifty hours e-mailing and talking on the phone getting to know each other before we actually met. That was five years ago and we've been married for four. We live in the state of Utah in the USA and I am classified as a permanent resident.

Dawne is an American citizen and she's worked as a member of the Peace Corps all over the world. For two people from such different backgrounds we hit it off really well. It seems to be working out just fine – Dawne being highly academic and me being, well, just a carpenter. Just a carpenter. Dawne was always too smart to know that wasn't the whole story. But then I was never too good at hiding the truth. That is what had got me here in the first place.

And here's the other thing. As far as I was concerned, I never wanted the story of what had happened to me to come out.

But risky as it might have seemed when everything else was being re-invented all those years ago, I had kept my name. No one had told me not to. And after all, it was all I had left of my former self.

Then, five years ago, I did something crazy. I as good as put up a sign saying 'Here I am'.

When I got a brand new MacBook in 2007, I opened a Facebook account in the name Robert Frank Teale. That's what the social network is for, isn't it, so old friends can find you, so the whole world can find you? And after so many years of hiding from the world, that is just what I wanted. At least I thought I did.

On this beautiful early summer morning with the sun getting up in the sky, I turned on my laptop and checked my e-mail.

When I opened the message I felt a rush of emotion just like a sixteen-year-old. Someone wanted to be my friend on Facebook. 'David Teale: Looking for Bobby.'

My heart was pounding. I had to get more breath into my lungs. I was shaking, sobbing, overwhelmed with emotion. It couldn't be him, it must be some nut-job. But I knew. I suppose I always knew that this moment would come.

I e-mailed back. 'What's your middle name? Where were you born?'

He came back straight away: 'Shut up. I'm your brother.'

No one but David could have responded like that. It really was him.

My son Jason was up and around. He found me sobbing like a kid. What could I tell him? How could I explain? I mumbled something about my brothers David and Alfie – people they'd never heard of. People I'd tried for so long to forget but couldn't. I said something about having to go back to London, something about detectives from Scotland Yard meeting me at Heathrow if I went through passport control and picking up where we left off in 1969. He looked at me as if I was crazy.

'That's not going to happen, Dad,' he said. What did he know? What did any of my children know about who I really was? But David Teale knew. And now he'd found me.

Now I'm in tears. Connections start to take place. I get an account going on Skype, and I start phoning every Sunday. I hear their voices, still strong, still with that London accent from the fifties I only get to hear (badly done) in movies. Mine, I guess, is some mid-Atlantic mash-up. We can all get over that.

David later told me what had led him to sending that 'look-ing for Bobby' message. In 2008 he had started helping people with drug problems. He was working with a female teacher named Lali who quickly became a friend. David told her about his childhood, and his association with some people called the Krays. Lali was amazed, and told him, 'Dave, you have got to write a book.' It was then that he confided to her that he could neither read nor write.

She told him to get a laptop, and where to go to attend an adult literacy class. She also asked him where I might be. David said they'd been told I was dead, although he had never really accepted that this was true.

David started going to classes twice a week. Lali also told him to start going to the library where he learned how to use the laptop. She also advised him to start looking for me via Facebook. She suggested he just put a note up: 'Looking for Bobby,' giving his own name but not much else.

In the meantime Alfie had suddenly been taken into hospital with a shadow on the lung that was suspected of being cancer. Alfie assumed the worst. He had an exploratory operation. He was clear. That's when David walked in to the hospital and said to Alfie that they were going to do this – that they were going to find their missing brother and write a book. And that's exactly what they did.

After that first amazing connection, we three brothers really let rip. We Skyped and we e-mailed, telling each other our stories with the Atlantic Ocean in the middle. We'd been so close when we were kids, yet circumstances had pulled us apart as young men. Then they had spun me out of Alfie and David's orbit completely.

How is everyone, I asked, how's Mum and Dad? I somehow thought everything would be the same as it was when I had left, just frozen in time. I realise now that was so dumb. Of course, my parents had both been dead for years now.

I remembered now that back in 1968 when I was in Maidstone Jail, I'd said to David that I didn't think I'd make it to Mum or Dad's funeral. David had looked surprised and asked 'Why?' and I told him I didn't know, just an instinct I had – which had now turned out to be right. The thought that I had missed Mum's death hurt most of all.

Now I knew I had to come back to England. Alfie meanwhile had told our oldest sister, Eileen, that they had managed to trace me. Eileen's response was: 'Oh my God, you haven't!'

Eileen then contacted my daughter, Traci. She still lived on the Isle of Wight. I hadn't seen her for forty-five years. Traci lovingly demanded that it was she who picked me up at the airport should I finally come over. Nothing was going to stop me now.

I arrived at Heathrow. I looked around expecting one person to be meeting me. I think I told her I'd be wearing a hat. Then I spotted Traci looking over in my direction. She was very shy when I first walked up to her and I got extremely tearful. Traci was with her own daughter, my granddaughter, Georgia. I felt incredibly emotional, not knowing who to hug or turn to first. The last time I had seen my Traci she was a little baby in her pram with her mother on the high street in Ryde in 1965. There she was. There I was.

All I wanted to do was to look at the daughter I hadn't seen for so long, and the grandchildren I'd never met. As Traci drove us away from the airport she kept saying: 'Don't look at me!' as she caught me staring at her. The strongest resemblance I could see was to her grandfather on her mother's side. And to my mother, her grandmother.

I remembered getting a visit when I was in prison from a solicitor, asking me to sign a paper to say that if I would guarantee never to see Traci ever again, she would be looked after like a princess. It came from her mother's family, the Readers, who had been working for this really from the time they'd become aware of my existence. Between them and the Krays, my marriage to Pat was never going to last.

If I didn't sign, they would have disowned Traci altogether. So I signed. I had lost my liberty and now I had lost my daughter. It was the most devastating time in my life and I'd tried to forget all of it. Now it was if it had happened yesterday.

Where should Alfie, David and I have the big meet? It would have to be London – the Holiday Inn in Holborn. Nice and anonymous. I was waiting in the restaurant and they were in the coffee shop, so even at the eleventh hour we were still missing each other. Then I saw them. No doubt about it. They were my long-lost brothers. Tears ran down our faces as we hugged one another.

What did I feel? It was all happening at once. Overwhelming love for my brothers for certain. But had I done the right thing in returning? For years I'd kept away, frightened of having to confront my past again. Easier, I'd believed, to force it down each time it briefly surfaced, along with the faces of those now long dead. But it wouldn't leave me alone, and even without my brother's message I sensed the truth would have finally sought me out.

We spent a long while simply being overjoyed at finding one another again. Then we began to open up even more to reveal the deepest secrets from long ago. It was not easy.

The big hurt was how I had vanished off the face of the earth and let everyone think I was dead. David explained the irony of it all – the deal they'd made with Ronnie just as I was getting ready to run, how much they trusted the intermediary, Patsy O'Mara, and were sure that it would stick.

And I didn't know. David then told me about taking our mum down to New Scotland Yard in the early seventies, going in to report me as a missing person. It broke my heart.

He told me they spoke to the officer on the desk first, and asked to see the inspector. They had to fill out some forms, and the police asked them if they had any idea what might have happened to me. They said they didn't and the officer promised to look into the matter and get back to them. No one ever did. So a few months later David took Mum back and they went through the whole thing again. They did this four or five times in the end.

David and Mum knew they were just being fobbed off and were getting very frustrated. The last time they went up there the police kept them waiting for over three hours. Each time they'd tell them: 'We understand your position', or 'We'll get back to you soon', but in the end our mother died without knowing what had happened to me.

The questions kept coming. Why did that happen? What did you do that for? In fact when the bad things were happening, we were kept forcibly apart (I was in prison, and after that I was under armed police guard) so we deliberately *couldn't* know what the others knew. Some of what the police and government were doing back then is still secret.

I was stunned to hear from David and Alfie how the Krays had been idolised, turned into heroes, and about the mythology that surrounded them. I still find it hard to comprehend. In fact I find it offensive. I felt that unless I could get the truth out about what happened, all that I had gone through at such a price, it was a life wasted. For all those years I didn't want to hear what had happened to the Krays – any of them. I shut it out. Now I wanted to know every detail.

So what was that crazy thing about our mother being arrested? Alfie reminded me that Ronnie Kray himself had stood up in open court at the Old Bailey and said the only reason we, the Teale brothers, were saying all this was to get our mother off the burglary charge.

Alfie told me that over the years he's sort of worked it out. Mum's arrest came out of the blue as far as we were concerned. It's just too far-fetched to think it was simply a coincidence. But Alfie said he can't help but think – and I have to agree with him – that it was the Krays who set our mother up deliberately, not the police. It doesn't fit with the rest of what Nipper was up to.

Ronnie was very clever in some things. If it looked like we were simply giving evidence for the prosecution to stop our mum going to prison, he'd be able to use this in his favour. It was Charlie Kray who was behind the burglary back in February 1968, but it might have been to do with the fact that the Krays knew we were due for release later that year, and wanted to have a hold over us when we came out. Anything we said after that would be tainted. It would look like a police fit-up. In fact it was a Kray-Boothby fit-up. It was still going on four years after all that madness at Cedra Court. And who had lived there then? Reggie and Ronnie, our mum and dad and the guy who did the burglary, Leslie Holt.

Then I heard from David what Ronnie did to him at Vallance Road.

And I was able to tell him he'd done the same thing to me.

Ronnie Kray raped me too.

It happened in Ryde on the Isle of Wight and still haunts me whenever I am there, anywhere, even today. We were all at a packed dance-hall when Albert Donoghue came to me and said Ronnie wanted us to have a party upstairs. We went up a narrow set of stairs, the Colonel in front of me, and two of the Firm behind me. When we reached the top of the stairs there was just a room with a bed and two chairs in it. The two sat down in the chairs and went to sleep, while Ronnie told me to take off my clothes and get into bed. I was about twenty-two years old and terrified. Then Ronnie raped me. Afterwards he kicked me so that I fell on the floor. I don't think telling David after all these years helped either of us. And nor could either of us explain, certainly not me, how we'd gone on doing their bidding after we'd been abused like that. When, after my marriage broke up and I left the island to go to London and be what I thought for a while was a proper gangster, it was Reggie who was my friend. It was Ronnie who wanted me dead. And he wanted Reggie to do the killing. Maybe it was an extension of rape. That's how crazy he was.

So these talks went on, with us comparing notes, filling in gaps. Remember that Alfie and David didn't really know what I was up to that summer after the Cornell killing. All they knew was that I was hanging out with Reggie, there'd been a police raid and the identity parade that followed had collapsed.

The Krays boasting about getting away with it was in all the papers on 6 August 1966, along with big, grinning photographs taken round their mum's. The next day, Alfie and David were both invited by me to this old guy's party where we stayed the night. He 'left by the rubbish chute' and turned up with a load of police on his own doorstep early the next morning. We were all arrested, didn't get bail – and ended up being charged with blackmail and going to prison, sentenced to three years. And I couldn't tell them why.

So all these years later, we worked it out between us. David was like a terrier at the British National Archives where the police and prosecution records had been released over the years.

He found all our original statements to Read and Mooney in July 1968, what we'd said at the committal and at the big Old Bailey trial. He found what Pogue had said. He found the Butler file that Read said in his book didn't exist (and may not have known existed), revealing that Butler gave up the pursuit of Ronnie and Reggie after the Lea Bridge Road raid and the Director of Public Prosecutions walked away – the week we were all arrested.

But a lot of it was still secret – and the dates on them for when they're allowed to be opened to the public are for after we'll all be long dead. The closed files include all the papers about our Old Bailey trial for blackmail. And why is that?

There are also boxes of evidence put together after the Cornell murder which still no one's allowed to see. Where are the pictures that we saw of us in Tintagel House? Where is the photograph I got of Scotch Ian? Where are the pictures of David's family with the Krays at Steeple Bay, the ones that the police took from Christine? Where are the surveillance photographs we saw of ourselves around Moresby Road? It's as if we never existed.

And you know, in the Kray biographies, neither Reggie nor Ronnie ever mention the time in the flat with the Firm and all the children. They go straight from the Blind Beggar to being lifted and put on Butler's identity parade. The three months in the middle aren't mentioned. What were they so ashamed of? I'll tell you. They were ashamed of hiding behind women and kids.

David thinks it was the police who were responsible for Moresby Road disappearing from the record and still being hidden. How would it look that they hadn't arrested them there and then when so many more murders followed? They knew Ronnie had done it. They surrounded David's place, Butler and his men. David says they told him at Tintagel afterwards that they planned to come in with all guns blazing. It was only down to the fact that the children were there that they didn't.

But Ronnie was told that at the time by his police contact inside the Yard. Ronnie told David when they were all in the flat that some copper had tipped him off: 'Where you are now, we won't come in, so don't worry about it.'

What with all the people coming in and going out, and Reggie and Charlie meeting up with police, the Old Bill was getting information all the time. No wonder the official files about all this are sealed for seventy years.

But David managed to get one file opened. It's a series of letters from July to August 1966 between officials in the Director of Public Prosecutions' office – David Hopkin and David Prys Jones – about whether or not to go after the Krays. There's a big note dated 18 July, reminding everyone that Butler, James Axon (the Whitechapel detective), and the commander of the CID, Ernest Millen (who had secretly investigated Leslie Holt's connection with Boothby two years before), had had a meeting in March to urgently discuss the Cornell killing.

That's what it says. March. Precisely when the Firm had taken over the flat and I'd made that first phone call to the Scotland Yard switchboard and asked to speak to Mr Butler.

In the note it's clear that everyone knows that it's Ronnie who did Cornell. Still these three very senior detectives think it's not going to work, that the twins can keep the East End intimidated, no one will talk and they're going to get off. And that will just boost Ronnie 'in the eyes of the underworld,' so they say. Which is exactly what happened, of course.

So their advice that March is to leave it alone. Just like always. But 'there are other matters in the melting pot which may be successful,' Butler says. That's me.

The police are saying they can do nothing, while the DPP is saying they should go after the Krays because they must be seen to be doing something. It's all political.

After that, there's the raid on Lea Bridge Road and the cock-up at the identity parade. Everyone's very embarrassed. But this law officer reports after it's all gone wrong that: 'One factor that has emerged is that Chief Superintendent Butler is satisfied from the description given to him *by his informant* that the second man involved is [Scotch Ian] Barrie.'

Well, that's me again. And now the law officers in the Department of Public Prosecutions know that he's got a spy in the Firm. That's not police, that's the government. Who else in the government knows?

Then a day later on 8 August, Butler says that there's nothing more he can do. Within a matter of hours of him saying that, the police know that I'm with Wallace in Dolphin Square, and that Alfie and David are with me.

And who or what was Wallace? I'd met him, it seemed, by chance. He was friendly, accommodating, he lent me his car and didn't mind too much when I got arrested in it. He was gay, but he didn't try anything on me. He just seemed to like me being around. And it was very handy to have somewhere to lie low.

It was Wallace who took me in when I had nowhere to hide after Epping and the Firm was looking for me at Steeple Bay. But what was he really? The operation to bring us in had to be primed – with him as the ready-made 'victim' to get us all nicked.

The three of us were invited to stay the night. Next thing we knew we were all arrested, dragged off to court, stitched up at the Old Bailey and dispatched to spend the next two years in prison as blackmailers of homosexuals. Who invented that one? The file on our trial is closed until the year 2037. I am told if I can produce my own death certificate (and Alfie's and David's) I might be allowed to see it.

So how, at the time, could I explain that to my brothers? How do I really explain it all these years later?

Of course there was suspicion and resentment between us after the initial joy of reunion, a sudden sidelong glance from David when he thought I wasn't looking, a questioning look as if even now he was wondering whether to trust me. Alfie, too, in spite of his obvious affection for me, remained puzzled about some of my actions. Worst of all for me was the look in their eyes when they asked, 'Why didn't you tell us, let us in on what you were doing? We are your brothers, for God's sake.' In the Teale family, that means a lot.

I understand why they feel like this. I would too, if it had been one of them who had disappeared. But as Ronnie would have said, 'What's done is done,' and all we can do is to look back and make some kind of sense of it.

Turning informer was one of the hardest decisions I ever had to make in my life. Having villains as our family friends at first had all seemed so glamorous, so exciting. But then I saw the violent reality, the fear, the cruelty. After Ronnie raped me on the Isle of Wight I couldn't deal with it. And when I saw what they were doing to David, his children and our little brother, I knew I had to act. So I did what I did.

In vain I tell David and Alfie that it is because they are my brothers that I did all this. That I was trying to protect them and their families from what the Krays might do. I knew Alfie and David were on Ron's dreaded list – we all were.

There is a quote from somewhere I've always remembered: 'All that is necessary for evil to triumph is that good men do nothing.'

I had to do something, and I did it, even at the terrible cost of losing my family for forty years. I'm not ashamed of that – I'm proud of it. And over the years to come I hope to be able to convince Alfie and David of it too.

NOTE

Ronnie Kray married twice while in prison. He divorced his second wife, Kate, in May 1994. On 17 March 1995 he died of a heart attack in Wexham Park Hospital, Slough. He was sixty-one. Reggie organised a quasi-state funeral for his twin from inside prison. He married his second wife, Roberta, while in Maidstone in July 1997. In June 1997 Charlie was sentenced to twelve years for conspiracy to supply cocaine. He died in April 2000. Then Reggie was diagnosed with stomach cancer and died on 1 October 2000. He was conveyed ten days later to Chingford Cemetery to be buried next to Ronnie with Frances besides them. Bobby was in America and did not follow events. Alfie and David Teale attended none of the Kray funerals.

ACKNOWLEDGEMENTS

My brothers and I would first and foremost like to thank our family for all of their love, support and encouragement: our mother Ellen, Dawne, Traci, Christine, Wendy, Mark and Michael. Special thanks go to Clare and Christy Campbell for all of their help. Without them this book wouldn't be half the book it is.

We are extremely grateful to Jonathan Lloyd, Felicity Blunt and everyone at Curtis Brown. We would also like to thank Kelly Ellis, Andrew Goodfellow and all of the team at Ebury.

Thank you to Kelly Whitfield and the team at Teacher Stern; Lali Gotich and, finally, to Rasolil Daitor at the Kings Cross Computer Centre.